The writings of Irenaeus

Irenaeus, Saint, Bishop of Lyon

Nabu Public Domain Reprints:

You are holding a reproduction of an original work published before 1923 that is in the public domain in the United States of America, and possibly other countries. You may freely copy and distribute this work as no entity (individual or corporate) has a copyright on the body of the work. This book may contain prior copyright references, and library stamps (as most of these works were scanned from library copies). These have been scanned and retained as part of the historical artifact.

This book may have occasional imperfections such as missing or blurred pages, poor pictures, errant marks, etc. that were either part of the original artifact, or were introduced by the scanning process. We believe this work is culturally important, and despite the imperfections, have elected to bring it back into print as part of our continuing commitment to the preservation of printed works worldwide. We appreciate your understanding of the imperfections in the preservation process, and hope you enjoy this valuable book.

T. and T. Clark's Publications.

CLARK'S FOREIGN THEOLOGICAL LIBRARY—Continued.

Dr. John H. A. Ebrard.—Commentary on the Epistles of St. John. By Dr. JOHN H. A. EBRARD, Professor of Theology in the University of Erlangen. In One Volume. (10s. 6d.)

Dr. J. P. Lange.—Theological and Homiletical Commentary on the Gospel of St. Matthew and Mark. Specially Designed and Adapted for the Use of Ministers and Students. By J. P. LANGE, D.D., Professor of Divinity in the University of Bonn. Three Volumes. (10s. 6d. each.)

Dr. J. A. Dorner.—History of the Development of the Doctrine of the Person of Christ. By Dr. J. A. DORNER, Professor of Theology in the University of Berlin. Five Volumes. (£2, 12s. 6d.)

Dr. J. J. Van Oosterzee.—Theological and Homiletical Commentary on the Gospel of St. Luke. Specially Designed and Adapted for the Use of Ministers and Students. Edited by J. P. LANGE, D.D. Two Volumes. (18s.)

Professor Kurtz.—The Sacrificial Worship of the Old Testament. One Volume. (10s. 6d.)

Professor Ebrard.—The Gospel History: A Compendium of Critical Investigations in support of the Historical Character of the Four Gospels. One Volume. (10s. 6d.)

Lechler and Gerok.—Theological and Homiletical Commentary on the Acts of the Apostles. Edited by Dr. LANGE. (Lange Series.) Two Volumes. (21s.)

Dr. Hengstenberg.—Commentary on the Gospel of St. John. Two Volumes. (21s.)

Professor Keil.—Biblical Commentary on the Pentateuch. Three Volumes. (31s. 6d.)

Professor Keil.—Commentary on Joshua, Judges, and Ruth. One Volume. (10s. 6d.)

Professor Keil.—Commentary on the Books of Samuel. One Volume. (10s. 6d.)

Professor Delitzsch.—Commentary on the Book of Job. Two Volumes. (21s.)

Bishop Martensen.—Christian Dogmatics. A Compendium of the Doctrines of Christianity. One Volume. (10s. 6d.)

And, in connection with the Series,—

Shedd's History of Christian Doctrine. Two Volumes. (21s.)
MacDonald's Introduction to the Pentateuch. Two Volumes. (21s.)
Hengstenberg's Egypt and the Books of Moses. (7s. 6d.)
Ackerman on the Christian Element in Plato. (7s. 6d.)
Robinson's Greek Lexicon of the New Testament. 8vo. (9s.)
Gerlach's Commentary on the Pentateuch. Demy 8vo. (10s. 6d.)

The above, in 102 Volumes (including 1870), price £26, 15s. 6d., form an *Apparatus*, without which it may be truly said *no Theological Library can be complete*, and the Publishers take the liberty of suggesting that no more appropriate gift could be presented to a Clergyman than the Series, in whole or in part.

⁎⁎ *In reference to the above, it must be noted that* NO DUPLICATES *can be included in the Selection of Twenty Volumes: and it will save trouble and correspondence if it be distinctly understood that* NO LESS *number than Twenty can be supplied, unless at non-subscription price.*

EDINBURGH: T. & T. CLARK.

LONDON: (*For Works at Non-subscription price only*) HAMILTON, ADAMS, & Co.

T. and T. Clark's Publications.

Ante-Nicene Christian Library.

A COLLECTION OF ALL THE WORKS OF THE FATHERS OF THE CHRISTIAN CHURCH, PRIOR TO THE COUNCIL OF NICÆA,

EDITED BY THE

REV. ALEXANDER ROBERTS, D.D.,

AND

JAMES DONALDSON, LL.D.

The Volumes of First Year—THE APOSTOLIC FATHERS, in One Volume; JUSTIN MARTYR and ATHENAGORAS, in One Volume; TATIAN, THEOPHILUS, and the CLEMENTINE RECOGNITIONS, in One Volume; and CLEMENT OF ALEXANDRIA, Volume First;—and the Volumes of Second Year—IRENÆUS, Volume First; HIPPOLYTUS, Volume First; TERTULLIAN AGAINST MARCION, in One Volume; and CYPRIAN, Volume First;—and the Volumes of the Third Year—the Completion of IRENÆUS and HIPPOLYTUS, in One Volume, the First Volume of the Writings of ORIGEN, CLEMENT OF ALEXANDRIA, Volume II., and the First Volume of the Writings of TERTULLIAN; and the Volumes of Fourth Year, viz., The Writings of METHODIUS, etc., One Volume, the Writings of CYPRIAN, etc., Volume II., APOCRYPHAL WRITINGS, One Volume, Writings of TERTULLIAN, Volume II.; and the First Issue of Fifth Year—The CLEMENTINE and the APOSTOLIC CONSTITUTIONS, in One Volume; and the WRITINGS of TERTULLIAN, Volume III.

The Subscription for 1st, 2d, 3d, 4th, and 5th Years is now due—£5, 5s.

The Subscription to the Series is at the rate of 21s. for Four Volumes when paid in advance (or 24s. when not so paid), and 10s. 6d. each Volume to Non-Subscribers.

'We give this series every recommendation in our power. The translation, so far as we have tested it, and that is pretty widely, appears to be thoroughly faithful and honest; the books are handsomely printed on good paper, and wonderfully cheap. . . . . The work being done so well, can any one wonder at our hoping that the Messrs. Clark will find a large body of supporters?'—*Literary Churchman.*

'The work of the different translators has been done with skill and spirit. To all students of Church history and of theology these books will be of great value. . . . . . We must add, also, that good print and good paper help to make these fit volumes for the library.'—*Church and State Review.*

'We promise our readers, those hitherto unaccustomed to the task, a most healthy exercise for mind and heart, if they procure these volumes and study them.'—*Clerical Journal.*

'For the critical care with which the translations have been prepared, the fulness of the introductory notices, the completeness of the collection, the beauty and clearness of the type, the accuracy of the indexes, they are incomparably the most satisfactory English edition of the Fathers we know.'—*Freeman.*

'It will be a reproach to the age if this scheme should break down for want of encouragement from the public.'—*Watchman.*

' The translations in these two volumes, as far as we have had opportunity of judging, are fairly executed.'—*Westminster Review.*

T. and T. Clark's Publications.

ANTE-NICENE CHRISTIAN LIBRARY.   OPINIONS OF THE PRESS—*continued.*

'There is everything about these volumes to recommend them, and we hope they will find a place in the libraries of all our ministers and students.'—*English Indpendent.*

'The translation is at once good and faithful.'—*Ecclesiastic.*

'The translations are, in our opinion, and in respect of all places that we have carefully examined, thoroughly satisfactory for exact truth and happy expressiveness; and the whole business of the editing has been done to perfection.'—*Nonconformist.*

'The entire undertaking, as revealed in this instalment, is nobly conceived. . . . . We can most heartily congratulate the editors on this noble commencement of their voluminous responsible undertaking, and on the highly attractive appearance of these volumes; and we most heartily commend them to the notice of all theological students who have neither time nor opportunity to consult the original authorities.'—*British Quarterly Review.*

'The whole getting up of the work deserves warm commendation, and we conclude by again recommending it to notice, and expressing the hope that it will attain the wide circulation that it well deserves.'—*Record.*

'This series ought to have a place in every ministerial and in every congregational library, as well as in the collections of those laymen, happily an increasing number, interested in theological studies.'—*Christian Spectator.*

'If the succeeding volumes are executed in the same manner as the two now before us, the series will be one of the most useful and valuable that can adorn the library of the theological student, whether lay or cleric.'—*Scotsman.*

'The editing is all that it should be. The translation is well executed, perspicuously and faithfully, so far as we have examined. . . . . . There is nothing in English to compete with it. Not only all ministers, but all intelligent laymen who take an interest in theological subjects, should enrich their libraries with this series of volumes.'—*Daily Review.*

MESSRS. CLARK have the honour to include in the Subscription List, amongst other distinguished names, both of Clergy and Laity—

His Grace the Archbishop of Canterbury.
His Grace the Archbishop of York.
His Grace the Archbishop of Armagh.
The Right Rev. the Bishop of Winchester.
The Right Rev. the Bishop of London.
The Right Rev. the Bishop of Oxford.
The Right Rev. the Bishop of Gloucester and Bristol.
The Right Rev. the Bishop of Ely.
The Right Rev. the Bishop of St. David's.
The Right Rev. the Bishop of Kilmore.
The Right Rev. the Bishop of Meath.
The Right Rev. the Bishop of Barbadoes.
The Right Rev. Bishop Eden of Moray.
The Right Rev. Bishop Wordsworth of St. Andrews.
The Rev. Principal, Cuddesdon College.
The Rev. President, Trinity College, Oxford.
The Rev. Canon Mansel, Christ Church.
The Rev. Canon Robinson, Bolton Abbey.
His Grace the Duke of Argyll.
His Grace the Duke of Buccleuch.
The Right Hon. the Marquis of Bute.
The Right Hon. the Earl of Strathmore.

The Works of St. Augustine.

MESSRS. CLARK beg to announce that they have in preparation Translations of a Selection from the WRITINGS OF ST. AUGUSTINE, on the plan of their ANTE-NICENE LIBRARY, and under the editorship of the Rev. MARCUS DODS, A.M. They append a list of the works which they intend to include in the Series, each work being given entire, unless otherwise specified.

> All the TREATISES in the PELAGIAN, and the four leading TREATISES in the DONATIST CONTROVERSY.
>
> The TREATISES against FAUSTUS the Manichæan; on CHRISTIAN DOCTRINE; the TRINITY; the HARMONY OF THE EVANGELISTS; the SERMON ON THE MOUNT.
>
> Also the LECTURES on the GOSPEL OF ST. JOHN, the CONFESSIONS, the CITY OF GOD, and a SELECTION from the LETTERS.

All these works are of first-rate importance, and only a small proportion of them have yet appeared in an English dress. The SERMONS and the COMMENTARIES ON THE PSALMS having been already given by the Oxford Translators, it is not intended, at least in the first instance, to publish them.

The Series will include a LIFE OF ST. AUGUSTINE, by ROBERT RAINY, D.D., Professor of Church History, New College, Edinburgh.

The Series will probably extend to Twelve or Fourteen Volumes. It will not be commenced for some time, so as to allow the ANTE-NICENE SERIES to approach nearer to completion; but the Publishers will be glad to receive the *Names* of Subscribers.

The form and mode of printing have not yet been finally settled; but in any case the quantity of matter will be equal to the subscription of Four Volumes for a Guinea, as in the case of the ANTE-NICENE SERIES.

ANTE-NICENE

CHRISTIAN LIBRARY

TRANSLATIONS OF
THE WRITINGS OF THE FATHERS
DOWN TO A.D. 325.

EDITED BY THE
REV. ALEXANDER ROBERTS, D.D.,
AND
JAMES DONALDSON, LL.D.

VOL. IX.
IRENÆUS, VOL. II.—HIPPOLYTUS, VOL. II.
—FRAGMENTS OF THIRD CENTURY.

EDINBURGH:
T. & T. CLARK, 38, GEORGE STREET.
MDCCCLXXI.

PRINTED BY MURRAY AND GIBB,
FOR
T. & T. CLARK, EDINBURGH.

LONDON,	. . . .	HAMILTON, ADAMS, AND CO.
DUBLIN,	. . . .	JOHN ROBERTSON AND CO.
NEW YORK,	. . .	C. SCRIBNER AND CO.

THE WRITINGS

OF

IRENÆUS.

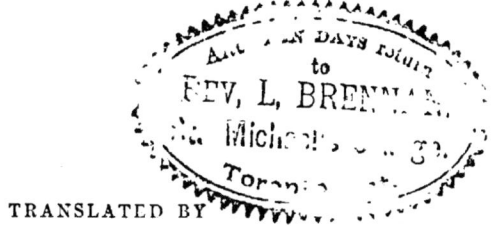

TRANSLATED BY

REV. ALEXANDER ROBERTS, D.D.,

AND

REV. W. H. RAMBAUT, A.B.

VOL. II.

EDINBURGH.
T. & T. CLARK, 38, GEORGE STREET.

MDCCCLXXI.

CONTENTS.

BOOK IV. (*continued.*)

CHAP.		PAGE
31.	We should not hastily impute as crimes to the men of old time those actions which the Scripture has not condemned, but should rather seek in them types of things to come: an example of this in the incest committed by Lot,	1
32.	That one God was the author of both testaments, is confirmed by the authority of a presbyter who had been taught by the apostles,	4
33.	Whosoever confesses that one God is the author of both testaments, and diligently reads the Scriptures in company with the presbyters of the church, is a true spiritual disciple; and he will rightly understand and interpret all that the prophets have declared respecting Christ and the liberty of the new testament,	6
34.	Proof against the Marcionites, that the prophets referred in all their predictions to our Christ,	18
35.	A refutation of those who allege that the prophets uttered some predictions under the inspiration of the Highest, others from the Demiurge. Disagreements of the Valentinians among themselves with regard to these same predictions,	22
36.	The prophets were sent from one and the same Father from whom the Son was sent,	26
37.	Men are possessed of free-will, and endowed with the faculty of making a choice. It is not true, therefore, that some are by nature good, and others bad,	36
38.	Why man was not made perfect from the beginning,	42

CONTENTS.

CHAP.		PAGE
39.	Man is endowed with the faculty of distinguishing good and evil; so that, without compulsion, he has the power, by his own will and choice, to perform God's commandments, by doing which he avoids the evils prepared for the rebellious,	45
40.	One and the same God the Father inflicts punishment on the reprobate, and bestows rewards on the elect,	48
41.	Those persons who do not believe in God, but who are disobedient, are angels and sons of the devil, not indeed by nature, but by imitation. Close of this book, and scope of the succeeding one,	50

BOOK V.

PREFACE,		54
1.	Christ alone is able to teach divine things, and to redeem us: He, the same, took flesh of the Virgin Mary, not merely in appearance, but actually, by the operation of the Holy Spirit, in order to renovate us. Strictures on the conceits of Valentinus and Ebion,	55
2.	When Christ visited us in His grace, He did not come to what did not belong to Him: also, by shedding His true blood for us, and exhibiting to us His true flesh in the Eucharist, He conferred upon our flesh the capacity of salvation,	58
3.	The power and glory of God shine forth in the weakness of human flesh, as He will render our body a participator of the resurrection and of immortality, although He has formed it from the dust of the earth; He will also bestow upon it the enjoyment of immortality, just as He grants it this short life in common with the soul,	61
4.	Those persons are deceived who feign another God the Father besides the Creator of the world; for he must have been feeble and useless, or else malignant and full of envy, if he be either unable or unwilling to extend eternal life to our bodies,	64
5.	The prolonged life of the ancients, the translation of Elijah and of Enoch in their own bodies, as well as the preservation of Jonah, of Shadrach, Meshach, and Abednego, in the midst of extreme peril, are clear demonstrations that God can raise up our bodies to life eternal,	65

CHAP.		PAGE
6.	God will bestow salvation upon the whole nature of man, consisting of body and soul in close union, since the Word took it upon Him, and adorned it with the gifts of the Holy Spirit, of whom our bodies are, and are termed, the temples,	67
7.	Inasmuch as Christ did rise in our flesh, it follows that we shall be also raised in the same; since the resurrection promised to us should not be referred to spirits naturally immortal, but to bodies in themselves mortal,	70
8.	The gifts of the Holy Spirit which we receive prepare us for incorruption, render us spiritual, and separate us from carnal men. These two classes are signified by the clean and unclean animals in the legal dispensation,	72
9.	Showing how that passage of the apostle which the heretics pervert, should be understood: viz., "Flesh and blood shall not possess the kingdom of God,"	75
10.	By a comparison drawn from the wild olive-tree, whose quality but not whose nature is changed by grafting, he proves more important things; he points out also that man without the Spirit is not capable of bringing forth fruit, or of inheriting the kingdom of God,	78
11.	Treats upon the actions of carnal and of spiritual persons; also, that the spiritual cleansing is not to be referred to the substance of our bodies, but to the manner of our former life,	80
12.	Of the difference between life and death; of the breath of life and the vivifying Spirit: also how it is that the substance of flesh revives which once was dead,	82
13.	In the dead who were raised by Christ we possess the highest proof of the resurrection; and our hearts are shown to be capable of life eternal, because they can now receive the Spirit of God,	87
14.	Unless the flesh were to be saved, the Word would not have taken upon Him flesh of the same substance as ours: from this it would follow that neither should we have been reconciled by Him,	91
15.	Proofs of the resurrection from Isaiah and Ezekiel; the same God who created us will also raise us up,	94
16.	Since our bodies return to the earth, it follows that they have their substance from it; also, by the advent of the Word, the image of God in us appeared in a clearer light,	98

CHAP.		PAGE
17.	There is but one Lord and one God, the Father and Creator of all things, who has loved us in Christ, given us commandments, and remitted our sins; whose Son and Word Christ proved Himself to be, when He forgave our sins,	100
18.	God the Father and His Word have formed all created things (which they use) by their own power and wisdom, not out of defect or ignorance. The Son of God, who received all power from the Father, would otherwise never have taken flesh upon Him,	103
19.	A comparison is instituted between the disobedient and sinning Eve and the Virgin Mary, her patroness. Various and discordant heresies are mentioned,	106
20.	Those pastors are to be heard to whom the apostles committed the churches, possessing one and the same doctrine of salvation; the heretics, on the other hand, are to be avoided. We must think soberly with regard to the mysteries of the faith,	108
21.	Christ is the Head of all things already mentioned. It was fitting that He should be sent by the Father, the Creator of all things, to assume human nature, and should be tempted by Satan, that He might fulfil the promises, and carry off a glorious and perfect victory,	110
22.	The true Lord and the one God is declared by the law, and manifested by Christ His Son in the gospel; whom alone we should adore, and from Him we must look for all good things, not from Satan,	114
23.	The devil is well practised in falsehood, by which Adam having been led astray, sinned on the sixth day of the creation, in which day also he has been renewed by Christ,	116
24.	Of the constant falsehood of the devil, and of the powers and governments of the world, which we ought to obey, inasmuch as they are appointed of God, not of the devil,	119
25.	The fraud, pride, and tyrannical kingdom of Antichrist, as described by Daniel and Paul,	121
26.	John and Daniel have predicted the dissolution and desolation of the Roman Empire, which shall precede the end of the world and the eternal kingdom of Christ. The Gnostics are refuted, those tools of Satan, who invent another Father different from the Creator,	125
27.	The future judgment by Christ. Communion with and	

CHAP.		PAGE
	separation from the Divine Being. The eternal punishment of unbelievers, ...	128
28.	The distinction to be made between the righteous and the wicked. The future apostasy in the time of Antichrist, and the end of the world, ...	130
29.	All things have been created for the service of man. The deceits, wickedness, and apostate power of Antichrist. This was prefigured at the deluge, as afterwards by the persecution of Shadrach, Meshach, and Abednego, .	133
30.	Although certain as to the number of the name of Antichrist, yet we should come to no rash conclusions as to the name itself, because this number is capable of being fitted to many names. Reasons for this point being reserved by the Holy Spirit. Antichrist's reign and death, ...	135
31.	The preservation of our bodies is confirmed by the resurrection and ascension of Christ: the souls of the saints during the intermediate period are in a state of expectation of that time when they shall receive their perfect and consummated glory, ...	139
32.	In that flesh in which the saints have suffered so many afflictions, they shall receive the fruits of their labours; especially since all creation waits for this, and God promises it to Abraham and his seed, . . .	141
33.	Further proofs of the same proposition, drawn from the promises made by Christ, when He declared that He would drink of the fruit of the vine with His disciples in His Father's kingdom, while at the same time He promised to reward them an hundred-fold, and to make them partake of banquets. The blessing pronounced by Jacob had pointed out this already, as Papias and the elders have interpreted it, ...	143
34.	He fortifies his opinions with regard to the temporal and earthly kingdom of the saints after their resurrection, by the various testimonies of Isaiah, Ezekiel, Jeremiah, and Daniel; also by the parable of the servants watching, to whom the Lord promised that He would minister, ...	147
35.	He contends that these testimonies already alleged cannot be understood allegorically of celestial blessings, but that they shall have their fulfilment after the coming of Antichrist, and the resurrection, in the terrestrial Jerusalem. To the former prophecies he subjoins others	

CHAP.		PAGE
	drawn from Isaiah, Jeremiah, and the Apocalypse of John,	151
36.	Men shall be actually raised: the world shall not be annihilated; but there shall be various mansions for the saints, according to the rank allotted to each individual. All things shall be subject to God the Father, and so shall He be all in all,	155

FRAGMENTS FROM THE LOST WRITINGS OF IRENÆUS 158

INDEX OF TEXTS, ... 189

INDEX OF PRINCIPAL SUBJECTS, ... 200

IRENÆUS AGAINST HERESIES.

BOOK IV.

CHAP. XXXI.—*We should not hastily impute as crimes to the men of old time those actions which the Scripture has not condemned, but should rather seek in them types of things to come: an example of this in the incest committed by Lot.*

1. WHEN recounting certain matters of this kind respecting them of old time, the presbyter [before mentioned] was in the habit of instructing us, and saying: "With respect to those misdeeds for which the Scriptures themselves blame the patriarchs and prophets, we ought not to inveigh against them, nor become like Ham, who ridiculed the shame of his father, and so fell under a curse; but we should [rather] give thanks to God in their behalf, inasmuch as their sins have been forgiven them through the advent of our Lord; for He said that they gave thanks [for us], and gloried in our salvation. With respect to those actions, again, on which the Scriptures pass no censure, but which are simply set down [as having occurred], we ought not to become the accusers [of those who committed them], for we are not more exact than God, nor can we be superior to our Master; but we should search for a type [in them]. For not one of those things which have been set down in Scripture without being condemned is without significance." An example is found in the case of Lot, who led forth his daughters from Sodom,

and these then conceived by their own father; and who left behind him within the confines [of the land] his wife, [who remains] a pillar of salt unto this day. For Lot, not acting under the impulse of his own will, nor at the prompting of carnal concupiscence, nor having any knowledge or thought of anything of the kind, did [in fact] work out a type [of future events]. As says the Scripture: "And that night the elder went in and lay with her father; and Lot knew not when she lay down, nor when she arose."[1] And the same thing took place in the case of the younger: "And he knew not," it is said, "when she slept with him, nor when she arose."[2] Since, therefore, Lot knew not [what he did], nor was a slave to lust [in his actions], the arrangement [designed by God] was carried out, by which the two daughters (that is, the two churches[3]), who gave birth to children begotten of one and the same father, were pointed out, apart from [the influence of] the lust of the flesh. For there was no other person, [as they supposed], who could impart to them quickening seed, and the means of their giving birth to children, as it is written: "And the elder said unto the younger, And there is not a man on the earth to enter in unto us after the manner of all the earth: come, let us make our father drunk with wine, and let us lie with him, and raise up seed from our father."[4]

2. Thus, after their simplicity and innocence, did these daughters [of Lot] so speak, imagining that all mankind had perished, even as the Sodomites had done, and that the anger of God had come down upon the whole earth. Wherefore also they are to be held excusable, since they supposed that they only, along with their father, were left for the preservation of the human race; and for this reason it was that they deceived their father. Moreover, by the words they used this fact was pointed out—that there is no other one who can confer upon the elder and younger church the

---

[1] Gen. xix. 33.   [2] Gen. xix. 35.
[3] "Id est duæ synagogæ," referring to the Jews and Gentiles. Some regard the words as a marginal gloss which has crept into the text
[4] Gen. xix. 31, 32.

[power of] giving birth to children, besides our Father. Now the father of the human race is the Word of God, as Moses points out when he says, "Is not He thy father who hath obtained thee [by generation], and formed thee, and created thee?"[1] At what time, then, did He pour out upon the human race the life-giving seed—that is, the Spirit of the remission of sins, through means of whom we are quickened? Was it not then, when He was eating with men, and drinking wine upon the earth? For it is said, "The Son of man came eating and drinking;"[2] and when He had lain down, He fell asleep, and took repose. As He does Himself say in David, "I slept, and took repose."[3] And because He used thus to act while He dwelt and lived among us, He says again, "And my sleep became sweet unto me."[4] Now this whole matter was indicated through Lot, that the seed of the Father of all—that is, of the Spirit of God, by whom all things were made—was commingled and united with flesh—that is, with His own workmanship; by which commixture and unity the two synagogues—that is, the two churches—produced from their own father living sons to the living God.

3. And while these things were taking place, his wife remained in [the territory of] Sodom, no longer corruptible flesh, but a pillar of salt which endures for ever;[5] and by those natural processes[6] which appertain to the human race, indicating that the church also, which is the salt of the earth,[7] has been left behind within the confines of the earth, and subject to human sufferings; and while entire members are

---

[1] Deut. xxxii. 6, LXX.
[2] Matt. xi. 19.
[3] Ps. iii. 6.
[4] Jer. xxxi. 26.
[5] Comp. Clem. Rom. chap. xi. Josephus (*Antiq.* i. 11, 4) testifies that he had himself seen this pillar.
[6] The Latin is "per naturalia," which words, according to Harvey, correspond to δι' ἐμμηνορροίας. There is a poem entitled *Sodoma* preserved among the works of Tertullian and Cyprian which contains the following lines:

"Dicitur et vivens, alio jam corpore, sexus
   Munificos solito dispungere sanguine menses."

[7] Matt. v. 13.

often taken away from it, the pillar of salt still endures,[1] thus typifying the foundation of the faith which maketh strong, and sends forward, children to their Father.

CHAP. XXXII.—*That one God was the author of both testaments, is confirmed by the authority of a presbyter who had been taught by the apostles.*

1. After this fashion also did a presbyter,[2] a disciple of the apostles, reason with respect to the two testaments, proving that both were truly from one and the same God. For [he maintained] that there was no other God besides Him who made and fashioned us, and that the discourse of those men has no foundation who affirm that this world of ours was made either by angels, or by any other power whatsoever, or by another God. For if a man be once moved away from the Creator of all things, and if he grant that this creation to which we belong was formed by any other or through any other [than the one God], he must of necessity fall into much inconsistency, and many contradictions of this sort; to which he will [be able to] furnish no explanations which can be regarded as either probable or true. And, for this reason, those who introduce other doctrines conceal from us the opinion which they themselves hold respecting God, because they are aware of the untenable[3] and absurd nature of their doctrine, and are afraid lest, should they be vanquished, they should have some difficulty in making good

---

[1] The poem just referred to also says in reference to this pillar:

"Ipsaque imago sibi formam sine corpore servans
Durat adhuc, et enim nuda statione sub æthram
Nec pluviis dilapsa situ, nec diruta ventis.
Quin etiam si quis mutilaverit advena formam,
Protinus ex sese suggestu vulnera complet."

[2] Harvey remarks here, that this can hardly be the same presbyter mentioned before, "who was only a hearer of those who had heard the apostles. Irenæus may here mean the venerable martyr Polycarp, bishop of Smyrna."

[3] "Quassum et futile." The text varies much in the MSS.

their escape. But if any one believes in [only] one God, who also made all things by the Word, as Moses likewise says, "God said, Let there be light: and there was light;"[1] and as we read in the Gospel, "All things were made by Him; and without Him was nothing made;"[2] and the Apostle Paul [says] in like manner, "There is one Lord, one faith, one baptism, one God and Father, who is above all, and through all, and in us all"[3]—this man will first of all "hold the head, from which the whole body is compacted and bound together, and, through means of every joint according to the measure of the ministration of each several part, maketh increase of the body to the edification of itself in love."[4] And then shall every word also seem consistent to him,[5] if he for his part diligently read the Scriptures in company with those who are presbyters in the church, among whom is the apostolic doctrine, as I have pointed out.

2. For all the apostles taught that there were indeed two testaments among the two peoples; but that it was one and the same God who appointed both for the advantage of those men (for whose[6] sakes the testaments were given) who were to believe in God, I have proved in the third book from the very teaching of the apostles; and that the first testament was not given without reason, or to no purpose, or in an accidental sort of manner; but that it subdued[7] those to whom it was given to the service of God, for their benefit (for God needs no service from men), and exhibited a type of heavenly things, inasmuch as man was not yet able to see the things of God through means of immediate vision;[8] and foreshadowed the images of those things which [now actually] exist in the church, in order that our faith might be firmly established; and contained a prophecy of things to come, in

---

[1] Gen. i. 3.   [2] John i. 3.   [3] Eph. iv. 5, 6.
[4] Eph. iv. 16; Col. ii. 19.   [5] "Constabit ei."
[6] We here read "secundum *quos*" with Massuet, instead of the usual "secundum *quod*."
[7] "Concurvans," corresponding to $\sigma\upsilon\gamma\kappa\acute{\alpha}\mu\pi\tau\omega\nu$, which, says Harvey, "would be expressive of those who were brought under the law, as the neck of the steer is bent to the yoke."
[8] The Latin is, "per proprium visum."

order that man might learn that God has foreknowledge of all things.

CHAP. XXXIII.—*Whosoever confesses that one God is the author of both testaments, and diligently reads the Scriptures in company with the presbyters of the church, is a true spiritual disciple; and he will rightly understand and interpret all that the prophets have declared respecting Christ and the liberty of the new testament.*

1. A spiritual disciple of this sort truly receiving the Spirit of God, who was from the beginning, in all the dispensations of God, present with mankind, and announced things future, revealed things present, and narrated things past—[such a man] does indeed judge all men, but is himself judged by no man.[1] For he judges the Gentiles, "who serve the creature more than the Creator,"[2] and with a reprobate mind spend all their labour on vanity. And he also judges the Jews, who do not accept of the word of liberty, nor are willing to go forth free, although they have a Deliverer present [with them]; but they pretend, at a time unsuitable [for such conduct], to serve, [with observances] beyond [those required by] the law, God who stands in need of nothing, and do not recognise the advent of Christ, which He accomplished for the salvation of men, nor are willing to understand that all the prophets announced His two advents: the one, indeed, in which He became a man subject to stripes, and knowing what it is to bear infirmity,[3] and sat upon the foal of an ass,[4] and was a stone rejected by the builders,[5] and was led as a sheep to the slaughter,[6] and by the stretching forth of His hands destroyed Amalek;[7] while He gathered from the ends of the earth into His Father's fold the children who were scattered abroad,[8] and remembered His own dead ones who had formerly fallen asleep,[9] and came down to them that He might deliver them: but the second in which

---

[1] 1 Cor. ii. 15.   [2] Rom. i. 21.   [3] Isa. liii. 3.
[4] Zech. ix. 9.   [5] Ps. cxviii. 22.   [6] Isa. liii. 7.
[7] Ex. xvii. 11.   [8] Isa. xi. 12.   [9] Comp. book iii. 20, 4.

He will come on the clouds,[1] bringing on the day which burns as a furnace,[2] and smiting the earth with the word of His mouth,[3] and slaying the impious with the breath of His lips, and having a fan in His hands, and cleansing His floor, and gathering the wheat indeed into His barn, but burning the chaff with unquenchable fire.[4]

2. Moreover, he shall also examine the doctrine of Marcion, [inquiring] how he holds that there are two gods, separated from each other by an infinite distance.[5] Or how can *he* be good who draws away men that do not belong to him from him who made them, and calls them into his own kingdom? And why is his goodness, which does not save all [thus], defective? Also, why does he, indeed, seem to be good as respects men, but most unjust with regard to him who made men, inasmuch as he deprives him of his possessions? Moreover, how could the Lord, with any justice, if He belonged to another father, have acknowledged the bread to be His body, while He took it from that creation to which we belong, and affirmed the mixed cup to be His blood?[6] And why did He acknowledge Himself to be the Son of man, if He had not gone through that birth which belongs to a human being? How, too, could He forgive us those sins for which we are answerable to our Maker and God? And how, again, supposing that He was not flesh, but was a man merely in appearance, could He have been crucified, and could blood and water have issued from His pierced side?[7] What body, moreover, was it that those who buried Him consigned to the tomb? And what was that which rose again from the dead?

3. [This spiritual man] shall also judge all the followers of Valentinus, because they do indeed confess with the tongue one God the Father, and that all things derive their existence

---

[1] Dan. vii. 13.   [2] Mal. iv. 1.
[3] Isa. xi. 4.   [4] Matt. iii. 12; Luke iii. 17.
[5] Harvey points this sentence interrogatively.
[6] "Temperamentum calicis:" on which Harvey remarks that "the mixture of water with the wine in the holy Eucharist was the universal practice of antiquity . . . the wine signifying the mystical Head of the church, the water the body."
[7] John xix. 34.

from Him, but do at the same time maintain that He who formed all things is the fruit of an apostasy or defect. [He shall judge them, too, because] they do in like manner confess with the tongue one Lord Jesus Christ, the Son of God, but assign in their [system of] doctrine a production of his own to the Only-begotten, one of his own also to the Word, another to Christ, and yet another to the Saviour; so that, according to them, all these beings are indeed said [in Scripture to be], as it were, one; [while they maintain], notwithstanding, that each one of them should be understood [to exist] separately [from the rest], and to have [had] his own special origin, according to his peculiar conjunction. [It appears], then,[1] that their tongues alone, forsooth, have conceded the unity [of God], while their [real] opinion and their understanding (by their habit of investigating profundities) have fallen away from [this doctrine of] unity, and taken up the notion of manifold deities,—[this, I say, must appear] when they shall be examined by Christ as to the points [of doctrine] which they have invented. Him, too, they affirm to have been born at a later period than the Pleroma of the Æons, and that His production took place after [the occurrence of] a degeneracy or apostasy; and they maintain that, on account of the passion which was experienced by Sophia, they themselves were brought to the birth. But their own special prophet Homer, listening to whom they have invented such doctrines, shall himself reprove them, when he expresses himself as follows:

"Hateful to me that man as Hades' gates,
Who one thing thinks, while he another states."[2]

[This spiritual man] shall also judge the vain speeches of the perverse Gnostics, by showing that they are the disciples of Simon Magus.

4. He will judge also the Ebionites; [for] how can they be saved unless it was God who wrought out their salvation upon earth? Or how shall man pass into God, unless God has [first] passed into man? And how shall he (man) escape

---

[1] This sentence is very obscure in the Latin text.
[2] *Iliad*, ix. 312, 313.

from the generation subject to death, if not by means¹ of a new generation, given in a wonderful and unexpected manner (but as a sign of salvation) by God—[I mean] that regeneration which flows from the virgin through faith?² Or how shall they receive adoption from God if they remain in this [kind of] generation, which is naturally possessed by man in this world? And how could He (Christ) have been greater than Solomon,³ or greater than Jonah, or have been the Lord of David,⁴ who was of the same substance as they were? How, too, could He have subdued⁵ him who was stronger than men,⁶ who had not only overcome man, but also retained him under his power, and conquered him who had conquered, while he set free mankind who had been conquered, unless He had been greater than man who had thus been vanquished? But who else is superior to, and more eminent than, that man who was formed after the likeness of God, except the Son of God, after whose image man was created? And for this reason He did in these last days⁷ exhibit the similitude; [for] the Son of God was made man, assuming the ancient production [of His hands] into His own nature,⁸ as I have shown in the immediately preceding book.

5. He shall also judge those who describe Christ as [having become man] only in [human] opinion. For how can they imagine that they do themselves carry on a real discussion, when their Master was a mere imaginary being? Or how can they receive anything stedfast from Him, if He was a merely imagined being, and not a verity? And how can these men really be partakers of salvation, if He in whom they profess to believe, manifested Himself as a merely imaginary being? Everything, therefore, connected with these men is unreal, and

---

¹ The text is obscure, and the construction doubtful.
² The Latin here is, "quæ est ex virgine per fidem regenerationem." According to Massuet, "virgine" here refers not to Mary, but to the church. Grabe suspects that some words have been lost.
³ Matt. xii. 41, 42.   ⁴ Matt. xxii. 43.
⁵ Matt. xxii. 29; Luke xi. 21, 22.
⁶ Literally, "who was strong against men."
⁷ In fine: lit. "in the end."
⁸ In semetipsum: lit. "unto Himself."

nothing [possessed of the character of] truth; and, in these circumstances, it may be made a question whether (since, perchance, they themselves in like manner are not men, but mere dumb animals) they do not present,[1] in most cases, simply a shadow of humanity.

6. He shall also judge false prophets, who, without having received the gift of prophecy from God, and not possessed of the fear of God, but either for the sake of vainglory, or with a view to some personal advantage, or acting in some other way under the influence of a wicked spirit, pretend to utter prophecies, while all the time they lie against God.

7. He shall also judge those who give rise to schisms, who are destitute of the love of God, and who look to their own special advantage rather than to the unity of the church; and who for trifling reasons, or any kind of reason which occurs to them, cut in pieces and divide the great and glorious body of Christ, and so far as in them lies, [positively] destroy it,— men who prate of peace while they give rise to war, and do in truth strain out a gnat, but swallow a camel.[2] For no reformation of so great importance can be effected by them, as will compensate for the mischief arising from their schism. He shall also judge all those who are beyond the pale of the truth, that is, who are outside the church; but he himself shall be judged by no one. For to him all things are consistent: he has a full faith in one God Almighty, of whom are all things; and in the Son of God, Jesus Christ our Lord, by whom are all things, and in the dispensations connected with Him, by means of which the Son of God became man; and a firm belief in the Spirit of God, who furnishes us with a knowledge of the truth, and has set forth the dispensations of the Father and the Son, in virtue of which He dwells with every generation of men,[3] according to the will of the Father.

---

[1] We here follow the reading "proferant:" the passage is difficult and obscure, but the meaning is as above.

[2] Matt. xxiii. 24.

[3] The Greek text here is σκηνοβατοῦν (lit. "to tabernacle:" comp. ἐσκήνωσεν, John i. 14) καθ᾽ ἑκάστην γενεὰν ἐν τοῖς ἀνθρώποις; the Latin is,

8. True knowledge[1] is [that which consists in] the doctrine of the apostles, and the ancient constitution[2] of the church throughout all the world, and the distinctive manifestation of the body[3] of Christ according to the successions of the bishops, by which they have handed down that church which exists in every place, and has come even unto us, being guarded and preserved,[4] without any forging of Scriptures, by a very complete system[5] of doctrine, and neither receiving addition nor [suffering] curtailment [in the truths which she believes]; and [it consists in] reading [the word of God] without falsification, and a lawful and diligent exposition in harmony with the Scriptures, both without danger and without blasphemy; and [above all, it consists in] the pre-eminent gift of love,[6] which is more precious than knowledge, more glorious than prophecy, and which excels all the other gifts [of God].

9. Wherefore the church does in every place, because of that love which she cherishes towards God, send forward, throughout all time, a multitude of martyrs to the Father; while all others[7] not only have nothing of this kind to point to among themselves, but even maintain that such witness-bearing is not at all necessary, for that their system of doctrines is the true witness [for Christ], with the exception, perhaps, that one or two among them, during the whole time

"Secundum quas (dispositiones) aderat generi humano." We have endeavoured to express the meaning of both.

[1] The following section is an important one, but very difficult to translate with undoubted accuracy. The editors differ considerably both as to the construction and the interpretation. We have done our best to represent the meaning in English, but may not have been altogether successful.

[2] The Greek is $\sigma \acute{v} \sigma \tau \eta \mu a$; the Latin text has "status."

[3] The Latin is, "character corporis."

[4] The text here is, "custodita sine fictione scripturarum;" some prefer joining "scripturarum" to the following words.

[5] We follow Harvey's text, "tractatione;" others read "tractatio." According to Harvey, the creed of the church is denoted by "tractatione;" but Massuet renders the clause thus: ["True knowledge consists in] a very complete *tractatio* of the Scriptures, which has come down to us by being preserved ('custoditione' being read instead of 'custodita') without falsification."

[6] Comp. 2 Cor. viii. 1; 1 Cor. xiii. [7] *i.e.* the heretics.

which has elapsed since the Lord appeared on earth, have occasionally, along with our martyrs, borne the reproach of the name (as if he too [the heretic] had obtained mercy), and have been led forth with them [to death], being, as it were, a sort of retinue granted unto them. For the church alone sustains with purity the reproach of those who suffer persecution for righteousness' sake, and endure all sorts of punishments, and are put to death because of the love which they bear to God, and their confession of His Son; often weakened indeed, yet immediately increasing her members, and becoming whole again, after the same manner as her type,[1] Lot's wife, who became a pillar of salt. Thus, too, [she passes through an experience] similar to that of the ancient prophets, as the Lord declares, "For so persecuted they the prophets who were before you;"[2] inasmuch as she does indeed, in a new fashion, suffer persecution from those who do not receive the word of God, while the self-same spirit rests upon her[3] [as upon these ancient prophets].

10. And indeed the prophets, along with other things which they predicted, also foretold this, that all those on whom the Spirit of God should rest, and who would obey the word of the Father, and serve Him according to their ability, should suffer persecution, and be stoned and slain. For the prophets prefigured in themselves all these things, because of their love to God, and on account of His word. For since they themselves were members of Christ, each one of them in his place as a member did, in accordance with this, set forth the prophecy [assigned him]; all of them, although many, prefiguring only one, and proclaiming the things which pertain to one. For just as the working of the whole body is exhibited through means of our members, while the figure of a complete man is not displayed by one member, but through means of all taken together, so also did all the prophets prefigure the one [Christ]; while every one of them, in his special place as a member, did, in accordance with this, fill up the [established] dispensation, and shadowed forth beforehand that particular working of Christ which was connected with that member.

[1] Comp. above, xxxi. 2. [2] Matt. v. 12. [3] Comp. 1 Pet. iv. 14.

11. For some of them, beholding Him in glory, saw His glorious life (*conversationem*) at the Father's right hand;[1] others beheld Him coming on the clouds as the Son of man;[2] and those who declared regarding Him, "They shall look on Him whom they have pierced,"[3] indicated His [second] advent, concerning which He Himself says, "Thinkest thou that when the Son of man cometh, He shall find faith on the earth?"[4] Paul also refers to this event when he says, "If, however, it is a righteous thing with God to recompense tribulation to them that trouble you, and to you that are troubled rest with us, at the revelation of the Lord Jesus from heaven, with His mighty angels, and in a flame of fire."[5] Others again, speaking of Him as a judge, and [referring], as if it were a burning furnace, [to] the day of the Lord, who "gathers the wheat into His barn, but will burn up the chaff with unquenchable fire,"[6] were accustomed to threaten those who were unbelieving, concerning whom also the Lord Himself declares, "Depart from me, ye cursed, into everlasting fire, which my Father has prepared for the devil and his angels."[7] And the apostle in like manner says [of them], "Who shall be punished with everlasting death from the face of the Lord, and from the glory of His power, when He shall come to be glorified in His saints, and to be admired in those who believe in Him."[8] There are also some [of them] who declare, "Thou art fairer than the children of men;"[9] and, "God, Thy God, hath anointed Thee with the oil of gladness above Thy fellows;"[10] and, "Gird Thy sword upon Thy thigh, O most Mighty, with Thy beauty and Thy fairness, and go forward and proceed prosperously; and rule Thou because of truth, and meekness, and righteousness."[11] And whatever other things of a like nature are spoken regarding Him, these indicated that beauty and splendour which exist in His

---

[1] Isa. vi. 1; Ps. cx. 1.   [2] Dan. vii. 13.   [3] Zech. xii. 10.
[4] Luke xviii. 8. There is nothing to correspond with "putas" in the received text.
[5] 2 Thess. i. 6–8.   [6] Matt. iii. 12.   [7] Matt. xxv. 41.
[8] 2 Thess. i. 9, 10.   [9] Ps. xlv. 2.   [10] Ps. xlv. 7.
[11] Ps. xlv. 3, 4.

kingdom, along with the transcendent and pre-eminent exaltation [belonging] to all who are under His sway, that those who hear might desire to be found there, doing such things as are pleasing to God. Again, there are those who say, "He is a man, and who shall know him?"[1] and, "I came unto the prophetess, and she bare a son, and His name is called Wonderful, Counsellor, the Mighty God;"[2] and those [of them] who proclaimed Him as Immanuel, [born] of the Virgin, exhibited the union of the Word of God with His own workmanship, [declaring] that the Word should become flesh, and the Son of God the Son of man (the pure One opening purely that pure womb which regenerates men unto God, and which He Himself made pure); and having become this which we also are, He [nevertheless] is the Mighty God, and possesses a generation which cannot be declared. And there are also some of them who say, "The Lord hath spoken in Zion, and uttered His voice from Jerusalem;"[3] and, "In Judah is God known;"[4]—these indicated His advent which took place in Judea. Those, again, who declare that "God comes from the south, and from a mountain thick with foliage,"[5] announced His advent at Bethlehem, as I have pointed out in the preceding book.[6] From that place, also, He who rules, and who feeds the people of His Father, has come. Those, again, who declare that at His coming "the lame man shall leap as an hart, and the tongue of the dumb shall [speak] plainly, and the eyes of the blind shall be opened, and the ears of the deaf shall hear,"[7] and that "the hands which hang down, and the feeble knees, shall be strengthened,"[8] and that "the dead which are in the grave shall arise,"[9] and that He Himself "shall take [upon Him] our weaknesses, and bear our sorrows,"[10]—[all these] pro-

---

[1] Jer. xvii. 9 (Sept.). Harvey here remarks: "The LXX read אֱנוֹשׁ instead of אֲנֻשׁ. Thus, from a text that teaches us that *the heart is deceitful above all things*, the fathers extract a proof of the manhood of Christ."
[2] Isa. viii. 3, ix. 6, vii. 14. [3] Joel iii. 16. [4] Ps. lxxvi. 1.
[5] Hab. iii. 3. [6] See III. xx. 4. [7] Isa. xxxv. 5, 6.
[8] Isa. xxxv. 3. [9] Isa. xxvi. 19. [10] Isa. liii. 4.

claimed those works of healing which were accomplished by Him.

12. Some of them, moreover—[when they predicted that] as a weak and inglorious man, and as one who knew what it was to bear infirmity,[1] and sitting upon the foal of an ass,[2] He should come to Jerusalem; and that He should give His back to stripes,[3] and His cheeks to palms [which struck Him]; and that He should be led as a sheep to the slaughter;[4] and that He should have vinegar and gall given Him to drink;[5] and that He should be forsaken by His friends and those nearest to Him;[6] and that He should stretch forth His hands the whole day long;[7] and that He should be mocked and maligned by those who looked upon Him;[8] and that His garments should be parted, and lots cast upon His raiment;[9] and that He should be brought down to the dust of death,[10] with all [the other] things of a like nature—prophesied His coming in the character of a man as He entered Jerusalem, in which by His passion and crucifixion He endured all the things which have been mentioned. Others, again, when they said, "The holy Lord remembered His own dead ones who slept in the dust, and came down to them to raise them up, that He might save them,"[11] furnished us with the reason on account of which He suffered all these things. Those, moreover, who said, "In that day, saith the Lord, the sun shall go down at noon, and there shall be darkness over the earth in the clear day; and I will turn your feast days into mourning, and all your songs into lamentation,"[12] plainly announced that obscuration of the sun which at the time of His crucifixion took place from the sixth hour onwards, and that after this event, those days which were their festivals according to the law, and their songs, should be changed into grief and lamentation when they were handed over to the Gentiles.

[1] Isa. liii. 3. [2] Zech. ix. 9. [3] Isa. l. 6.
[4] Isa. liii. 7. [5] Ps. lxix. 21. [6] Ps. xxxviii. 11.
[7] Isa. lxv. 2. [8] Ps. xxii. 7. [9] Ps. xxii. 18.
[10] Ps. xxii. 15.
[11] Compare vol. i. of our translation, pp. 350, 454.
[12] Amos viii. 9, 10.

Jeremiah, too, makes this point still clearer, when he thus speaks concerning Jerusalem: "She that hath born [seven] languisheth; her soul hath become weary; her sun hath gone down while it was yet noon; she hath been confounded, and suffered reproach: the remainder of them will I give to the sword in the sight of their enemies."[1]

13. Those of them, again, who spoke of His having slumbered and taken sleep, and of His having risen again because the Lord sustained Him,[2] and who enjoined the principalities of heaven to set open the everlasting doors, that the King of glory might go in,[3] proclaimed beforehand His resurrection from the dead through the Father's power, and His reception into heaven. And when they expressed themselves thus, " His going forth is from the height of heaven, and His returning even to the highest heaven; and there is no one who can hide himself from His heat,"[4] they announced that very truth of His being taken up again to the place from which He came down, and that there is no one who can escape His righteous judgment. And those who said, "The Lord hath reigned; let the people be enraged: [even] He who sitteth upon the cherubim; let the earth be moved,"[5] were thus predicting partly that wrath from all nations which after His ascension came upon those who believed in Him, with the movement of the whole earth against the church; and partly the fact that, when He comes from heaven with His mighty angels, the whole earth shall be shaken, as He Himself declares, "There shall be a great earthquake, such as has not been from the beginning."[6] And again, when one says, "Whosoever is judged, let him stand opposite; and whosoever is justified, let him draw near to the servant[7] of God;"[8] and, "Woe unto you, for ye shall all wax old as doth a garment, and the moth shall eat you up;" and, "All flesh shall be humbled, and the Lord alone shall be exalted in the highest,"[9]—it is thus indicated that, after His passion and ascension, God shall cast down under His feet all who were

---

[1] Jer. xv. 9.   [2] Ps. iii. 5.   [3] Ps. xxiv. 7.
[4] Ps. xix. 6.   [5] Ps. xcix. 1.   [6] Matt. xxiv. 21.
[7] Or "son."   [8] Isa. l. 8, 9 (loosely quoted).   [9] Isa. ii. 17.

opposed to Him, and He shall be exalted above all, and there shall be no one who can be justified or compared to Him.

14. And those of them who declare that God would make a new covenant[1] with men, not such as that which He made with the fathers at Mount Horeb, and would give to men a new heart and a new spirit;[2] and again, "And remember ye not the things of old: behold, I make new things which shall now arise, and ye shall know it; and I will make a way in the desert, and rivers in a dry land, to give drink to my chosen people, my people whom I have acquired, that they may show forth my praise,"[3]—plainly announced that liberty which distinguishes the new covenant, and the new wine which is put into new bottles,[4] [that is], the faith which is in Christ, by which He has proclaimed the way of righteousness sprung up in the desert, and the streams of the Holy Spirit in a dry land, to give water to the elect people of God, whom He has acquired, that they might show forth His praise, but not that they might blaspheme Him who made these things, that is, God.

15. And all those other points which I have shown the prophets to have uttered by means of so long a series of Scriptures, he who is truly spiritual will interpret by pointing out, in regard to every one of the things which have been spoken, to what special point in the dispensation of the Lord it referred, and [by thus exhibiting] the entire system of the work of the Son of God, knowing always the same God, and always acknowledging the same Word of God, although He has [but] now been manifested to us; acknowledging also at all times the same Spirit of God, although He has been poured out upon us after a new fashion in these last times, [knowing that He descends] even from the creation of the world to its end upon the human race simply as such, from whom those who believe God and follow His word receive that salvation which flows from Him. Those, on the other hand, who depart from Him, and despise His precepts, and by their deeds bring dishonour on Him who made them, and

[1] Jer. xxxi. 31, 32.
[2] Ezek. xxxvi. 26.
[3] Isa. xliii. 19-21.
[4] Matt. ix. 17.

by their opinions blaspheme Him who nourishes them, heap up against themselves most righteous judgment.[1] He therefore (*i.e.* the spiritual man) sifts and tries them all, but he himself is tried by no man:[2] he neither blasphemes his Father, nor sets aside His dispensations, nor inveighs against the fathers, nor dishonours the prophets, by maintaining that they were [sent] from another God [than he worships], or again, that their prophecies were derived from different sources.[3]

CHAP. XXXIV.—*Proof against the Marcionites, that the prophets referred in all their predictions to our Christ.*

1. Now I shall simply say, in opposition to all the heretics, and principally against the followers of Marcion, and against those who are like to these, in maintaining that the prophets were from another God [than He who is announced in the gospel], read with earnest care that gospel which has been conveyed to us by the apostles, and read with earnest care the prophets, and you will find that the whole conduct, and all the doctrine, and all the sufferings of our Lord, were predicted through them. But if a thought of this kind should then suggest itself to you, to say, What then did the Lord bring to us by His advent?—know ye that He brought all [possible] novelty, by bringing Himself who had been announced. For this very thing was proclaimed beforehand, that a novelty should come to renew and quicken mankind. For the advent of the King is previously announced by those servants who are sent [before Him], in order to the preparation and equipment of those men who are to entertain their Lord. But when the King has actually come, and those who are His subjects have been filled with that joy which was proclaimed beforehand, and have attained to that liberty which He bestows, and share in the sight of Him, and have listened to His words, and have enjoyed the gifts which He confers, the question will not then be asked by any that are

---

[1] Rom. ii. 5.   [2] 1 Cor. ii. 15.
[3] "Ex alia et alia substantia fuisse prophetias."

possessed of sense what new thing the King has brought beyond [that proclaimed by] those who announced His coming. For He has brought Himself, and has bestowed on men those good things which were announced beforehand, which things the angels desired to look into.[1]

2. But the servants would then have been proved false, and not sent by the Lord, if Christ on His advent, by being found exactly such as He was previously announced, had not fulfilled their words. Wherefore He said, "Think not that I have come to destroy the law or the prophets; I came not to destroy, but to fulfil. For verily I say unto you, Until heaven and earth pass away, one jot or one tittle shall not pass from the law and the prophets till all come to pass."[2] For by His advent He Himself fulfilled all things, and does still fulfil in the church the new covenant foretold by the law, onwards to the consummation [of all things]. To this effect also Paul, His apostle, says in the Epistle to the Romans, "But now,[3] without the law, has the righteousness of God been manifested, being witnessed by the law and the prophets; for the just shall live by faith."[4] But this fact, that the just shall live by faith, had been previously announced[5] by the prophets.

3. But whence could the prophets have had power to predict the advent of the King, and to preach beforehand that liberty which was bestowed by Him, and previously to announce all things which were done by Christ, His words, His works, and His sufferings, and to predict the new covenant, if they had received prophetical inspiration from another God [than He who is revealed in the gospel], they being ignorant, as ye allege, of the ineffable Father, of His kingdom, and His dispensations, which the Son of God fulfilled when He came upon earth in these last times? Neither are ye in a position to say that these things came to pass by a certain kind of chance, as if they were spoken by the prophets in regard to some other person, while like events happened to

---

[1] 1 Pet. i. 12.
[2] Matt. v. 17, 18.
[3] Rom. iii. 21.
[4] Rom. i. 17.
[5] Hab. ii. 4.

the Lord. For all the prophets prophesied these same things, but they never came to pass in the case of any one of the ancients. For if these things had happened to any man among them of old time, those [prophets] who lived subsequently would certainly not have prophesied that these events should come to pass in the last times. Moreover, there is in fact none among the fathers, nor the prophets, nor the ancient kings, in whose case any one of these things properly and specifically took place. For all indeed prophesied as to the sufferings of Christ, but they themselves were far from enduring sufferings similar to what was predicted. And the points connected with the passion of the Lord, which were foretold, were realized in no other case. For neither did it happen at the death of any man among the ancients that the sun set at mid-day, nor was the veil of the temple rent, nor did the earth quake, nor were the rocks rent, nor did the dead rise up, nor was any one of these men [of old] raised up on the third day, nor received into heaven, nor at his assumption were the heavens opened, nor did the nations believe in the name of any other; nor did any from among them, having been dead and rising again, lay open the new covenant of liberty. Therefore the prophets spake not of any one else but of the Lord, in whom all these aforesaid tokens concurred.

4. If any one, however, advocating the cause of the Jews, do maintain that this new covenant consisted in the rearing of that temple which was built under Zerubbabel after the emigration to Babylon, and in the departure of the people from thence after the lapse of seventy years, let him know that the temple constructed of stones was indeed then rebuilt (for as yet that law was observed which had been made upon tables of stone), yet no new covenant was given, but they used the Mosaic law until the coming of the Lord; but from the Lord's advent, the new covenant which brings back peace, and the law which gives life, has gone forth over the whole earth, as the prophets said: "For out of Zion shall go forth the law, and the word of the Lord from Jerusalem; and He shall rebuke many people; and they shall break down their swords into ploughshares, and their spears into pruning-

hooks, and they shall no longer learn to fight."[1] If therefore another law and word, going forth from Jerusalem, brought in such a [reign of] peace among the Gentiles which received it (the word), and convinced, through them, many a nation of its folly, then [only] it appears that the prophets spake of some other person. But if the law of liberty, that is, the word of God, preached by the apostles (who went forth from Jerusalem) throughout all the earth, caused such a change in the state of things, that these [nations] did form the swords and war-lances into ploughshares, and changed them into pruning-hooks for reaping the corn, [that is], into instruments used for peaceful purposes, and that they are now unaccustomed to fighting, but when smitten, offer also the other cheek,[2] then the prophets have not spoken these things of any other person, but of Him who effected them. This person is our Lord, and in Him is that declaration borne out; since it is He Himself who has made the plough, and introduced the pruning-hook, that is, the first semination of man, which was the creation exhibited in Adam,[3] and the gathering in of the produce in the last times by the Word; and, for this reason, since He joined the beginning to the end, and is the Lord of both, He has finally displayed the plough, in that the wood has been joined on to the iron, and has thus cleansed His land; because the Word, having been firmly united to flesh, and in its mechanism fixed with pins,[4] has reclaimed the savage earth. In the beginning, He figured forth the pruning-hook by means of Abel, pointing out that there should be a gathering in of a righteous race of men. He says, "For behold how the just man perishes, and no man considers it; and righteous men are taken away, and no man layeth it to heart."[5] These things were acted beforehand in Abel, were also previously declared by the prophets,

---

[1] Isa. ii. 3, 4; Mic. iv. 2, 3.   [2] Matt. v. 39.   [3] Vol. i. p. 40.
[4] This is following Harvey's conjectural emendation of the text, viz. "taleis" for "talis." He considers the *pins* here as symbolical of the *nails* by which our Lord was fastened to the cross. The whole passage is almost hopelessly obscure, though the general meaning may be guessed.
[5] Isa. lvii. 1.

but were accomplished in the Lord's person; and the same [is still true] with regard to us, the body following the example of the Head.

5. Such are the arguments proper [to be used] in opposition to those who maintain that the prophets [were inspired] by a different God, and that our Lord [came] from another Father, if perchance [these heretics] may at length desist from such extreme folly. This is my earnest object in adducing these scriptural proofs, that confuting them, as far as in me lies, by these very passages, I may restrain them from such great blasphemy, and from insanely fabricating a multitude of gods.

CHAP. XXXV.—*A refutation of those who allege that the prophets uttered some predictions under the inspiration of the Highest, others from the Demiurge. Disagreements of the Valentinians among themselves with regard to these same predictions.*

1. Then again, in opposition to the Valentinians, and the other Gnostics, falsely so called, who maintain that some parts of Scripture were spoken at one time from the Pleroma (*a summitate*) through means of the seed [derived] from that place, but at another time from the intermediate abode through means of the audacious mother Prunica, but that many are due to the Creator of the world, from whom also the prophets had their mission, we say that it is altogether irrational to bring down the Father of the universe to such straits, as that He should not be possessed of His own proper instruments, by which the things in the Pleroma might be perfectly proclaimed. For of whom was He afraid, so that He should not reveal His will after His own way and independently, freely, and without being involved with that spirit which came into being in a state of degeneracy and ignorance? Was it that He feared that very many would be saved, when more should have listened to the unadulterated truth? Or, on the other hand, was He incapable of preparing for Himself those who should announce the Saviour's advent?

2. But if, when the Saviour came to this earth, He sent

His apostles into the world to proclaim with accuracy His advent, and to teach the Father's will, having nothing in common with the doctrine of the Gentiles or of the Jews, much more, while yet existing in the Pleroma, would He have appointed His own heralds to proclaim His future advent into this world, and having nothing in common with those prophecies originating from the Demiurge. But if, when within the Pleroma, He availed Himself of those prophets who were under the law, and declared His own matters through their instrumentality; much more would He, upon His arrival hither, have made use of these same teachers, and have preached the gospel to us by their means. Therefore let them not any longer assert that Peter and Paul and the other apostles proclaimed the truth, but that it was the scribes and Pharisees, and the others, through whom the law was propounded. But if, at His advent, He sent forth His own apostles in the spirit of truth, and not in that of error, He did the very same also in the case of the prophets; for the Word of God was always the selfsame: and if the Spirit from the Pleroma was, according to these men's system, the Spirit of light, the Spirit of truth, the Spirit of perfection, and the Spirit of knowledge, while that from the Demiurge was the spirit of ignorance, degeneracy, and error, and the offspring of obscurity; how can it be, that in one and the same being there exist perfection and defect, knowledge and ignorance, error and truth, light and darkness? But if it was impossible that such should happen in the case of the prophets, for they preached the word of the Lord from one God, and proclaimed the advent of His Son, much more would the Lord Himself never have uttered words, on one occasion from above, but on another from degeneracy below, thus becoming the teacher at once of knowledge and of ignorance; nor would He have ever glorified as Father at one time the Founder of the world, and at another Him who is above this one, as He does Himself declare: "No man putteth a piece of a new garment upon an old one, nor do they put new wine into old bottles."[1] Let these men, there-

[1] Luke v. 36, 37.

fore, either have nothing whatever to do with the prophets, as with those that are ancients, and allege no longer that these men, being sent beforehand by the Demiurge, spake certain things under that new influence which pertains to the Pleroma; or, on the other hand, let them be convinced by our Lord, when He declares that new wine cannot be put into old bottles.

3. But from what source could the offspring of their mother derive his knowledge of the mysteries within the Pleroma, and power to discourse regarding them? Suppose that the mother, while beyond the Pleroma, did bring forth this very offspring; but what is beyond the Pleroma they represent as being beyond the pale of knowledge, that is, ignorance. How, then, could that seed, which was conceived in ignorance, possess the power of declaring knowledge? Or how did the mother herself, a shapeless and undefined being, one cast out of doors as an abortion, obtain knowledge of the mysteries within the Pleroma, she who was organized outside it and given a form there, and prohibited by Horos from entering within, and who remains outside the Pleroma till the consummation [of all things], that is, beyond the pale of knowledge? Then, again, when they say that the Lord's passion is a type of the extension of the Christ above, which he effected through Horos, and so imparted a form to their mother, they are refuted in the other particulars [of the Lord's passion], for they have no semblance of a type to show with regard to them. For when did the Christ above have vinegar and gall given him to drink? Or when was his raiment parted? Or when was he pierced, and blood and water came forth? Or when did he sweat great drops of blood? And [the same may be demanded] as to the other particulars which happened to the Lord, of which the prophets have spoken. From whence, then, did the mother or her offspring divine the things which had not yet taken place, but which should occur afterwards?

4. They affirm that certain things still, besides these, were spoken from the Pleroma, but are confuted by those which are referred to in the Scriptures as bearing on the advent of Christ.

But what these are [that are spoken from the Pleroma] they are not agreed, but give different answers regarding them. For if any one, wishing to test them, do question one by one with regard to any passage those who are their leading men, he shall find one of them referring the passage in question to the Propator—that is, to Bythus; another attributing it to Arche—that is, to the Only-begotten; another to the Father of all—that is, to the Word; while another, again, will say that it was spoken of that one Æon who was [formed from the joint contributions] of the Æons in the Pleroma;[1] others [will regard the passage] as referring to Christ, while another [will refer it] to the Saviour. One, again, more skilled than these,[2] after a long protracted silence, declares that it was spoken of Horos; another that it signifies the Sophia which is within the Pleroma; another that it announces the mother outside the Pleroma; while another will mention the God who made the world (the Demiurge). Such are the variations existing among them with regard to one [passage], holding discordant opinions as to the same Scriptures; and when the same identical passage is read out, they all begin to purse up their eyebrows, and to shake their heads, and they say that they might indeed utter a discourse transcendently lofty, but that all cannot comprehend the greatness of that thought which is implied in it; and that, therefore, among the wise the chief thing is silence. For that Sige (*silence*) which is above must be typified by that silence which they preserve. Thus do they, as many as they are, all depart [from each other], holding so many opinions as to one thing, and bearing about their clever notions in secret within themselves. When, therefore, they shall have agreed among themselves as to the things predicted in the Scriptures, then also shall they be confuted by us. For, though holding wrong opinions, they do in the meanwhile, however, convict themselves, since they are not of one mind with regard to the same words. But as we follow for our teacher the one and only true God, and possess His words as the rule of truth, we do all speak alike with

---

[1] Vol. i. p. 11.

[2] Illorum; following the Greek form of the comparative degree.

regard to the same things, knowing but one God, the Creator of this universe, who sent the prophets, who led forth the people from the land of Egypt, who in these last times manifested His own Son, that He might put the unbelievers to confusion, and search out the fruit of righteousness.

CHAP. XXXVI.—*The prophets were sent from one and the same Father from whom the Son was sent.*

1. Which [God] the Lord does not reject, nor does He say that the prophets [spake] from another god than His Father; nor from any other essence, but from one and the same Father; nor that any other being made the things in the world, except His own Father, when He speaks as follows in His teaching: "There was a certain householder, and he planted a vineyard, and hedged it round about, and digged in it a winepress, and built a tower, and let it out to husbandmen, and went into a far country: And when the time of the fruit drew near, he sent his servants unto the husbandmen, that they might receive the fruits of it. And the husbandmen took his servants: they cut one to pieces, stoned another, and killed another. Again he sent other servants more than the first: and they did unto them likewise. But last of all he sent unto them his only son, saying, Perchance they will reverence my son. But when the husbandmen saw the son, they said among themselves, This is the heir; come, let us kill him, and we shall possess his inheritance. And they caught him, and cast him out of the vineyard, and slew him. When, therefore, the lord of the vineyard shall come, what will he do unto these husbandmen? They say unto him, He will miserably destroy these wicked men, and will let out his vineyard to other husbandmen, who shall render him the fruits in their seasons."[1] Again does the Lord say: "Have ye never read, The stone which the builders rejected, the same is become the head of the corner: this is the Lord's doing, and it is marvellous in our eyes? Therefore I say unto you, that the kingdom of God shall be

[1] Matt. xxi. 33–41.

taken from you, and given to a nation bringing forth the fruits thereof."[1] By these words He clearly points out to His disciples one and the same Householder—that is, one God the Father, who made all things by Himself; while [He shows] that there are various husbandmen, some obstinate, and proud, and worthless, and slayers of the Lord, but others who render Him, with all obedience, the fruits in their seasons; and that it is the same Householder who sends at one time His servants, at another His Son. From that Father, therefore, from whom the Son was sent to those husbandmen who slew Him, from Him also were the servants [sent]. But the Son, as coming from the Father with supreme authority (*principali auctoritate*), used to express Himself thus: "But I say unto you."[2] The servants, again, [who came] as from their Lord, spake after the manner of servants, [delivering a message]; and they therefore used to say, "Thus saith the Lord."

2. Whom these men did therefore preach to the unbelievers as Lord, Him did Christ teach to those who obey Him; and the God who had called those of the former dispensation, is the same as He who has received those of the latter. In other words, He who at first used that law which entails bondage, is also He who did in after times [call His people] by means of adoption. For God planted the vineyard of the human race when at the first He formed Adam and chose the fathers; then He let it out to husbandmen when He established the Mosaic dispensation: He hedged it round about, that is, He gave particular instructions with regard to their worship: He built a tower, [that is], He chose Jerusalem: He digged a winepress, that is, He prepared a receptacle of the prophetic Spirit. And thus did He send prophets prior to the transmigration to Babylon, and after that event others again in greater number than the former, to seek the fruits, saying thus to them (the Jews): "Thus saith the Lord, Cleanse your ways and your doings, execute just judgment, and look each one with pity and compassion on his brother: oppress not the widow nor the orphan, the proselyte nor the

[1] Matt. xxi. 42-44.   [2] Matt. v. 22.

poor, and let none of you treasure up evil against his brother in your hearts, and love not false swearing. Wash you, make ye clean, put away evil from your hearts, learn to do well, seek judgment, protect the oppressed, judge the fatherless (*pupillo*), plead for the widow; and come, let us reason together, saith the Lord."[1] And again: "Keep thy tongue from evil, and thy lips that they speak no guile; depart from evil, and do good; seek peace, and pursue it."[2] In preaching these things, the prophets sought the fruits of righteousness. But last of all He sent to those unbelievers His own Son, our Lord Jesus Christ, whom the wicked husbandmen cast out of the vineyard when they had slain Him. Wherefore the Lord God did even give it up (no longer hedged around, but thrown open throughout all the world) to other husbandmen, who render the fruits in their seasons,—the beautiful elect tower being also raised everywhere. For the illustrious church is [now] everywhere, and everywhere is the winepress digged: because those who do receive the Spirit are everywhere. For inasmuch as the former have rejected the Son of God, and cast Him out of the vineyard when they slew Him, God has justly rejected them, and given to the Gentiles outside the vineyard the fruits of its cultivation. This is in accordance with what Jeremiah says, "The Lord hath rejected and cast off the nation which does these things; for the children of Judah have done evil in my sight, saith the Lord."[3] And again in like manner does Jeremiah speak: "I set watchmen over you; hearken to the sound of the trumpet; and they said, We will not hearken. Therefore have the Gentiles heard, and they who feed the flocks in them."[4] It is therefore one and the same Father who planted the vineyard, who led forth the people, who sent the prophets, who sent His own Son, and who gave the vineyard to those other husbandmen that render the fruits in their season.

3. And therefore did the Lord say to His disciples, to make us become good workmen: "Take heed to yourselves, and watch continually upon every occasion, lest at any time your

---

[1] Jer. vii. 3; Zech. vii. 9, 10, viii. 17; Isa. i. 17-19.
[2] Ps. xxxiv. 13, 14.   [3] Jer. vii. 29, 30.   [4] Jer. vi. 17, 18.

hearts be overcharged with surfeiting and drunkenness, and cares of this life, and that day shall come upon you unawares; for as a snare shall it come upon all dwelling upon the face of the earth."[1] "Let your loins, therefore, be girded about, and your lights burning, and ye like to men who wait for their lord, when he shall return from the wedding."[2] "For as it was in the days of Noe, they did eat and drink, they bought and sold, they married and were given in marriage, and they knew not, until Noe entered into the ark, and the flood came and destroyed them all; as also it was in the days of Lot, they did eat and drink, they bought and sold, they planted and builded, until the time that Lot went out of Sodom.; it rained fire from heaven, and destroyed them all: so shall it also be at the coming of the Son of man."[3] "Watch ye therefore, for ye know not in what day your Lord shall come."[4] [In these passages] He declares one and the same Lord, who in the times of Noah brought the deluge because of men's disobedience, and who also in the days of Lot rained fire from heaven because of the multitude of sinners among the Sodomites, and who, on account of this same disobedience and similar sins, will bring on the day of judgment at the end of time (*in novissimo*); on which day He declares that it shall be more tolerable for Sodom and Gomorrah than for that city and house which shall not receive the word of His apostles. "And thou, Capernaum," He said, "is it that thou shalt be exalted to heaven?[5] Thou shalt go down to hell. For if the mighty works which have been done in thee had been done in Sodom, it would have remained unto this day. Verily I say unto you, that it shall be more tolerable for Sodom in the day of judgment than for you."[6]

4. Since the Son of God is always one and the same, He gives to those who believe on Him a well of water[7] [springing

---

[1] Luke xxi. 34, 35.   [2] Luke xii. 35, 36.
[3] Luke xvii. 26, etc.   [4] Matt. xxiv. 42.
[5] No other of the Greek fathers quotes this text as above; from which fact Grabe infers that the old Latin translator, or his transcribers, altered the words of Irenæus to suit the Latin versions.
[6] Matt. xi. 23, 24.   [7] John iv. 14.

up] to eternal life, but He causes the unfruitful fig-tree immediately to dry up; and in the days of Noah He justly brought on the deluge for the purpose of extinguishing that most infamous race of men then existent, who could not bring forth fruit to God, since the angels that sinned had commingled with them, and [acted as He did] in order that He might put a check upon the sins of these men, but [that at the same time] He might preserve the archetype,[1] the formation of Adam. And it was He who rained fire and brimstone from heaven, in the days of Lot, upon Sodom and Gomorrah, "an example of the righteous judgment of God,"[2] that all may know, "that every tree that bringeth not forth good fruit shall be cut down, and cast into the fire."[3] And it is He who uses [the words], that it will be more tolerable for Sodom in the general judgment than for those who beheld His wonders, and did not believe on Him, nor receive His doctrine.[4] For as He gave by His advent a greater privilege to those who believed on Him, and who do His will, so also did He point out that those who did not believe on Him should have a more severe punishment in the judgment; thus extending equal justice to all, and being to exact more from those to whom He gives the more; the more, however, not because He reveals the knowledge of another Father, as I have shown so fully and so repeatedly, but because He has, by means of His advent, poured upon the human race the greater gift of paternal grace.

5. If, however, what I have stated be insufficient to convince any one that the prophets were sent from one and the same Father, from whom also our Lord was sent, let such a one, opening the mouth of his heart, and calling upon the Master, Christ Jesus the Lord, listen to Him when He says,

---

[1] This is Massuet's conjectural emendation of the text, viz. *archetypum* for *arcætypum*. Grabe would insert *per* before *arcæ*, and he thinks the passage to have a reference to 1 Pet. iii. 20. Irenæus, in common with the other ancient fathers, believed that the fallen angels were the "sons of God" who commingled with "the daughters of men," and thus produced a race of spurious men.

[2] Jude 7.   [3] Matt. iii. 10.   [4] Matt. xi. 24; Luke x. 12.

"The kingdom of heaven is like unto a king who made a marriage for his son, and he sent forth his servants to call them who were bidden to the marriage." And when they would not obey, He goes on to say, "Again he sent other servants, saying, Tell them that are bidden, Come ye, I have prepared my dinner; my oxen and all the fatlings are killed, and everything is ready; come unto the wedding. But they made light of it, and went their way, some to their farm, and others to their merchandize; but the remnant took his servants, and some they treated despitefully, while others they slew. But when the king heard this, he was wroth, and sent his armies and destroyed these murderers, and burned up their city, and said to his servants, The wedding is indeed ready, but they which were bidden were not worthy. Go out therefore into the highways, and as many as ye shall find, gather in to the marriage. So the servants went out, and collected together as many as they found, bad and good, and the wedding was furnished with guests. But when the king came in to see the guests, he saw there a man not having on a wedding garment; and he said unto him, Friend, how camest thou hither, not having on a wedding garment? But he was speechless. Then said the king to his servants, Take him away, hand and foot, and cast him into outer darkness: there shall be weeping and gnashing of teeth. For many are called, but few are chosen."[1] Now, by these words of His, does the Lord clearly show all [these points, viz.] that there is one King and Lord, the Father of all, of whom He had previously said, "Neither shalt thou swear by Jerusalem, for it is the city of the great King;"[2] and that He had from the beginning prepared the marriage for His Son, and used, with the utmost kindness, to call, by the instrumentality of His servants, the men of the former dispensation to the wedding feast; and when they would not obey, He still invited them by sending out other servants, yet that even then they did not obey Him, but even stoned and slew

---

[1] Matt. xxii. 1, etc.

[2] Matt. v. 35. Instead of placing a period here, as the editors do, it seems to us preferable to carry on the construction.

those who brought them the message of invitation. He accordingly sent forth His armies and destroyed them, and burned down their city; but He called together from all the highways, that is, from all nations, [guests] to the marriage feast of His Son, as also He says by Jeremiah: "I have sent also unto you my servants the prophets to say, Return ye now, every man, from his very evil way, and amend your doings."[1] And again He says by the same prophet: "I have also sent unto you my servants the prophets throughout the day and before the light; yet they did not obey me, nor incline their ears unto me. And thou shalt speak this word to them: This is a people that obeyeth not the voice of the Lord, nor receiveth correction; faith has perished from their mouth."[2] The Lord, therefore, who has called us everywhere by the apostles, is He who called those of old by the prophets, as appears by the words of the Lord; and although they preached to various nations, the prophets were not from one God, and the apostles from another; but, [proceeding] from one and the same, some of them announced the Lord, others preached the Father, and others again foretold the advent of the Son of God, while yet others declared Him as already present to those who then were afar off.

6. Still further did He also make it manifest, that we ought, after our calling, to be also adorned with works of righteousness, so that the Spirit of God may rest upon us; for this is the wedding garment, of which also the apostle speaks, "Not for that we would be unclothed, but clothed upon, that mortality might be swallowed up by immortality."[3] But those who have indeed been called to God's supper, yet have not received the Holy Spirit, because of their wicked conduct "shall be," He declares, "cast into outer darkness."[4] He thus clearly shows that the very same King who gathered from all quarters the faithful to the marriage of His Son, and who grants them the incorruptible banquet, [also] orders that man to be cast into outer darkness who has not on a wedding garment, that is, one who despises it. For as in

[1] Jer. xxxv. 15.   [2] Jer. vii. 25, etc.
[3] 2 Cor. v. 4.   [4] Matt. xxii. 13.

the former covenant, "with many of them was He not well pleased;"[1] so also is it the case here, that "many are called, but few chosen."[2] It is not, then, one God who judges, and another Father who calls us together to salvation; nor one, forsooth, who confers eternal light, but another who orders those who have not on the wedding garment to be sent into outer darkness. But it is one and the same God, the Father of our Lord, from whom also the prophets had their mission, who does indeed, through His infinite kindness, call the unworthy; but He examines those who are called, [to ascertain] if they have on the garment fit and proper for the marriage of His Son, because nothing unbecoming or evil pleases Him. This is in accordance with what the Lord said to the man who had been healed: "Behold, thou art made whole; sin no more, lest a worse thing come unto thee." For He who is good, and righteous, and pure, and spotless, will endure nothing evil, nor unjust, nor detestable in His wedding chamber. This is the Father of our Lord, by whose providence all things consist, and all are administered by His command; and He confers His free gifts upon those who should [receive them]; but the most righteous Retributor metes out [punishment] according to their deserts, most deservedly, to the ungrateful and to those that are insensible of His kindness; and therefore does He say, "He sent His armies, and destroyed those murderers, and burned up their city."[4] He says here, "His armies," because all men are the property of God. For "the earth is the Lord's, and the fulness thereof; the world, and all that dwell therein."[5] Wherefore also the Apostle Paul says in the Epistle to the Romans, "For there is no power but of God; the powers that be are ordained of God. Whosoever resisteth the power, resisteth the ordinance of God; and they that resist shall receive unto themselves condemnation. For rulers are not for a terror to a good work, but to an evil. Wilt thou then not be afraid of the power? Do that which is good, and thou shalt have praise of the same; for he is the minister of God to thee for good. But if thou do that

[1] 1 Cor. x. 5.   [2] Matt. xxii. 14.   [3] John v. 14.
[4] Matt. xxii. 7.   [5] Ps. xxiv. 1.

which is evil, be afraid; for he beareth not the sword in vain: for he is the minister of God, the avenger for wrath upon him that doeth evil. Wherefore ye must needs be subject, not only for wrath, but also for conscience sake. For this cause pay ye tribute also; for they are God's ministers, attending continually upon this very thing."[1] Both the Lord, then, and the apostles announce as the one only God the Father, Him who gave the law, who sent the prophets, who made all things; and therefore does He say " He sent His armies," because every man, inasmuch as he is a man, is His workmanship, although he may be ignorant of his God. For He gives existence to all; He, " who maketh His sun to rise upon the evil and the good, and sendeth rain upon the just and unjust."[2]

7. And not alone by what has been stated, but also by the parable of the two sons, the younger of whom consumed his substance by living luxuriously with harlots, did the Lord teach one and the same Father, who did not even allow a kid to his elder son; but for him who had been lost, [namely] his younger son, he ordered the fatted calf to be killed, and he gave him the best robe.[3] Also by the parable of the workmen who were sent into the vineyard at different periods of the day, one and the same God is declared[4] as having called some in the beginning, when the world was first created; but others afterwards, and others during the intermediate period, others after a long lapse of time, and others again in the end of time; so that there are many workmen in their generations, but only one householder who calls them together. For there is but one vineyard, since there is also but one righteousness, and one dispensator, for there is one Spirit of God who arranges all things; and in like manner is there one hire, for they all received a penny each man, having [stamped upon it] the royal image and superscription, the knowledge of the Son of God, which is immortality. And therefore He began by giving the hire to those [who were engaged] last, because in the last times, when the Lord was revealed, He presented Himself to all [as their reward].

8. Then, in the case of the publican, who excelled the

[1] Rom. xiii. 1-7. [2] Matt. v. 45. [3] Luke xv. 11. [4] Matt. xx. 1, etc.

Pharisee in prayer, [we find] that it was not because he worshipped another Father that he received testimony from the Lord that he was justified rather [than the other]; but because with great humility, apart from all boasting and pride, he made confession to the same God.[1] The parable of the two sons also: those who are sent into the vineyard, of whom one indeed opposed his father, but afterwards repented, when repentance profited him nothing; the other, however, promised to go, at once assuring his father, but he did not go (for "every man is a liar;"[2] "to will is present with him, but he finds not means to perform"[3]),—[this parable, I say], points out one and the same Father. Then, again, this truth was clearly shown forth by the parable of the fig-tree, of which the Lord says, "Behold, now these three years I come seeking fruit on this fig-tree, but I find none"[4] (pointing onwards, by the prophets, to His advent, by whom He came from time to time, seeking the fruit of righteousness from them, which he did not find), and also by the circumstance that, for the reason already mentioned, the fig-tree should be hewn down. And, without using a parable, the Lord said to Jerusalem, "O Jerusalem, Jerusalem, thou that killest the prophets, and stonest those that are sent unto thee; how often would I have gathered thy children together, as a hen gathereth her chickens under her wings, and ye would not! Behold, your house shall be left unto you desolate."[5] For that which had been said in the parable, "Behold, for three years I come seeking fruit," and in clear terms, again, [where He says], "How often would I have gathered thy children together," shall be [found] a falsehood, if we do not understand His advent, which is [announced] by the prophets—if, in fact, He came to them but once, and then for the first time. But since He who chose the patriarchs and those [who lived under the first covenant], is the same Word of God who did both visit them through the prophetic Spirit, and us also who have been called together from all quarters by His advent; in addition to what has been already said, He truly declared,

---

[1] Luke xviii. 10.　　[2] Ps. cxvi. 2.　　[3] Rom. vii. 18.
[4] Luke xiii. 6.　　[5] Luke xiii. 34; Matt. xxiii. 37.

"Many shall come from the east and from the west, and shall recline with Abraham, and Isaac, and Jacob, in the kingdom of heaven. But the children of the kingdom shall go into outer darkness; there shall be weeping and gnashing of teeth."[1] If, then, those who do believe in Him through the preaching of His apostles throughout the east and west shall recline with Abraham, Isaac, and Jacob, in the kingdom of heaven, partaking with them of the [heavenly] banquet, one and the same God is set forth as He who did indeed choose the patriarchs, visited also the people, and called the Gentiles.

CHAP. XXXVII.—*Men are possessed of free will, and endowed with the faculty of making a choice. It is not true, therefore, that some are by nature good, and others bad.*

1. This expression [of our Lord], "How often would I have gathered thy children together, and thou wouldest not,"[2] set forth the ancient law of human liberty, because God made man a free [agent] from the beginning, possessing his own power, even as he does his own soul, to obey the behests (*ad utendum sententia*) of God voluntarily, and not by compulsion of God. For there is no coercion with God, but a good will [towards us] is present with Him continually. And therefore does He give good counsel to all. And in man, as well as in angels, He has placed the power of choice (for angels are rational beings), so that those who had yielded obedience might justly possess what is good, given indeed by God, but preserved by themselves. On the other hand, they who have not obeyed shall, with justice, be not found in possession of the good, and shall receive condign punishment: for God did kindly bestow on them what was good; but they themselves did not diligently keep it, nor deem it something precious, but poured contempt upon His supereminent goodness. Rejecting therefore the good, and as it were spuing it out, they shall all deservedly incur the just judgment of God, which also the Apostle Paul testifies in his Epistle to the Romans, where he says, "But dost thou despise the riches of His goodness, and patience, and long-

---

[1] Matt. viii. 11, 12.   [2] Matt. xxiii. 37.

suffering, being ignorant that the goodness of God leadeth thee to repentance? But according to thy hardness and impenitent heart, thou treasurest to thyself wrath against the day of wrath, and the revelation of the righteous judgment of God." "But glory and honour," he says, "to every one that doeth good."[1] God therefore has given that which is good, as the apostle tells us in this epistle, and they who work it shall receive glory and honour, because they have done that which is good when they had it in their power not to do it; but those who do it not shall receive the just judgment of God, because they did not work good when they had it in their power so to do.

2. But if some had been made by nature bad, and others good, these latter would not be deserving of praise for being good, for such were they created; nor would the former be reprehensible, for thus they were made [originally]. But since all men are of the same nature, able both to hold fast and to do what is good; and, on the other hand, having also the power to cast it from them and not to do it,—some do justly receive praise even among men who are under the control of good laws (and much more from God), and obtain deserved testimony of their choice of good in general, and of persevering therein; but the others are blamed, and receive a just condemnation, because of their rejection of what is fair and good. And therefore the prophets used to exhort men to what was good, to act justly and to work righteousness, as I have so largely demonstrated, because it is in our power so to do, and because by excessive negligence we might become forgetful, and thus stand in need of that good counsel which the good God has given us to know by means of the prophets.

3. For this reason the Lord also said, "Let your light so shine before men, that they may see your good deeds, and glorify your Father who is in heaven."[2] And, "Take heed to yourselves, lest perchance your hearts be overcharged with surfeiting, and drunkenness, and worldly cares."[3] And, "Let your loins be girded about, and your lamps burning, and ye like unto men that wait for their Lord, when He

[1] Rom. ii. 4, 5, 7.   [2] Matt. v. 16.   [3] Luke xxi. 34.

returns from the wedding, that when He cometh and knocketh, they may open to Him. Blessed is that servant whom his Lord, when He cometh, shall find so doing."[1] And again, "The servant who knows his Lord's will, and does it not, shall be beaten with many stripes."[2] And, "Why call ye me, Lord, Lord, and do not the things which I say?"[3] And again, "But if the servant say in his heart, The Lord delayeth, and begin to beat his fellow-servants, and to eat, and drink, and to be drunken, his Lord will come in a day on which he does not expect Him, and shall cut him in sunder, and appoint his portion with the hypocrites."[4] All such passages demonstrate the independent will[5] of man, and at the same time the counsel which God conveys to him, by which He exhorts us to submit ourselves to Him, and seeks to turn us away from [the sin of] unbelief against Him, without, however, in any way coercing us.

4. No doubt, if any one is unwilling to follow the gospel itself, it is in his power [to reject it], but it is not expedient. For it is in man's power to disobey God, and to forfeit what is good; but [such conduct] brings no small amount of injury and mischief. And on this account Paul says, "All things are lawful to me, but all things are not expedient;"[6] referring both to the liberty of man, in which respect "all things are lawful," God exercising no compulsion in regard to him; and [by the expression] "not expedient" pointing out that we "should not use our liberty as a cloak of maliciousness,"[7] for this is not expedient. And again he says, "Speak ye every man truth with his neighbour."[8] And, "Let no corrupt communication proceed out of your mouth, neither filthiness, nor foolish talking, nor scurrility, which are not convenient, but rather giving of thanks."[9] And, "For ye were sometimes darkness, but now are ye light in the Lord; walk honestly as children of the light, not in rioting and drunkenness, not in chambering and wantonness, not in anger and

---

[1] Luke xii. 35, 36. [2] Luke xii. 47. [3] Luke vi. 46.
[4] Luke xii. 45, 46; Matt. xxiv. 48-51. [5] τὸ αὐτεξούσιον.
[6] 1 Cor. vi. 12. [7] 1 Pet. ii. 16. [8] Eph. iv. 25.
[9] Eph. iv. 29.

jealousy. And such were some of you; but ye have been washed, but ye have been sanctified in the name of our Lord."[1] If then it were not in our power to do or not to do these things, what reason had the apostle, and much more the Lord Himself, to give us counsel to do some things, and to abstain from others? But because man is possessed of free will from the beginning, and God is possessed of free will, in whose likeness man was created, advice is always given to him to keep fast the good, which thing is done by means of obedience to God.

5. And not merely in works, but also in faith, has God preserved the will of man free and under his own control, saying, "According to thy faith be it unto thee;"[2] thus showing that there is a faith specially belonging to man, since he has an opinion specially his own. And again, "All things are possible to him that believeth;"[3] and, "Go thy way; and as thou hast believed, so be it done unto thee."[4] Now all such expressions demonstrate that man is in his own power with respect to faith. And for this reason, "he that believeth in Him has eternal life; while he who believeth not the Son hath not eternal life, but the wrath of God shall remain upon him."[5] In the same manner therefore the Lord, both showing His own goodness, and indicating that man is in his own free will and his own power, said to Jerusalem, "How often have I wished to gather thy children together, as a hen [gathereth] her chickens under her wings, and ye would not! Wherefore your house shall be left unto you desolate."[6]

6. Those, again, who maintain the opposite to these [conclusions], do themselves present the Lord as destitute of power, as if, forsooth, He were unable to accomplish what He willed; or, on the other hand, as being ignorant that they were by nature "material," as these men express it, and such as cannot receive His immortality. "But He should not," say they, "have created angels of such a nature that they were capable of transgression, nor men who immediately proved ungrateful towards Him; for they were made

---

[1] 1 Cor. vi. 11.   [2] Matt. ix. 29.   [3] Mark ix. 23.
[4] Matt. viii. 13.   [5] John iii. 36.   [6] Matt. xxiii. 37, 38.

rational beings, endowed with the power of examining and judging, and were not [formed] as things irrational or of a [merely] animal nature, which can do nothing of their own will, but are drawn by necessity and compulsion to what is good, in which things there is one mind and one usage, working mechanically in one groove (*inflexibiles et sine judicio*), who are incapable of being anything else except just what they had been created." But upon this supposition, neither would what is good be grateful to them, nor communion with God be precious, nor would the good be very much to be sought after, which would present itself without their own proper endeavour, care, or study, but would be implanted of its own accord and without their concern. Thus it would come to pass, that their being good would be of no consequence, because they were so by nature rather than by will, and are possessors of good spontaneously, not by choice; and for this reason they would not understand this fact, that good is a comely thing, nor would they take pleasure in it. For how can those who are ignorant of good enjoy it? Or what credit is it to those who have not aimed at it? And what crown is it to those who have not followed in pursuit of it, like those victorious in the contest?

7. On this account, too, did the Lord assert that the kingdom of heaven was the portion of "the violent;" and He says, "The violent take it by force;"[1] that is, those who by strength and earnest striving are on the watch to snatch it away on the moment. On this account also Paul the Apostle says to the Corinthians, "Know ye not, that they who run in a racecourse, do all indeed run, but one receiveth the prize? So run, that ye may obtain. Every one also who engages in the contest is temperate in all things: now these men [do it] that they may obtain a corruptible crown, but we an incorruptible. But I so run, not as uncertainly; I fight, not as one beating the air; but I make my body livid, and bring it into subjection, lest by any means, when preaching to others, I may myself be rendered a castaway."[2] This able wrestler, therefore, exhorts us to the struggle for im-

[1] Matt. xi. 12.   [2] 1 Cor. ix. 24-27.

mortality, that we may be crowned, and may deem the crown precious, namely, that which is acquired by our struggle, but which does not encircle us of its own accord (*sed non ultro coalitam*). And the harder we strive, so much is it the more valuable; while so much the more valuable it is, so much the more should we esteem it. And indeed those things are not esteemed so highly which come spontaneously, as those which are reached by much anxious care. Since, then, this power has been conferred upon us, both the Lord has taught and the apostle has enjoined us the more to love God, that we may reach this [prize] for ourselves by striving after it. For otherwise, no doubt, this our good would be [virtually] irrational, because not the result of trial. Moreover, the faculty of seeing would not appear to be so desirable, unless we had known what a loss it were to be devoid of sight; and health, too, is rendered all the more estimable by an acquaintance with disease; light, also, by contrasting it with darkness; and life with death. Just in the same way is the heavenly kingdom honourable to those who have known the earthly one. But in proportion as it is more honourable, so much the more do we prize it; and if we have prized it more, we shall be the more glorious in the presence of God. The Lord has therefore endured all these things on our behalf, in order that we, having been instructed by means of them all, may be in all respects circumspect for the time to come, and that, having been rationally taught to love God, we may continue in His perfect love: for God has displayed long-suffering in the case of man's apostasy; while man has been instructed by means of it, as also the prophet says, "Thine own apostasy shall heal thee;"[1] God thus determining all things beforehand for the bringing of man to perfection, for his edification, and for the revelation of His dispensations, that goodness may both be made apparent, and righteousness perfected, and that the church may be fashioned after the image of His Son, and that man may finally be brought to maturity at some future time, becoming ripe through such privileges to see and comprehend God.

[1] Jer. ii. 19.

CHAP. XXXVIII.—*Why man was not made perfect from the beginning.*

1. If, however, any one say, "What then? Could not God have exhibited man as perfect from the beginning?" let him know that, inasmuch as God is indeed always the same and unbegotten as respects Himself, all things are possible to Him. But created things must be inferior to Him who created them, from the very fact of their later origin; for it was not possible for things recently created to have been uncreated. But inasmuch as they are not uncreated, for this very reason do they come short of the perfect. Because, as these things are of later date, so are they infantile; so are they unaccustomed to, and unexercised in, perfect discipline. For as it certainly is in the power of a mother to give strong food to her infant, [but she does not do so], as the child is not yet able to receive more substantial nourishment; so also it was possible for God Himself to have made man perfect from the first, but man could not receive this [perfection], being as yet an infant. And for this cause our Lord, in these last times, when He had summed up all things into Himself, came to us, not as He might have come, but as we were capable of beholding Him. He might easily have come to us in His immortal glory, but in that case we could never have endured the greatness of the glory; and therefore it was that He, who was the perfect bread of the Father, offered Himself to us as milk, [because we were] as infants. He did this when He appeared as a man, that we, being nourished, as it were, from the breast of His flesh, and having, by such a course of milk-nourishment, become accustomed to eat and drink the Word of God, may be able also to contain in ourselves the Bread of immortality, which is the Spirit of the Father.

2. And on this account does Paul declare to the Corinthians, "I have fed you with milk, not with meat, for hitherto ye were not able to bear it."[1] That is, ye have indeed learned the advent of our Lord as a man; nevertheless, because of your infirmity, the Spirit of the Father has not as yet rested

[1] 1 Cor. iii. 2.

upon you. "For when envying and strife," he says, "and dissensions are among you, are ye not carnal, and walk as men?"[1] That is, that the Spirit of the Father was not yet with them, on account of their imperfection and the shortcomings of their walk in life. As, therefore, the apostle had the power to give them strong meat—for those upon whom the apostles laid hands received the Holy Spirit, who is the food of life [eternal]—but they were not capable of receiving it, because they had the sentient faculties of the soul still feeble and undisciplined in the practice of things pertaining to God; so, in like manner, God had power at the beginning to grant perfection to man; but as the latter was only recently created, he could not possibly have received it, or even if he had received it, could he have contained it, or containing it, could he have retained it. It was for this reason that the Son of God, although He was perfect, passed through the state of infancy in common with the rest of mankind, partaking of it thus not for His own benefit, but for that of the infantile stage of man's existence, in order that man might be able to receive Him. There was nothing, therefore, impossible to and deficient in God, [implied in the fact] that man was not an uncreated being; but this merely applied to him who was lately created, [namely] man.

3. With God there are simultaneously exhibited power, wisdom, and goodness. His power and goodness [appear] in this, that of His own will He called into being and fashioned things having no previous existence; His wisdom [is shown] in His having made created things parts of one harmonious and consistent whole; and those things which, through His super-eminent kindness, receive growth and a long period of existence, do reflect the glory of the uncreated One, of that God who bestows what is good ungrudgingly. For from the very fact of these things having been created, [it follows] that they are not uncreated; but by their continuing in being throughout a long course of ages, they shall receive a faculty of the Uncreated, through the gratuitous bestowal of eternal existence upon them by God. And thus in all things God has

[1] 1 Cor. iii. 3.

the pre-eminence, who alone is uncreated, the first of all things, and the primary cause of the existence of all, while all other things remain under God's subjection. But being in subjection to God is continuance in immortality, and immortality is the glory of the uncreated One. By this arrangement, therefore, and these harmonics, and a sequence of this nature, man, a created and organized being, is rendered after the image and likeness of the uncreated God,—the Father planning everything well and giving His commands, the Son carrying these into execution and performing the work of creating, and the Spirit nourishing and increasing [what is made], but man making progress day by day, and ascending towards the perfect, that is, approximating to the uncreated One. For the Uncreated is perfect, that is, God. Now it was necessary that man should in the first instance be created; and having been created, should receive growth; and having received growth, should be strengthened; and having been strengthened, should abound; and having abounded, should recover [from the disease of sin]; and having recovered, should be glorified; and being glorified, should see his Lord. For God is He who is yet to be seen, and the beholding of God is productive of immortality, but immortality renders one nigh unto God.

4. Irrational, therefore, in every respect, are they who await not the time of increase, but ascribe to God the infirmity of their nature. Such persons know neither God nor themselves, being insatiable and ungrateful, unwilling to be at the outset what they have also been created—men subject to passions; but go beyond the law of the human race, and before that they become men, they wish to be even now like God their Creator, and they who are more destitute of reason than dumb animals [insist] that there is no distinction between the uncreated God and man, a creature of to-day. For these, [the dumb animals], bring no charge against God for not having made them men; but each one, just as he has been created, gives thanks that he has been created. For we cast blame upon Him, because we have not been made gods from the beginning, but at first merely men,

then at length gods; although God has adopted this course out of His pure benevolence, that no one may impute to Him invidiousness or grudgingness. He declares, "I have said, Ye are gods; and ye are all sons of the Highest."[1] But since we could not sustain the power of divinity, He adds, "But ye shall die like men," setting forth both truths—the kindness of His free gift, and our weakness, and also that we were possessed of power over ourselves. For after His great kindness He graciously conferred good [upon us], and made men like to Himself, [that is] in their own power; while at the same time by His prescience He knew the infirmity of human beings, and the consequences which would flow from it; but through [His] love and [His] power, He shall overcome the substance of created nature.[2] For it was necessary, at first, that nature should be exhibited; then, after that, that what was mortal should be conquered and swallowed up by immortality, and the corruptible by incorruptibility, and that man should be made after the image and likeness of God, having received the knowledge of good and evil.

CHAP. XXXIX.—*Man is endowed with the faculty of distinguishing good and evil; so that, without compulsion, he has the power, by his own will and choice, to perform God's commandments, by doing which he avoids the evils prepared for the rebellious.*

1. Man has received the knowledge of good and evil. It is good to obey God, and to believe in Him, and to keep His commandment, and this is the life of man; as not to obey God is evil, and this is his death. Since God, therefore, gave [to man] such mental power (*magnanimitatem*), man knew both the good of obedience and the evil of disobedience, that the eye of the mind, receiving experience of both, may with judgment make choice of the better things; and that he may never become indolent or neglectful of God's com-

---

[1] Ps. lxxxii. 6, 7.
[2] That is, that man's human nature should not prevent him from becoming a partaker of the divine.

mand; and learning by experience that it is an evil thing which deprives him of life, that is, disobedience to God, may never attempt it at all, but that, knowing that what preserves his life, namely, obedience to God, is good, he may diligently keep it with all earnestness. Wherefore he has also had a twofold experience, possessing knowledge of both kinds, that with discipline he may make choice of the better things. But how, if he had no knowledge of the contrary, could he have had instruction in that which is good? For there is thus a surer and an undoubted comprehension of matters submitted to us than the mere surmise arising from an opinion regarding them. For just as the tongue receives experience of sweet and bitter by means of tasting, and the eye discriminates between black and white by means of vision, and the ear recognises the distinctions of sounds by hearing; so also does the mind, receiving through the experience of both the knowledge of what is good, become more tenacious of its preservation, by acting in obedience to God: in the first place, casting away, by means of repentance, disobedience, as being something disagreeable and nauseous; and afterwards coming to understand what it really is, that it is contrary to goodness and sweetness, so that the mind may never even attempt to taste disobedience to God. But if any one do shun the knowledge of both these kinds of things, and the twofold perception of knowledge, he unawares divests himself of the character of a human being.

2. How, then, shall he be a God, who has not as yet been made a man? Or how can he be perfect who was but lately created? How, again, can he be immortal, who in his mortal nature did not obey his Maker? For it must be that thou, at the outset, shouldest hold the rank of a man, and then afterwards partake of the glory of God. For thou dost not make God, but God thee. If, then, thou art God's workmanship, await the hand of thy Maker which creates everything in due time; in due time as far as thou art concerned, whose creation is being carried out.[1] Offer to Him thy heart in a soft and tractable state, and preserve the form in

[1] Efficeris.

which the Creator has fashioned thee, having moisture in thyself, lest, by becoming hardened, thou lose the impressions of His fingers. But by preserving the framework thou shalt ascend to that which is perfect, for the moist clay which is in thee is hidden [there] by the workmanship of God. His hand fashioned thy substance; He will cover thee over [too] within and without with pure gold and silver, and He will adorn thee to such a degree, that even "the King Himself shall have pleasure in thy beauty."[1] But if thou, being obstinately hardened, dost reject the operation of His skill, and show thyself ungrateful towards Him, because thou wert created a [mere] man, by becoming thus ungrateful to God, thou hast at once lost both His workmanship and life. For creation is an attribute of the goodness of God; but to be created is that of human nature. If, then, thou shalt deliver up to Him what is thine, that is, faith towards Him and subjection, thou shalt receive His handiwork, and shalt be a perfect work of God.

3. If, however, thou wilt not believe in Him, and wilt flee from His hands, the cause of imperfection shall be in thee who didst not obey, but not in Him who called [thee]. For He commissioned [messengers] to call people to the marriage, but they who did not obey Him deprived themselves of the royal supper.[2] The skill of God, therefore, is not defective, for He has power of the stones to raise up children to Abraham;[3] but the man who does not obtain it, is the cause to himself of his own imperfection. Nor, [in like manner], does the light fail because of those who have blinded themselves; but while it remains the same as ever, those who are [thus] blinded are involved in darkness through their own fault. The light does never enslave any one by necessity; nor, again, does God exercise compulsion upon any one unwilling to accept the exercise of His skill. Those persons, therefore, who have apostatized from the light given by the Father, and transgressed the law of liberty, have done so through their own fault, since they have been created free agents, and possessed of power over themselves.

[1] Ps. xlv. 11.   [2] Matt xxii. 3, etc.   [3] Matt. iii. 9.

4. But God, foreknowing all things, prepared fit habitations for both, kindly conferring that light which they desire on those who seek after the light of incorruption, and resort to it; but for the despisers and mockers who avoid and turn themselves away from this light, and who do, as it were, blind themselves, He has prepared darkness suitable to persons who oppose the light, and He has inflicted an appropriate punishment upon those who try to avoid being subject to Him. Submission to God is eternal rest, so that they who shun the light have a place worthy of their flight; and those who fly from eternal rest, have a habitation in accordance with their fleeing. Now, since all good things are with God, they who by their own determination fly from God, do defraud themselves of all good things; and having been [thus] defrauded of all good things with respect to God, they shall consequently fall under the just judgment of God. For those persons who shun rest shall justly incur punishment, and those who avoid the light shall justly dwell in darkness. For as in the case of this temporal light, those who shun it do deliver themselves over to darkness, so that they do themselves become the cause to themselves that they are destitute of light, and do inhabit darkness; and, as I have already observed, the light is not the cause of such an [unhappy] condition of existence to them; so those who fly from the eternal light of God, which contains in itself all good things, are themselves the cause to themselves of their inhabiting eternal darkness, destitute of all good things, having become to themselves the cause of [their consignment to] an abode of that nature.

CHAP. XL.—*One and the same God the Father inflicts punishment on the reprobate, and bestows rewards on the elect.*

1. It is therefore one and the same God the Father who has prepared good things with Himself for those who desire His fellowship, and who remain in subjection to Him; and who has prepared the eternal fire for the ringleader of the apostasy, the devil, and those who revolted with him, into which [fire] the Lord[1] has declared those men shall be sent

[1] Matt. xxv. 41.

who have been set apart by themselves on His left hand. And this is what has been spoken by the prophet, "I am a jealous God, making peace, and creating evil things;"[1] thus making peace and friendship with those who repent and turn to Him, and bringing [them to] unity, but preparing for the impenitent, those who shun the light, eternal fire and outer darkness, which are evils indeed to those persons who fall into them.

2. If, however, it were truly one Father who confers rest, and another God who has prepared the fire, their sons would have been equally different [one from the other]; one, indeed, sending [men] into the Father's kingdom, but the other into eternal fire. But inasmuch as one and the same Lord has pointed out that the whole human race shall be divided at the judgment, "as a shepherd divideth the sheep from the goats,"[2] and that to some He will say, "Come, ye blessed of my Father, receive the kingdom which has been prepared for you,"[3] but to others, "Depart from me, ye cursed, into everlasting fire, which my Father has prepared for the devil and his angels,"[4] one and the same Father is manifestly declared [in this passage], "making peace and creating evil things," preparing fit things for both; as also there is one Judge sending both into a fit place, as the Lord sets forth in the parable of the tares and the wheat, where He says, "As therefore the tares are gathered together, and burned in the fire, so shall it be at the end of the world. The Son of man shall send His angels, and they shall gather from His kingdom everything that offendeth, and those who work iniquity, and shall send them into a furnace of fire: there shall be weeping and gnashing of teeth. Then shall the just shine forth as the sun in the kingdom of their Father."[5] The Father, therefore, who has prepared the kingdom for the righteous, into which the Son has received those worthy of it, is He who has also prepared the furnace of fire, into which these angels commissioned by the Son of man shall send those persons who deserve it, according to God's command.

---

[1] Isa. xlv. 7.   [2] Matt. xxv. 32.   [3] Matt. xxv. 34.
[4] Matt. xxv. 41.   [5] Matt. xiii. 40–43.

3. The Lord, indeed, sowed good seed in His own field;[1] and He says, "The field is the world." But while men slept, the enemy came, and "sowed tares in the midst of the wheat, and went his way."[2] Hence we learn that this was the apostate angel and the enemy, because he was envious of God's workmanship, and took in hand to render this [workmanship] at enmity with God. For this cause also God has banished from His presence him who did of his own accord stealthily sow the tares, that is, him who brought about the transgression;[3] but He took compassion upon man, who, through want of care no doubt, but still wickedly [on the part of another], became involved in disobedience; and He turned the enmity by which [the devil] had designed to make [man] the enemy of God, against the author of it, by removing His own anger from man, turning it in another direction, and sending it instead upon the serpent. As also the Scripture tells us that God said to the serpent, "And I will place enmity between thee and the woman, and between thy seed and her seed. He[4] shall bruise thy head, and thou shalt bruise his heel."[5] And the Lord summed up in Himself this enmity, when He was made man from a woman, and trod upon his [the serpent's] head, as I have pointed out in the preceding book.

CHAP. XLI.—*Those persons who do not believe in God, but who are disobedient, are angels and sons of the devil, not indeed by nature, but by imitation. Close of this book, and scope of the succeeding one.*

1. Inasmuch as the Lord has said that there are certain angels, [viz. those] of the devil, for whom eternal fire is prepared; and as, again, He declares with regard to the tares,

---

[1] Matt. xiii. 34. [2] Matt. xiii. 28.
[3] The old Latin translator varies from this (the Greek of which was recovered by Grabe from two ancient *Catenæ Patrum*), making the clause run thus, *that is, the transgression which he had himself introduced*, making the explanatory words to refer to the *tares*, and not, as in the Greek, to the *sower of the tares*.
[4] Following the reading of the LXX., αὐτός σου τηρήσει κεφαλήν.
[5] Gen. iii. 15.

"The tares are the children of the wicked one,"[1] it must be affirmed that He has ascribed all who are of the apostasy to him who is the ringleader of this transgression. But He made neither angels nor men so by nature. For we do not find that the devil created anything whatsoever, since indeed he is himself a creature of God, like the other angels. For God made all things, as also David says with regard to all things of the kind: "For He spake the word, and they were made; He commanded, and they were created."[2]

2. Since, therefore, all things were made by God, and since the devil has become the cause of apostasy to himself and others, justly does the Scripture always term those who remain in a state of apostasy "sons of the devil" and "angels of the wicked one" (*maligni*). For [the word] "son," as one before me has observed, has a twofold meaning: one [is a son] in the order of nature, because he was born a son; the other, in that he was made so, is reputed a son, although there be a difference between being born so and being made so. For the first is indeed born from the person referred to; but the second is made so by him, whether as respects his creation or by the teaching of his doctrine. For when any person has been taught from the mouth of another, he is termed the son of him who instructs him, and the latter [is called] his father. According to nature, then—that is, according to creation, so to speak—we are all sons of God, because we have all been created by God. But with respect to obedience and doctrine we are not all the sons of God: those only are so who believe in Him and do His will. And those who do not believe, and do not obey His will, are sons and angels of the devil, because they do the works of the devil. And that such is the case He has declared in Isaiah: "I have begotten and brought up children, but they have rebelled against me."[3] And again, where He says that these children are aliens: "Strange children have lied unto me."[4] According to nature, then, they are [His] children, because they have been so created; but with regard to their works, they are not His children.

[1] Matt. xiii. 38.
[2] Ps. cxlix. 5.
[3] Isa. i. 2.
[4] Ps. xviii. 45.

3. For as, among men, those sons who disobey their fathers, being disinherited, are still their sons in the course of nature, but by law are disinherited, for they do not become the heirs of their natural parents; so in the same way is it with God,—those who do not obey Him being disinherited by Him, have ceased to be His sons. Wherefore they cannot receive His inheritance: as David says, "Sinners are alienated from the womb; their anger is after the likeness of a serpent."[1] And therefore did the Lord term those whom He knew to be the offspring of men "a generation of vipers;"[2] because after the manner of these animals they go about in subtilty, and injure others. For He said, "Beware of the leaven of the Pharisees and of the Sadducees."[3] Speaking of Herod, too, He says, "Go ye and tell that fox,"[4] aiming at his wicked cunning and deceit. Wherefore the prophet David says, "Man, being placed in honour, is made like unto cattle."[5] And again Jeremiah says, "They are become like horses, furious about females; each one neighed after his neighbour's wife."[6] And Isaiah, when preaching in Judea, and reasoning with Israel, termed them "rulers of Sodom" and "people of Gomorrah;"[7] intimating that they were like the Sodomites in wickedness, and that the same description of sins was rife among them, calling them by the same name, because of the similarity of their conduct. And inasmuch as they were not by nature so created by God, but had power also to act rightly, the same person said to them, giving them good counsel, "Wash ye, make you clean; take away iniquity from your souls before mine eyes; cease from your iniquities."[8] Thus, no doubt, since they had transgressed and sinned in the same manner, so did they receive the same reproof as did the Sodomites. But when they should be converted and come to repentance, and cease from evil, they should have power to become the sons of God, and to receive the inheritance of immortality which is given by Him. For this reason, therefore, He has termed those "angels of the

---

[1] Ps. lviii. 3, 4.   [2] Matt. xxiii. 33.   [3] Matt. xvi. 6.
[4] Luke xiii. 32.   [5] Ps. xlix. 21.   [6] Jer. v. 8.
[7] Isa. i. 10.   [8] Isa. i. 16.

devil," and "children of the wicked one,"[1] who give heed to the devil, and do his works. But these are, at the same time, all created by the one and the same God. When, however, they believe and are subject to God, and go on and keep His doctrine, they are the sons of God; but when they have apostatized and fallen into transgression, they are ascribed to their chief, the devil—to him who first became the cause of apostasy to himself, and afterwards to others.

4. Inasmuch as the words of the Lord are numerous, while they all proclaim one and the same Father, the Creator of this world, it was incumbent also upon me, for their own sake, to refute by many [arguments] those who are involved in many errors, if by any means, when they are confuted by many [proofs], they may be converted to the truth and saved. But it is necessary to subjoin to this composition, in what follows, also the doctrine of Paul after the words of the Lord, to examine the opinion of this man, and expound the apostle, and to explain whatsoever [passages] have received other interpretations from the heretics, who have altogether misunderstood what Paul has spoken, and to point out the folly of their mad opinions; and to demonstrate from that same Paul, from whose [writings] they press questions upon us, that they are indeed utterers of falsehood, but that the apostle was a preacher of the truth, and that he taught all things agreeable to the preaching of the truth; [to the effect that] it was one God the Father who spake with Abraham, who gave the law, who sent the prophets beforehand, who in the last times sent His Son, and conferred salvation upon His own handiwork—that is, the substance of flesh. Arranging, then, in another book, the rest of the words of the Lord, which He taught concerning the Father not by parables, but by expressions taken in their obvious meaning (*sed simpliciter ipsis dictionibus*), and the exposition of the epistles of the blessed apostle, I shall, with God's aid, furnish thee with the complete work of the exposure and refutation of knowledge, falsely so called; thus practising myself and thee in [these] five books for presenting opposition to all heretics.

[1] Matt. xxv. 41, xiii. 38.

BOOK V.

PREFACE.

IN the four preceding books, my very dear friend, which I put forth to thee, all the heretics have been exposed, and their doctrines brought to light, and these men refuted who have devised irreligious opinions. [I have accomplished this by adducing] something from the doctrine peculiar to each of these men, which they have left in their writings, as well as by using arguments of a more general nature, and applicable to them all.[1] Then I have pointed out the truth, and shown the preaching of the church, which the prophets proclaimed (as I have already demonstrated), but which Christ brought to perfection, and the apostles have handed down, from whom the church, receiving [these truths], and throughout all the world alone preserving them in their integrity (*bene*), has transmitted them to her sons. Then also—having disposed of all questions which the heretics propose to us, and having explained the doctrine of the apostles, and clearly set forth many of those things which were said and done by the Lord in parables—I shall endeavour, in this the fifth book of the entire work which treats of the exposure and refutation of knowledge falsely so called, to exhibit proofs from the rest of the Lord's doctrine and the apostolical epistles: [thus] complying with thy demand, as thou didst request of me (since indeed I have been assigned a place in the ministry of the word); and, labouring by every means in my power to

---

[1] Ex ratione universis ostensionibus procedente. The words are very obscure.

furnish thee with large assistance against the contradictions of the heretics, as also to reclaim the wanderers and convert them to the church of God, to confirm at the same time the minds of the neophytes, that they may preserve stedfast the faith which they have received, guarded by the church in its integrity, in order that they be in no way perverted by those who endeavour to teach them false doctrines, and lead them away from the truth. It will be incumbent upon thee, however, and all who may happen to read this writing, to peruse with great attention what I have already said, that thou mayest obtain a knowledge of the subjects against which I am contending. For it is thus that thou wilt both controvert them in a legitimate manner, and wilt be prepared to receive the proofs brought forward against them, casting away their doctrines as filth by means of the celestial faith; but following the only true and stedfast teacher, the Word of God, our Lord Jesus Christ, who did, through His transcendent love, become what we are, that He might bring us to be even what He is Himself.

CHAP. I.—*Christ alone is able to teach divine things, and to redeem us: He, the same, took flesh of the Virgin Mary, not merely in appearance, but actually, by the operation of the Holy Spirit, in order to renovate us. Strictures on the conceits of Valentinus and Ebion.*

1. For in no other way could we have learned the things of God, unless our Master, existing as the Word, had become man. For no other being had the power of revealing to us the things of the Father, except His own proper Word. For what other person "knew the mind of the Lord," or who else "has become His counsellor?"[1] Again, we could have learned in no other way than by seeing our Teacher, and hearing His voice with our own ears, that, having become imitators of His works as well as doers of His words, we may have communion with Him, receiving increase from the perfect One, and from Him who is prior to all creation. We—who were but lately

[1] Rom. xi. 34.

created by the only best and good Being, by Him also who has the gift of immortality, having been formed after His likeness (predestinated, according to the prescience of the Father, that we, who had as yet no existence, might come into being), and made the first-fruits of creation [1]—have received, in the times known beforehand, [the blessings of salvation] according to the ministration of the Word, who is perfect in all things, as the mighty Word, and very man, who, redeeming us by His own blood in a manner consonant to reason, gave Himself as a redemption for those who had been led into captivity. And since the apostasy tyrannized over us unjustly, and, though we were by nature the property of the omnipotent God, alienated us contrary to nature, rendering us its own disciples, the Word of God, powerful in all things, and not defective with regard to His own justice, did righteously turn against that apostasy, and redeem from it His own property, not by violent means, as the [apostasy] had obtained dominion over us at the beginning, when it insatiably snatched away what was not its own, but by means of persuasion, as became a God of counsel, who does not use violent means to obtain what He desires; so that neither should justice be infringed upon, nor the ancient handiwork of God go to destruction. Since the Lord thus has redeemed us through His own blood, giving His soul for our souls, and His flesh for our flesh, and has also poured out the Spirit of the Father for the union and communion of God and man, imparting indeed God to men by means of the Spirit, and, on the other hand, attaching man to God by His own incarnation, and bestowing upon us at His coming immortality durably and truly, by means of communion with God,—all the doctrines of the heretics fall to ruin.

2. Vain indeed are those who allege that He appeared in mere seeming. For these things were not done in appearance only, but in actual reality. But if He did appear as a man, when He was not a man, neither could the Holy Spirit have rested upon Him,—an occurrence which did actually take

---

[1] "Initium facturæ," which Grabe thinks should be thus translated with reference to Jas. i. 18.

place—as the Spirit is invisible; nor, [in that case], was there any degree of truth in Him, for He was not that which He seemed to be. But I have already remarked that Abraham and the other prophets beheld Him after a prophetical manner, foretelling in vision what should come to pass. If, then, such a being has now appeared in outward semblance different from what he was in reality, there has been a certain prophetical vision made to men; and another advent of His must be looked forward to, in which He shall be such as He has now been seen in a prophetic manner. And I have proved already, that it is the same thing to say that He appeared merely to outward seeming, and [to affirm] that He received nothing from Mary. For He would not have been one truly possessing flesh and blood, by which He redeemed us, unless He had summed up in Himself the ancient formation of Adam. Vain therefore are the disciples of Valentinus who put forth this opinion, in order that they may exclude the flesh from salvation, and cast aside what God has fashioned.

3. Vain also are the Ebionites, who do not receive by faith into their soul the union of God and man, but who remain in the old leaven of [the natural] birth, and who do not choose to understand that the Holy Ghost came upon Mary, and the power of the Most High did overshadow her:[1] wherefore also what was generated is a holy thing, and the Son of the Most High God the Father of all, who effected the incarnation of this being, and showed forth a new [kind of] generation; that as by the former generation we inherited death, so by this new generation we might inherit life. Therefore do these men reject the commixture of the heavenly wine,[2] and wish it to be water of the world only, not receiving God so as to have union with Him, but they remain in that Adam who had been conquered and was expelled from Paradise: not considering that as, at the beginning

---

[1] Luke i. 35.

[2] In allusion to the mixture of water in the eucharistic cup, as practised in these primitive times. The Ebionites and others used to consecrate the element of water alone.

of our formation in Adam, that breath of life which proceeded from God, having been united to what had been fashioned, animated the man, and manifested him as a being endowed with reason; so also, in [the times of] the end, the Word of the Father and the Spirit of God, having become united with the ancient substance of Adam's formation, rendered man living and perfect, receptive of the perfect Father, in order that as in the natural [Adam] we all were dead, so in the spiritual we may all be made alive.[1] For never at any time did Adam escape the *hands*[2] of God, to whom the Father speaking, said, "Let us make man in our image, after our likeness." And for this reason in the last times (*fine*), not by the will of the flesh, nor by the will of man, but by the good pleasure of the Father,[3] His hands formed a living man, in order that Adam might be created [again] after the image and likeness of God.

CHAP. II.—*When Christ visited us in His grace, He did not come to what did not belong to Him: also, by shedding His true blood for us, and exhibiting to us His true flesh in the Eucharist, He conferred upon our flesh the capacity of salvation.*

1. And vain likewise are those who say that God came to those things which did not belong to Him, as if covetous of another's property; in order that He might deliver up that man who had been created by another, to that God who had neither made nor formed anything, but who also was deprived from the beginning of His own proper formation of men. The advent, therefore, of Him whom these men represent as coming to the things of others, was not righteous; nor did He truly redeem us by His own blood, if He did not really become man, restoring to His own handiwork what was said [of it] in the beginning, that man was made after the image and likeness of God; not snatching away by stratagem the property of another, but taking possession of His own in a righteous and gracious manner. As far as concerned the

---

[1] 1 Cor. xv. 22.   [2] Viz. the Son and the Spirit.   [3] John i. 13.

apostasy, indeed, He redeems us righteously from it by His own blood; but as regards us who have been redeemed, [He does this] graciously. For we have given nothing to Him previously, nor does He desire anything from us, as if He stood in need of it; but we do stand in need of fellowship with Him. And for this reason it was that He graciously poured Himself out, that He might gather us into the bosom of the Father.

2. But vain in every respect are they who despise the entire dispensation of God, and disallow the salvation of the flesh, and treat with contempt its regeneration, maintaining that it is not capable of incorruption. But if this indeed do not attain salvation, then neither did the Lord redeem us with His blood, nor is the cup of the Eucharist the communion of His blood, nor the bread which we break the communion of His body.[1] For blood can only come from veins and flesh, and whatsoever else makes up the substance of man, such as the Word of God was actually made. By His own blood He redeemed us, as also His apostle declares, "In whom we have redemption through His blood, even the remission of sins."[2] And as we are His members, we are also nourished by means of the creation (and He Himself grants the creation to us, for He causes His sun to rise, and sends rain when He wills[3]). He has acknowledged the cup (which is a part of the creation) as His own blood, from which He bedews our blood; and the bread (also a part of the creation) He has established as His own body, from which He gives increase to our bodies.

3. When, therefore, the mingled cup and the manufactured bread receives the Word of God, and the Eucharist of the blood and the body of Christ is made,[4] from which things the substance of our flesh is increased and supported, how can they affirm that the flesh is incapable of receiving the gift of God, which is life eternal, which [flesh] is nourished from the body and blood of the Lord, and is a member of Him?—

---

[1] 1 Cor. x. 16.   [2] Col. i. 14.   [3] Matt. v. 45.
[4] The Greek text, of which a considerable portion remains here, would give, "and the Eucharist becomes the body of Christ."

even as the blessed Paul declares in his Epistle to the Ephesians, that "we are members of His body, of His flesh, and of His bones."[1] He does not speak these words of some spiritual and invisible man, for a spirit has not bones nor flesh;[2] but [he refers to] that dispensation [by which the Lord became] an actual man, consisting of flesh, and nerves, and bones,—that [flesh] which is nourished by the cup which is His blood, and receives increase from the bread which is His body. And just as a cutting from the vine planted in the ground fructifies in its season, or as a corn of wheat falling into the earth and becoming decomposed, rises with manifold increase by the Spirit of God, who contains all things, and then, through the wisdom of God, serves for the use of men, and having received the Word of God, becomes the Eucharist, which is the body and blood of Christ; so also our bodies, being nourished by it, and deposited in the earth, and suffering decomposition there, shall rise at their appointed time, the Word of God granting them resurrection to the glory of God, even the Father, who freely gives to this mortal immortality, and to this corruptible incorruption,[3] because the strength of God is made perfect in weakness,[4] in order that we may never become puffed up, as if we had life from ourselves, and exalted against God, our minds becoming ungrateful; but learning by experience that we possess eternal duration from the excelling power of this Being, not from our own nature, we may neither undervalue that glory which surrounds God as He is, nor be ignorant of our own nature, but that we may know what God can effect, and what benefits man receives, and thus never wander from the true comprehension of things as they are, that is, both with regard to God and with regard to man. And might it not be the case, perhaps, as I have already observed, that for this purpose God permitted our resolution into the common dust of mortality,[5] that we, being instructed by every mode, may be

---

[1] Eph. v. 30. [2] Luke xxiv. 39. [3] 1 Cor. xv. 53. [4] 2 Cor. xii. 3.

[5] This is Harvey's free rendering of the passage, which is in the Greek (as preserved in the Catena of John of Damascus): καὶ διὰ τοῦτο ἠνέσχετο ὁ Θεὸς τὴν εἰς τὴν γῆν ἡμῶν ἀνάλυσιν. In the Latin: Propter

accurate in all things for the future, being ignorant neither of God nor of ourselves?

CHAP. III.—*The power and glory of God shine forth in the weakness of human flesh, as He will render our body a participator of the resurrection and of immortality, although He has formed it from the dust of the earth; He will also bestow upon it the enjoyment of immortality, just as He grants it this short life in common with the soul.*

1. The Apostle Paul has, moreover, in the most lucid manner, pointed out that man has been delivered over to his own infirmity, lest, being uplifted, he might fall away from the truth. Thus he says in the second [Epistle] to the Corinthians: "And lest I should be lifted up by the sublimity of the revelations, there was given unto me a thorn in the flesh, the messenger of Satan to buffet me. And upon this I besought the Lord three times, that it might depart from me. But He said unto me, My grace is sufficient for thee; for strength is made perfect in weakness. Gladly therefore shall I rather glory in infirmities, that the power of Christ may dwell in me."[1] What, therefore? (as some may exclaim:) did the Lord wish, in that case, that His apostle should thus undergo buffeting, and that he should endure such infirmity? Even so it was; the word says it. For strength is made perfect in weakness, rendering him a better man who by means of his infirmity becomes acquainted with the power of God. For how could a man have learned that he is himself an infirm being, and mortal by nature, but that God is immortal and powerful, unless he had learned by experience what is in both? For there is nothing evil in learning one's infirmities by endurance; yea, rather, it has even the beneficial effect of preventing him from forming an undue opinion of his own nature (*non aberrare in natura sua*). But the

hoc passus est Deus fieri in nobis resolutionem. See the former volume, p. 348.

[1] 2 Cor. xii. 7–9.

being lifted up against God, and taking His glory to one's self, rendering man ungrateful, has brought much evil upon him. [And thus, I say, man must learn both things by experience], that he may not be destitute of truth and love either towards himself or his Creator.[1] But the experience of both confers upon him the true knowledge as to God and man, and increases his love towards God. Now, where there exists an increase of love, there a greater glory is wrought out by the power of God for those who love Him.

2. Those men, therefore, set aside the power of God, and do not consider what the word declares, when they dwell upon the infirmity of the flesh, but do not take into consideration the power of Him who raises it up from the dead. For if He does not vivify what is mortal, and does not bring back the corruptible to incorruption, He is not a God of power. But that He is powerful in all these respects, we ought to perceive from our origin, inasmuch as God, taking dust from the earth, formed man. And surely it is much more difficult and incredible, from non-existent bones, and nerves, and veins, and the rest of man's organization, to bring it about that all this should be, and to make man an animated and rational creature, than to reintegrate again that which had been created and then afterwards decomposed into earth (for the reasons already mentioned), having thus passed into those [elements] from which man, who had no previous existence, was formed. For He who in the beginning caused him to have being who as yet was not, just when He pleased, shall much more reinstate again those who had a former existence, when it is His will [that they should inherit] the life granted by Him. And that flesh shall also be found fit for and capable of receiving the power of God, which at the beginning received the skilful touches of God; so that one part became the eye for seeing; another, the ear for hearing; another, the hand for feeling and working; another, the

---

[1] We have adopted here the explanation of Massuet, who considers the preceding period as merely parenthetical. Both Grabe and Harvey, however, would make conjectural emendations in the text, which seem to us to be inadmissible.

sinews stretched out everywhere, and holding the limbs together; another, arteries and veins, passages for the blood and the air;[1] another, the various internal organs; another, the blood, which is the bond of union between soul and body. But why go [on in this strain]? Numbers would fail to express the multiplicity of parts in the human frame, which was made in no other way than by the great wisdom of God. But those things which partake of the skill and wisdom of God, do also partake of His power.

3. The flesh, therefore, is not destitute [of participation] in the constructive wisdom and power of God. But if the power of Him who is the bestower of life is made perfect in weakness—that is, in the flesh—let them inform us, when they maintain the incapacity of flesh to receive the life granted by God, whether they do say these things as being living men at present, and partakers of life, or acknowledge that, having no part in life whatever, they are at the present moment dead men. And if they really are dead men, how is it that they move about, and speak, and perform those other functions which are not the actions of the dead, but of the living? But if they are now alive, and if their whole body partakes of life, how can they venture the assertion that the flesh is not qualified to be a partaker of life, when they do confess that they have life at the present moment? It is just as if anybody were to take up a sponge full of water, or a torch on fire, and to declare that the sponge could not possibly partake of the water, or the torch of the fire. In this very manner do those men, by alleging that they are alive and bear life about in their members, contradict themselves afterwards, when they represent these members as not being capable of [receiving] life. But if the present temporal life, which is of such an inferior nature to eternal life, can nevertheless effect so much as to quicken our mortal members, why should not eternal life, being much more powerful than this, vivify the flesh, which has already held converse with, and

---

[1] The ancients erroneously supposed that the arteries were *air-vessels*, from the fact that these organs, after death, appear quite empty, from all the blood stagnating in the veins when death supervenes.

been accustomed to sustain, life? For that the flesh can really partake of life, is shown from the fact of its being alive; for it lives on, as long as it is God's purpose that it should do so. It is manifest, too, that God has the power to confer life upon it, inasmuch as He grants life to us who are in existence. And, therefore, since the Lord has power to infuse life into what He has fashioned, and since the flesh is capable of being quickened, what remains to prevent its participating in incorruption, which is a blissful and never-ending life granted by God?

CHAP. IV.—*Those persons are deceived who feign another God the Father besides the Creator of the world; for he must have been feeble and useless, or else malignant and full of envy, if he be either unable or unwilling to extend eternal life to our bodies.*

1. Those persons who feign the existence of another Father beyond the Creator, and who term him the good God, do deceive themselves; for they introduce him as a feeble, worthless, and negligent being, not to say malign and full of envy, inasmuch as they affirm that our bodies are not quickened by him. For when they say of things which it is manifest to all do remain immortal, such as the spirit and the soul, and such other things, that they are quickened by the Father, but that another thing [viz. the body] which is quickened in no different manner than by God granting [life] to it, is abandoned by life,—[they must either confess] that this proves their Father to be weak and powerless, or else envious and malignant. For since the Creator does even here quicken our mortal bodies, and promises them resurrection by the prophets, as I have pointed out; who [in that case] is shown to be more powerful, stronger, or truly good? Whether is it the Creator who vivifies the whole man, or is it their Father, falsely so called? He feigns to be the quickener of those things which are immortal by nature, to which things life is always present by their very nature; but he does not benevolently quicken those things which required his

assistance, that they might live, but leaves them carelessly to fall under the power of death. Whether is it the case, then, that their Father does not bestow life upon them when he has the power of so doing, or is it that he does not possess the power? If, on the one hand, it is because he cannot, he is, upon that supposition, not a powerful being, nor is he more perfect than the Creator; for the Creator grants, as we must perceive, what *He* is unable to afford. But if, on the other hand, [it be that he does not grant this] when he has the power of so doing, then he is proved to be not a good, but an envious and malignant Father.

2. If, again, they refer to any cause on account of which their Father does not impart life to bodies, then that cause must necessarily appear superior to the Father, since it restrains Him from the exercise of His benevolence; and His benevolence will thus be proved weak, on account of that cause which they bring forward. Now every one must perceive that bodies are capable of receiving life. For they live to the extent that God pleases that they should live; and that being so, the [heretics] cannot maintain that [these bodies] are utterly incapable of receiving life. If, therefore, on account of necessity and any other cause, those [bodies] which are capable of participating in life are not vivified, their Father shall be the slave of necessity and that cause, and not therefore a free agent, having His will under His own control.

CHAP. V.—*The prolonged life of the ancients, the translation of Elijah and of Enoch in their own bodies, as well as the preservation of Jonah, of Shadrach, Meshach, and Abednego, in the midst of extreme peril, are clear demonstrations that God can raise up our bodies to life eternal.*

1. [In order to learn] that bodies did continue in existence for a lengthened period, as long as it was God's good pleasure that they should flourish, let [these heretics] read the Scriptures, and they will find that our predecessors advanced beyond seven hundred, eight hundred, and nine hundred

years of age; and that their bodies kept pace with the protracted length of their days, and participated in life as long as God willed that they should live. But why do I refer to these men? For Enoch, when he pleased God, was translated in the same body in which he did please Him, thus pointing out by anticipation the translation of the just. Elijah, too, was caught up [when he was yet] in the substance of the [natural] form; thus exhibiting in prophecy the assumption of those who are spiritual, and that nothing stood in the way of their body being translated and caught up. For by means of the very same hands through which they were moulded at the beginning, did they receive this translation and assumption. For in Adam the hands of God had become accustomed to set in order, to rule, and to sustain His own workmanship, and to bring it and place it where they pleased. Where, then, was the first man placed? In paradise certainly, as the Scripture declares: "And God planted a garden [*paradisum*] eastward in Eden, and there He placed the man whom He had formed."[1] And then afterwards, when [man] proved disobedient, he was cast out thence into this world. Wherefore also the elders who were disciples of the apostles tell us that those who were translated were transferred to that place (for paradise has been prepared for righteous men, such as have the Spirit; in which place also Paul the apostle, when he was caught up, heard words which are unspeakable as regards us in our present condition[2]), and that there shall they who have been translated remain until the consummation [of all things], as a prelude to immortality.

2. If, however, any one imagine it impossible that men should survive for such a length of time, and that Elias was not caught up in the flesh, but that his flesh was consumed in the fiery chariot, let him consider that Jonah, when he had been cast into the deep, and swallowed down into the whale's belly, was by the command of God again thrown out safe upon the land.[3] And then, again, when Ananias, Azarias, and Misaël were cast into the furnace of fire sevenfold heated, they sustained no harm whatever, neither was the smell of

---

[1] Gen. ii. 8.   [2] 2 Cor. xii. 4.   [3] Jonah ii. 11.

fire perceived upon them. As, therefore, the hand of God was present with them, working out marvellous things in their case —[things] impossible [to be accomplished] by man's nature— what wonder was it, if also in the case of those who were translated it performed something wonderful, working in obedience to the will of God, even the Father? Now this is the Son of God, as the Scripture represents Nebuchadnezzar the king as having said, "Did not we cast three men bound into the furnace? and, lo, I do see four walking in the midst of the fire, and the fourth is like the Son of God."[1] Neither the nature of any created thing, therefore, nor the weakness of the flesh, can prevail against the will of God. For God is not subject to created things, but created things to God; and all things yield obedience to His will. Wherefore also the Lord declares, "The things which are impossible with men, are possible with God."[2] As, therefore, it might seem to the men of the present day, who are ignorant of God's appointment, to be a thing incredible and impossible that any man could live for such a number of years, yet those who were before us did live [to such an age], and those who were translated do live as an earnest of the future length of days; and [as it might also appear impossible] that from the whale's belly and from the fiery furnace men issued forth unhurt, yet they nevertheless did so, led forth as it were by the hand of God, for the purpose of declaring His power: so also now, although some, not knowing the power and promise of God, may oppose their own salvation, deeming it impossible for God, who raises up the dead, to have power to confer upon them eternal duration, yet the scepticism of men of this stamp shall not render the faithfulness of God of none effect.

CHAP. VI.—*God will bestow salvation upon the whole nature of man, consisting of body and soul in close union, since the Word took it upon Him, and adorned it with the gifts of the Holy Spirit, of whom our bodies are, and are termed, the temples.*

1. Now God shall be glorified in His handiwork, fitting it

[1] Dan. iii. 19–25.   [2] Luke xviii. 27.

so as to be conformable to, and modelled after, His own Son. For by the hands of the Father, that is, by the Son and the Holy Spirit, man, and not [merely] a part of man, was made in the likeness of God. Now the soul and the spirit are certainly a *part* of the man, but certainly not *the* man; for the perfect man consists in the commingling and the union of the soul receiving the spirit of the Father, and the admixture of that fleshly nature which was moulded after the image of God. For this reason does the apostle declare, "We speak wisdom among them that are perfect,"[1] terming those persons "perfect" who have received the Spirit of God, and who through the Spirit of God do speak in all languages, as he used himself also to speak. In like manner we do also hear[2] many brethren in the church, who possess prophetic gifts, and who through the Spirit speak all kinds of languages, and bring to light for the general benefit the hidden things of men, and declare the mysteries of God, whom also the apostle terms "spiritual," they being spiritual because they partake of the Spirit, and not because their flesh has been stripped off and taken away, and because they have become purely spiritual. For if any one take away the substance of flesh, that is, of the handiwork [of God], and understand that which is purely spiritual, such then would not be a spiritual man, but would be the spirit of a man, or the Spirit of God. But when the spirit here blended with the soul is united to [God's] handiwork, the man is rendered spiritual and perfect because of the outpouring of the Spirit, and this is he who was made in the image and likeness of God. But if the Spirit be wanting to the soul, he who is such is indeed of an animal nature, and being left carnal, shall be an imperfect being, possessing indeed the image [of God] in his formation (*in plasmate*), but not receiving the similitude through the Spirit; and thus is this being imperfect. Thus also, if any one take away the image and set aside the handiwork, he cannot then understand this as being a man, but as either some part of a man, as I have already said, or as something else than a man. For that flesh which has been moulded is not a perfect man in itself,

---

[1] 1 Cor. ii. 6 [2] The old Latin has "audivimus," *have heard*.

but the body of a man, and part of a man. Neither is the soul itself, considered apart by itself, the man; but it is the soul of a man, and part of a man. Neither is the spirit a man, for it is called the spirit, and not a man; but the commingling and union of all these constitutes the perfect man. And for this cause does the apostle, explaining himself, make it clear that the saved man is a complete man as well as a spiritual man; saying thus in the first Epistle to the Thessalonians, "Now the God of peace sanctify you perfect (*perfectos*); and may your spirit, and soul, and body be preserved whole without complaint to the coming of the Lord Jesus Christ."[1] Now what was his object in praying that these three—that is, soul, body, and spirit—might be preserved to the coming of the Lord, unless he was aware of the [future] reintegration and union of the three, and [that they should be heirs of] one and the same salvation? For this cause also he declares that those are "the perfect" who present unto the Lord the three [component parts] without offence. Those, then, are the perfect who have had the Spirit of God remaining in them, and have preserved their souls and bodies blameless, holding fast the faith of God, that is, that faith which is [directed] towards God, and maintaining righteous dealings with respect to their neighbours.

2. Whence also he says, that this handiwork is "the temple of God," thus declaring: "Know ye not that ye are the temple of God, and that the Spirit of God dwelleth in you? If any man, therefore, will defile the temple of God, him will God destroy: for the temple of God is holy, which [temple] ye are."[2] Here he manifestly declares the body to be the temple in which the Spirit dwells. As also the Lord speaks in reference to Himself, "Destroy this temple, and in three days I will raise it up. He spake this, however," it is said, "of the temple of His body."[3] And not only does he (the apostle) acknowledge our bodies to be a temple, but even the temple of Christ, saying thus to the Corinthians, "Know ye not that your bodies are members of Christ? Shall I then take the members of Christ, and make them the

[1] 1 Thess. v. 23. [2] 1 Cor. iii. 16. [3] John ii. 19–21.

members of an harlot?"¹ He speaks these things, not in reference to some other spiritual man; for a being of such a nature could have nothing to do with an harlot: but he declares "our body," that is, the flesh which continues in sanctity and purity, to be "the members of Christ;" but that when it becomes one with an harlot, it becomes the members of an harlot. And for this reason he said, "If any man defile the temple of God, him will God destroy." How then is it not the utmost blasphemy to allege, that the temple of God, in which the Spirit of the Father dwells, and the members of Christ, do not partake of salvation, but are reduced to perdition? Also, that our bodies are raised not from their own substance, but by the power of God, he says to the Corinthians, "Now the body is not for fornication, but for the Lord, and the Lord for the body. But God hath both raised up the Lord, and shall raise us up by His own power."²

CHAP. VII.—*Inasmuch as Christ did rise in our flesh, it follows that we shall be also raised in the same; since the resurrection promised to us should not be referred to spirits naturally immortal, but to bodies in themselves mortal.*

1. In the same manner, therefore, as Christ did rise in the substance of flesh, and pointed out to His disciples the mark of the nails and the opening in His side³ (now these are the tokens of that flesh which rose from the dead), so " shall He also," it is said, "raise us up by His own power."⁴ And again to the Romans he says, "But if the Spirit of Him that raised up Jesus from the dead dwell in you, He that raised up Christ from the dead shall also quicken your mortal bodies."⁵ What, then, are mortal bodies? Can they be souls? Nay, for souls are incorporeal when put in comparison with mortal bodies; for God "breathed into the face of man the breath of life, and man became a living soul." Now the breath

---

¹ 1 Cor. iii. 17. ² 1 Cor. vi. 13, 14. ³ John xx. 20, 25, 27.
⁴ 1 Cor. vi. 14. ⁵ Rom. viii. 11.

of life is an incorporeal thing. And certainly they cannot maintain that the very breath of life is mortal. Therefore David says, "My soul also shall live to Him,"[1] just as if its substance were immortal. Neither, on the other hand, can they say that the spirit is the mortal body. What therefore is there left to which we may apply the term "mortal body," unless it be the thing that was moulded, that is, the flesh, of which it is also said that God will vivify it? For this it is which dies and is decomposed, but not the soul or the spirit. For to die is to lose vital power, and to become henceforth breathless, inanimate, and devoid of motion, and to melt away into those [component parts] from which also it derived the commencement of [its] substance. But this event happens neither to the soul, for it is the breath of life; nor to the spirit, for the spirit is simple and not composite, so that it cannot be decomposed, and is itself the life of those who receive it. We must therefore conclude that it is in reference to the flesh that death is mentioned; which [flesh], after the soul's departure, becomes breathless and inanimate, and is decomposed gradually into the earth from which it was taken. This, then, is what is mortal. And it is this of which he also says, "He shall also quicken your mortal bodies." And therefore in reference to it he says, in the first [Epistle] to the Corinthians: "So also is the resurrection of the dead: it is sown in corruption, it rises in incorruption."[2] For he declares, "That which thou sowest cannot be quickened, unless first it die."[3]

2. But what is that which, like a grain of wheat, is sown in the earth and decays, unless it be the bodies which are laid in the earth, into which seeds are also cast? And for this reason he said, "It is sown in dishonour, it rises in glory."[4] For what is more ignoble than dead flesh? Or, on the other hand, what is more glorious than the same when it arises and partakes of incorruption? "It is sown in weakness, it is raised in power:"[5] in its own weakness certainly, because since it is earth it goes to earth; but [it is quickened]

[1] Ps. xxii. 31, LXX.   [2] 1 Cor. xv. 42.   [3] 1 Cor. xv. 36.
[4] 1 Cor. xv. 43.   [5] 1 Cor. xv. 43.

by the power of God, who raises it from the dead. "It is sown an animal body, it rises a spiritual body."[1] He has taught, beyond all doubt, that such language was not used by him, either with reference to the soul or to the spirit, but to bodies that have become corpses. For these are animal bodies, that is, [bodies] which partake of life, which when they have lost, they succumb to death; then, rising through the Spirit's instrumentality, they become spiritual bodies, so that by the Spirit they possess a perpetual life. "For now," he says, "we know in part, and we prophesy in part, but then face to face."[2] And this it is which has been said also by Peter: "Whom having not seen, ye love; in whom now also, not seeing, ye believe; and believing, ye shall rejoice with joy unspeakable."[3] For our face shall see the face of the Lord,[4] and shall rejoice with joy unspeakable,—that is to say, when it shall behold its own Delight.

CHAP. VIII.—*The gifts of the Holy Spirit which we receive prepare us for incorruption, render us spiritual, and separate us from carnal men. These two classes are signified by the clean and unclean animals in the legal dispensation.*

1. But we do now receive a certain portion of His Spirit, tending towards perfection, and preparing us for incorruption, being little by little accustomed to receive and bear God; which also the apostle terms "an earnest," that is, a part of the honour which has been promised us by God, where he says in the Epistle to the Ephesians, "In which ye also, having heard the word of truth, the gospel of your salvation, believing in which ye have been sealed with the Holy Spirit of promise, which is the earnest of our inheritance."[5] This earnest, therefore, thus dwelling in us, renders

---

[1] 1 Cor. xv. 44.   [2] 1 Cor. xiii. 9, 12.   [3] 1 Pet. i. 8.
[4] Grabe, Massuet, and Stieren prefer to read, "the face of the living God;" while Harvey adopts the above, reading merely "Domini," and not "Dei vivi."
[5] Eph. i. 13, etc.

us spiritual even now, and the mortal is swallowed up by immortality.[1] "For ye," he declares, "are not in the flesh, but in the Spirit, if so be that the Spirit of God dwell in you."[2] This, however, does not take place by a casting away of the flesh, but by the impartation of the Spirit. For those to whom he was writing were not without flesh, but they were those who had received the Spirit of God, "by which we cry, Abba, Father."[3] If therefore, at the present time, having the earnest, we do cry, "Abba, Father," what shall it be when, on rising again, we behold Him face to face; when all the members shall burst out into a continuous hymn of triumph, glorifying Him who raised them from the dead, and gave the gift of eternal life? For if the earnest, gathering man into itself, does even now cause him to cry, "Abba, Father," what shall the complete grace of the Spirit effect, which shall be given to men by God? It will render us like unto Him, and accomplish the will[4] of the Father; for it shall make man after the image and likeness of God.

2. Those persons, then, who possess the earnest of the Spirit, and who are not enslaved by the lusts of the flesh, but are subject to the Spirit, and who in all things walk according to the light of reason, does the apostle properly term "spiritual," because the Spirit of God dwells in them. Now, spiritual men shall not be incorporeal spirits; but our substance, that is, the union of flesh and spirit, receiving the Spirit of God, makes up the spiritual man. But those who do indeed reject the Spirit's counsel, and are the slaves of fleshly lusts, and lead lives contrary to reason, and who, without restraint, plunge headlong into their own desires, having no longing after the Divine Spirit, do live after the manner of swine and of dogs; these men, [I say], does the apostle very properly term "carnal," because they have no thought of anything else except carnal things.

3. For the same reason, too, do the prophets compare them to irrational animals, on account of the irrationality of

---

[1] 2 Cor. v. 4.   [2] Rom. viii. 9.   [3] Rom. viii. 15.
[4] This is adopting Harvey's emendation of "voluntatem" for "voluntate."

their conduct, saying, "They have become as horses raging for the females; each one of them neighing after his neighbour's wife."[1] And again, "Man, when he was in honour, was made like unto cattle."[2] This denotes that, for his own fault, he is likened to cattle, by rivalling their irrational life. And we also, as the custom is, do designate men of this stamp as cattle and irrational beasts.

3. Now the law has figuratively predicted all these, delineating man by the [various] animals:[3] whatsoever of these, says [the Scripture], have a double hoof and ruminate, it proclaims as clean; but whatsoever of them do not possess one or other of these [properties], it sets aside by themselves as unclean. Who then are the clean? Those who make their way by faith steadily towards the Father and the Son; for this is denoted by the steadiness of those which divide the hoof; and they meditate day and night upon the words of God,[4] that they may be adorned with good works: for this is the meaning of the ruminants. The unclean, however, are those which do neither divide the hoof nor ruminate; that is, those persons who have neither faith in God, nor do meditate on His words: and such is the abomination of the Gentiles. But as to those animals which do indeed chew the cud, but have not the double hoof, and are themselves unclean, we have in them a figurative description of the Jews, who certainly have the words of God in their mouth, but who do not fix their rooted stedfastness in the Father and in the Son; wherefore they are an unstable generation. For those animals which have the hoof all in one piece easily slip: but those which have it divided are more sure-footed, their cleft hoofs succeeding each other as they advance, and the one hoof supporting the other. In like manner, too, those are unclean which have the double hoof but do not ruminate: this is plainly an indication of all heretics, and of those who do not meditate on the words of God, neither are adorned with works of righteousness; to whom also the Lord says, " Why call ye me Lord, Lord, and do not the things which

[1] Jer. v. 3.
[2] Ps. xlix. 20.
[3] Lev. xi. 2; Deut. xiv. 3, etc.
[4] Ps. i. 2.

I say to you?"[1] For men of this stamp do indeed say that they believe in the Father and the Son, but they never meditate as they should upon the things of God, neither are they adorned with works of righteousness; but, as I have already observed, they have adopted the lives of swine and of dogs, giving themselves over to filthiness, to gluttony, and recklessness of all sorts. Justly, therefore, did the apostle call all such " carnal " and " animal,"[2]—[all those, namely], who through their own unbelief and luxury do not receive the Divine Spirit, and in their various phases cast out from themselves the life-giving Word, and walk stupidly after their own lusts: the prophets, too, spake of them as beasts of burden and wild beasts; custom likewise has viewed them in the light of cattle and irrational creatures; and the law has pronounced them unclean.

CHAP. IX.—*Showing how that passage of the apostle which the heretics pervert, should be understood; viz., " Flesh and blood shall not possess the kingdom of God."*

1. Among the other [truths] proclaimed by the apostle, there is also this one, "That flesh and blood cannot inherit the kingdom of God."[3] This is [the passage] which is adduced by all the heretics in support of their folly, with an attempt to annoy us, and to point out that the handiwork of God is not saved. They do not take this fact into consideration, that there are three things out of which, as I have shown, the complete man is composed—flesh, soul, and spirit. One of these does indeed preserve and fashion [the man]— this is the spirit; while as to another it is united and formed —that is the flesh; then [comes] that which is between these two—that is the soul, which sometimes indeed, when it follows the spirit, is raised up by it, but sometimes it sympathizes with the flesh, and falls into carnal lusts. Those then, as many as they be, who have not that which saves and forms [us] into life [eternal], shall be, and shall be called, [mere] flesh and blood; for these are they who have not the Spirit

[1] Luke vi. 46.   [2] 1 Cor. ii. 14, iii. 1, etc.   [3] 1 Cor. xv. 50.

of God in themselves. Wherefore men of this stamp are spoken of by the Lord as "dead;" for, says He, "Let the dead bury their dead,"[1] because they have not the Spirit which quickens man.

2. On the other hand, as many as fear God and trust in His Son's advent, and who through faith do establish the Spirit of God in their hearts,—such men as these shall be properly called both "pure," and "spiritual," and "those living to God," because they possess the Spirit of the Father, who purifies man, and raises him up to the life of God. For as the Lord has testified that "the flesh is weak," so [does He also say] that "the spirit is willing."[2] For this latter is capable of working out its own suggestions. If, therefore, any one admix the ready inclination of the Spirit to be, as it were, a stimulus to the infirmity of the flesh, it inevitably follows that what is strong will prevail over the weak, so that the weakness of the flesh will be absorbed by the strength of the Spirit; and that the man in whom this takes place cannot in that case be carnal, but spiritual, because of the fellowship of the Spirit. Thus it is, therefore, that the martyrs bear their witness, and despise death, not after the infirmity of the flesh, but because of the readiness of the Spirit. For when the infirmity of the flesh is absorbed, it exhibits the Spirit as powerful; and again, when the Spirit absorbs the weakness [of the flesh], it possesses the flesh as an inheritance in itself, and from both of these is formed a living man,—living, indeed, because he partakes of the Spirit, but man, because of the substance of flesh.

3. The flesh, therefore, when destitute of the Spirit of God, is dead, not having life, and cannot possess the kingdom of God: [it is as] irrational blood, like water poured out upon the ground. And therefore he says, "As is the earthy, such are they that are earthy."[3] But where the Spirit of the Father is, there is a living man; [there is] the rational blood preserved by God for the avenging [of those that shed it]; [there is] the flesh possessed by the Spirit, forgetful indeed of what belongs to it, and adopting the quality of the Spirit,

---

[1] Luke x. 60.   [2] Matt. xxvi. 41.   [3] 1 Cor. xv. 48.

being made conformable to the Word of God. And on this account he (the apostle) declares, "As we have borne the image of him who is of the earth, we shall also bear the image of Him who is from heaven."[1] What, therefore, is the earthly? That which was fashioned. And what is the heavenly? The Spirit. As therefore he says, when we were destitute of the celestial Spirit, we walked in former times in the oldness of the flesh, not obeying God; so now let us, receiving the Spirit, walk in newness of life, obeying God. Inasmuch, therefore, as without the Spirit of God we cannot be saved, the apostle exhorts us through faith and chaste conversation to preserve the Spirit of God, lest, having become non-participators of the Divine Spirit, we lose the kingdom of heaven; and he exclaims, that flesh in itself, and blood, cannot possess the kingdom of God.

4. If, however, we must speak strictly, [we would say that] the flesh *does not* inherit, but *is* inherited; as also the Lord declares, "Blessed are the meek, for they shall possess the earth by inheritance;"[2] as if in the [future] kingdom, the earth, from whence exists the substance of our flesh, is to be possessed by inheritance. This is the reason for His wishing the temple (*i.e.* the flesh) to be clean, that the Spirit of God may take delight therein, as a bridegroom with a bride. As, therefore, the bride cannot [be said] to wed, but to be wedded, when the bridegroom comes and takes her, so also the flesh cannot by itself possess the kingdom of God by inheritance; but it can be taken *for* an inheritance into the kingdom of God. For a living person inherits the goods of the deceased; and it is one thing to inherit, another to be inherited. The former rules, and exercises power over, and orders the things inherited at his will; but the latter things are in a state of subjection, are under orders, and are ruled over by him who has obtained the inheritance. What, therefore, is it that lives? The Spirit of God, doubtless. What, again, are the possessions of the deceased? The various parts of the man, surely, which rot in the earth. But these are inherited by the Spirit when they are translated into the kingdom of heaven. For

[1] 1 Cor. xv. 49. [2] Matt. v. 5.

this cause, too, did Christ die, that the gospel covenant being manifested and known to the whole world, might in the first place set free His slaves; and then afterwards, as I have already shown, might constitute them heirs of His property, when the Spirit possesses them by inheritance. For he who lives inherits, but the flesh is inherited. In order that we may not lose life by losing that Spirit which possesses us, the apostle, exhorting us to the communion of the Spirit, has said, according to reason, in those words already quoted, "That flesh and blood cannot inherit the kingdom of God." Just as if he were to say, "Do not err; for unless the Word of God dwell with, and the Spirit of the Father be in you, and if ye shall live frivolously and carelessly as if ye were this only, viz. mere flesh and blood, ye cannot inherit the kingdom of God."

CHAP. X.—*By a comparison drawn from the wild olive-tree, whose quality but not whose nature is changed by grafting, he proves more important things; he points out also that man without the Spirit is not capable of bringing forth fruit, or of inheriting the kingdom of God.*

1. This truth, therefore, [he declares], in order that we may not reject the engrafting of the Spirit while pampering the flesh. "But thou, being a wild olive-tree," he says, "hast been grafted into the good olive-tree, and been made a partaker of the fatness of the olive-tree."[1] As, therefore, when the wild olive has been engrafted, if it remain in its former condition, viz. a wild olive, it is "cut off, and cast into the fire;"[2] but if it takes kindly to the graft, and is changed into the good olive-tree, it becomes a fruit-bearing olive, planted, as it were, in a king's park (*paradiso*): so likewise men, if they do truly progress by faith towards better things, and receive the Spirit of God, and bring forth the fruit thereof, shall be spiritual, as being planted in the paradise of God. But if they cast out the Spirit, and remain in their former condition, desirous of being of the flesh rather

[1] Rom. xi. 17.   [2] Matt. vii. 19.

than of the Spirit, then it is very justly said with regard to men of this stamp, "That flesh and blood shall not inherit the kingdom of God;"[1] just as if any one were to say that the wild olive is not received into the paradise of God. Admirably therefore does the apostle exhibit our nature, and God's universal appointment, in his discourse about flesh and blood and the wild olive. For as the good olive, if neglected for a certain time, if left to grow wild and to run to wood, does itself become a wild olive; or again, if the wild olive be carefully tended and grafted, it naturally reverts to its former fruit-bearing condition: so men also, when they become careless, and bring forth for fruit the lusts of the flesh like woody produce, are rendered, by their own fault, unfruitful in righteousness. For when men sleep, the enemy sows the material of tares;[2] and for this cause did the Lord command His disciples to be on the watch.[3] And again, those persons who are not bringing forth the fruits of righteousness, and are, as it were, covered over and lost among brambles, if they use diligence, and receive the word of God as a graft,[4] arrive at the pristine nature of man—that which was created after the image and likeness of God.

2. But as the engrafted wild olive does not certainly lose the substance of its wood, but changes the quality of its fruit, and receives another name, being now not a wild olive, but a fruit-bearing olive, and is called so; so also, when man is grafted in by faith and receives the Spirit of God, he certainly does not lose the substance of flesh, but changes the quality of the fruit [brought forth, *i.e.*] of his works, and receives another name,[5] showing that he has become changed for the better, being now not [mere] flesh and blood, but a spiritual man, and is called such. Then, again, as the wild olive, if it be not grafted in, remains useless to its lord because of its woody quality, and is cut down as a tree bearing no fruit, and cast into the fire; so also man, if he does not receive through faith the engrafting of the Spirit, remains in his old condi-

---

[1] 1 Cor. xv. 50.
[2] Matt. xiii. 25.
[3] Matt. xxiv. 42, xxv. 13; Mark xiii. 33.
[4] Jas. i. 21.
[5] Rev. ii. 17.

tion, and being [mere] flesh and blood, he cannot inherit the kingdom of God. Rightly therefore does the apostle declare, "Flesh and blood cannot inherit the kingdom of God;"[1] and, "Those who are in the flesh cannot please God:"[2] not repudiating [by these words] the substance of flesh, but showing that into it the Spirit must be infused.[3] And for this reason he says, "This mortal must put on immortality, and this corruptible must put on incorruption."[4] And again he declares, "But ye are not in the flesh, but in the Spirit, if so be that the Spirit of God dwell in you."[5] He sets this forth still more plainly, where he says, "The body indeed is dead, because of sin; but the Spirit is life, because of righteousness. But if the Spirit of Him who raised up Jesus from the dead dwell in you, He that raised up Christ from the dead shall also quicken your mortal bodies, because of His Spirit dwelling in you."[6] And again he says, in the Epistle to the Romans, "For if ye live after the flesh, ye shall die."[7] [Now by these words] he does not prohibit them from living their lives in the flesh, for he was himself in the flesh when he wrote to them; but he cuts away the lusts of the flesh, those which bring death upon a man. And for this reason he says in continuation, "But if ye through the Spirit do mortify the works of the flesh, ye shall live. For whosoever are led by the Spirit of God, these are the sons of God."

CHAP. XI.—*Treats upon the actions of carnal and of spiritual persons; also, that the spiritual cleansing is not to be referred to the substance of our bodies, but to the manner of our former life.*

1. [The apostle], foreseeing the wicked speeches of unbelievers, has particularized the works which he terms carnal; and he explains himself, lest any room for doubt be left to

---

[1] 1 Cor. xv. 50.　　　　　　　[2] Rom. viii. 8.
[3] The Latin has, " sed infusionem Spiritus attrahens."
[4] 1 Cor. xv. 53.　　　　　　　[5] Rom. viii. 9.
[6] Rom. viii. 10, etc.　　　　　　[7] Rom. viii. 13.

those who do dishonestly pervert his meaning, thus saying in the Epistle to the Galatians: "Now the works of the flesh are manifest, which are: adulteries, fornications, uncleanness, luxuriousness, idolatries, witchcrafts,[1] hatreds, contentions, jealousies, wraths, emulations, animosities, irritable speeches, dissensions, heresies, envyings, drunkenness, carousings, and such like; of which I warn you, as also I have warned you, that they who do such things shall not inherit the kingdom of God."[2] Thus does he point out to his hearers in a more explicit manner what it is [he means when he declares], "Flesh and blood shall not inherit the kingdom of God." For they who do these things, since they do indeed walk after the flesh, have not the power of living unto God. And then, again, he proceeds to tell us the spiritual actions which vivify a man, that is, the engrafting of the Spirit; thus saying, "But the fruit of the Spirit is love, joy, peace, long-suffering, goodness, benignity, faith, meekness, continence, chastity: against these there is no law."[3] As, therefore, he who has gone forward to the better things, and has brought forth the fruit of the Spirit, is saved altogether because of the communion of the Spirit; so also he who has continued in the aforesaid works of the flesh, being truly reckoned as carnal, because he did not receive the Spirit of God, shall not have power to inherit the kingdom of heaven. As, again, the same apostle testifies, saying to the Corinthians, "Know ye not that the unrighteous shall not inherit the kingdom of God? Do not err," he says: "neither fornicators, nor idolaters, nor adulterers, nor effeminate, nor abusers of themselves with mankind, nor thieves, nor covetous, nor revilers, nor rapacious persons, shall inherit the kingdom of God. And these ye indeed have been; but ye have been washed, but ye have been sanctified, but ye have been justified in the name of the Lord Jesus Christ, and in the Spirit of our God."[4] He shows in the clearest manner through what things it is that man goes to destruction, if he has continued to live after the flesh; and then, on the other hand, [he points out]

---

[1] Or, "poisonings."   [2] Gal. v. 19, etc.
[3] Gal. v. 22.   [4] 1 Cor. vi. 9-11.

through what things he is saved. Now he says that the things which save are the name of our Lord Jesus Christ, and the Spirit of our God.

2. Since, therefore, in that passage he recounts those works of the flesh which are without the Spirit, which bring death [upon their doers], he exclaimed at the end of his epistle, in accordance with what he had already declared, "And as we have borne the image of him who is of the earth, we shall also bear the image of Him who is from heaven. For this I say, brethren, that flesh and blood cannot inherit the kingdom of God."[1] Now this which he says, "as we have borne the image of him who is of the earth," is analogous to what has been declared, "And such indeed ye were; but ye have been washed, but ye have been sanctified, but ye have been justified in the name of our Lord Jesus Christ, and in the Spirit of our God." When, therefore, did we bear the image of him who is of the earth? Doubtless it was when those actions spoken of as "works of the flesh" used to be wrought in us. And then, again, when [do we bear] the image of the heavenly? Doubtless when he says, "Ye have been washed," believing in the name of the Lord, and receiving His Spirit. Now we have washed away, not the substance of our body, nor the image of our [primary] formation, but the former vain conversation. In these members, therefore, in which we were going to destruction by working the works of corruption, in these very members are we made alive by working the works of the Spirit.

CHAP. XII.—*Of the difference between life and death; of the breath of life and the vivifying Spirit: also how it is that the substance of flesh revives which once was dead.*

1. For as the flesh is capable of corruption, so is it also of incorruption; and as it is of death, so is it also of life. These two do mutually give way to each other; and both cannot remain in the same place, but one is driven out by the other, and the presence of the one destroys that of the other. If,

[1] 1 Cor. xv. 49, etc.

then, when death takes possession of a man, it drives life away from him, and proves him to be dead, much more does life, when it has obtained power over the man, drive out death, and restore him as living unto God. For if death brings mortality, why should not life, when it comes, vivify man? Just as Esaias the prophet says, "Death devoured when it had prevailed."[1] And again, "God has wiped away every tear from every face." Thus that former life is expelled, because it was not given by the Spirit, but by the breath.

2. For the breath of life, which also rendered man an animated being, is one thing, and the vivifying Spirit another, which also caused him to become spiritual. And for this reason Isaiah said, "Thus saith the Lord, who made heaven and established it, who founded the earth and the things therein, and gave breath to the people upon it, and Spirit to those walking upon it;"[2] thus telling us that breath is indeed given in common to all people upon earth, but that the Spirit is theirs alone who tread down earthly desires. And therefore Isaiah himself, distinguishing the things already mentioned, again exclaims, "For the Spirit shall go forth from me, and I have made every breath."[3] Thus does he attribute the Spirit as peculiar to God, which in the last times He pours forth upon the human race by the adoption of sons; but [he shows] that breath was common throughout the creation, and points it out as something created. Now what has been made is a different thing from him who makes it. The breath, then, is temporal, but the Spirit eternal. The breath, too, increases [in strength] for a short period, and continues for a certain time; after that it takes its departure, leaving its former abode destitute of breath. But when the Spirit pervades the man within and without, inasmuch as it continues there, it never leaves him. "But that is not first which is spiritual," says the apostle, speaking this as if with reference to us human beings; "but that is first which is animal, afterwards that which is spiritual,"[4] in accordance with reason. For there had been a necessity that, in the

---

[1] Isa. xxv. 8, LXX.
[2] Isa. xlii. 5.
[3] Isa. lvii. 16.
[4] 1 Cor. xv. 46.

being driven out by his subsequent knowledge: just as the blind men whom the Lord healed did certainly lose their blindness, but received the substance of their eyes perfect, and obtained the power of vision in the very same eyes with which they formerly did not see; the darkness being merely driven away by the power of vision, while the substance of the eyes was retained, in order that, by means of those eyes through which they had not seen, exercising again the visual power, they might give thanks to Him who had restored them again to sight. And thus, also, he whose withered hand was healed, and all who were healed generally, did not change those parts of their bodies which had at their birth come forth from the womb, but simply obtained these anew in a healthy condition.

6. For the Maker of all things, the Word of God, who did also from the beginning form man, when He found His handiwork impaired by wickedness, performed upon it all kinds of healing. At one time [He did so], as regards each separate member, as it is found in His own handiwork; and at another time He did once for all restore man sound and whole in all points, preparing him perfect for Himself unto the resurrection. For what was His object in healing [different] portions of the flesh, and restoring them to their original condition, if those parts which had been healed by Him were not in a position to obtain salvation? For if it was [merely] a temporary benefit which He conferred, He granted nothing of importance to those who were the subjects of His healing. Or how can they maintain that the flesh is incapable of receiving the life which flows from Him, when it received healing from Him? For life is brought about through healing, and incorruption through life. He, therefore, who confers healing, the same does also confer life; and He [who gives] life, also surrounds His own handiwork with incorruption.

CHAP. XIII.—*In the dead who were raised by Christ we possess the highest proof of the resurrection; and our hearts are shown to be capable of life eternal, because they can now receive the Spirit of God.*

1. Let our opponents—that is, they who speak against their own salvation—inform us [as to this point]: The deceased daughter of the high priest;[1] the widow's dead son, who was being carried out [to burial] near the gate [of the city];[2] and Lazarus, who had lain four days in the tomb,[3]—in what bodies did they rise again? In those same, no doubt, in which they had also died. For if it were not in the very same, then certainly those same individuals who had died did not rise again. For [the Scripture] says, "The Lord took the hand of the dead man, and said to him, Young man, I say unto thee, Arise. And the dead man sat up, and He commanded that something should be given him to eat; and He delivered him to his mother."[4] Again, He called Lazarus "with a loud voice, saying, Lazarus, come forth; and he that was dead came forth bound with bandages, feet and hands." This was symbolical of that man who had been bound in sins. And therefore the Lord said, "Loose him, and let him depart." As, therefore, those who were healed were made whole in those members which had in times past been afflicted; and the dead rose in the identical bodies, their limbs and bodies receiving health, and that life which was granted by the Lord, who prefigures eternal things by temporal, and shows that it is He who is Himself able to extend both healing and life to His handiwork, that His words concerning its [future] resurrection may also be believed; so also at the end, when the Lord utters His voice "by the last trumpet,"[5] the dead shall be raised, as He Him-

---

[1] Mark v. 22. Irenæus confounds the ruler of the synagogue with the high priest.
[2] Luke vii. 12. [3] John ix. 30.
[4] The two miracles of raising the widow's son and the rabbi's daughter are here amalgamated.
[5] 1 Cor. xv. 52.

self declares: "The hour shall come, in which all the dead which are in the tombs shall hear the voice of the Son of man, and shall come forth; those that have done good to the resurrection of life, and those that have done evil to the resurrection of judgment."[1]

2. Vain, therefore, and truly miserable, are those who do not choose to see what is so manifest and clear, but shun the light of truth, blinding themselves like the tragic Œdipus. And as those who are not practised in wrestling, when they contend with others, laying hold with a determined grasp of some part of [their opponent's] body, really fall by means of that which they grasp, yet when they fall, imagine that they are gaining the victory, because they have obstinately kept their hold upon that part which they seized at the outset, and besides falling, become subjects of ridicule; so is it with respect to that [favourite] expression of the heretics: "Flesh and blood cannot inherit the kingdom of God;" while taking two expressions of Paul's, without having perceived the apostle's meaning, or examined critically the force of the terms, but keeping fast hold of the mere expressions by themselves, they die in consequence of their influence ($\pi\epsilon\rho\grave{\iota}$ $\alpha\grave{\upsilon}\tau\grave{\alpha}\varsigma$), overturning as far as in them lies the entire dispensation of God.

3. For thus they will allege that this passage refers to the flesh strictly so called, and not to fleshly works, as I have pointed out, so representing the apostle as contradicting himself. For immediately following, in the same epistle, he says conclusively, speaking thus in reference to the flesh: "For this corruptible must put on incorruption, and this mortal must put on immortality. So, when this mortal shall have put on immortality, then shall be brought to pass the saying which is written, Death is swallowed up in victory. O death, where is thy sting? O death, where is thy victory?"[2] Now these words shall be appropriately said at the time when this mortal and corruptible flesh, which is subject to death, which also is pressed down by a certain dominion of death, rising up into life, shall put on incorruption and immortality.

[1] John v. 28.   [2] 1 Cor. xv. 53.

For then, indeed, shall death be truly vanquished, when that flesh which is held down by it shall go forth from under its dominion. And again, to the Philippians he says: "But our conversation is in heaven, from whence also we look for the Saviour, the Lord Jesus, who shall transfigure the body of our humiliation conformable to the body of His glory, even as He is able (*ita ut possit*) according to the working of His own power."[1] What, then, is this "body of humiliation" which the Lord shall transfigure, [so as to be] conformed to "the body of His glory?" Plainly it is this body composed of flesh, which is indeed humbled when it falls into the earth. Now its transformation [takes place thus], that while it is mortal and corruptible, it becomes immortal and incorruptible, not after its own proper substance, but after the mighty working of the Lord, who is able to invest the mortal with immortality, and the corruptible with incorruption. And therefore he says,[2] "that mortality may be swallowed up of life. He who has perfected us for this very thing is God, who also has given unto us the earnest of the Spirit."[3] He uses these words most manifestly in reference to the flesh; for the soul is not mortal, neither is the spirit. Now, what is mortal shall be swallowed up of life, when the flesh is dead no longer, but remains living and incorruptible, hymning the praises of God, who has perfected us for this very thing. In order, therefore, that we may be perfected for this, aptly does he say to the Corinthians, "Glorify God in your body."[4] Now God is He who gives rise to immortality.

4. That he uses these words with respect to the body of flesh, and to none other, he declares to the Corinthians manifestly, indubitably, and free from all ambiguity: "Always bearing about in our body the dying of Jesus,[5] that also the

[1] Phil. iii. 29, etc.
[2] The original Greek text is preserved here, as above; the Latin translator inserts, "in secunda ad Corinthios." Harvey observes: "The interpolation of the scriptural reference by the translator suggests the suspicion that the greater number of such references have come in from the margin."
[3] 2 Cor. v. 4.   [4] 1 Cor. vi. 20.
[5] Agreeing with the Syriac version in omitting "the Lord" before the

life of Jesus Christ might be manifested in our body. For if we who live are delivered unto death for Jesus' sake, it is that the life of Jesus may also be manifested in our mortal flesh."[1] And that the Spirit lays hold on the flesh, he says in the same epistle, "That ye are the epistle of Christ, ministered by us, inscribed not with ink, but with the Spirit of the living God, not in tables of stone, but in the fleshly tables of the heart."[2] If, therefore, in the present time, fleshly hearts are made partakers of the Spirit, what is there astonishing if, in the resurrection, they receive that life which is granted by the Spirit? Of which resurrection the apostle speaks in the Epistle to the Philippians: "Having been made conformable to His death, if by any means I might attain to the resurrection which is from the dead."[3] In what other mortal flesh, therefore, can life be understood as being manifested, unless in that substance which is also put to death on account of that confession which is made of God?—as he has himself declared, "If, as a man, I have fought with beasts[4] at Ephesus, what advantageth it me if the dead rise not? For if the dead rise not, neither has Christ risen. Now, if Christ has not risen, our preaching is vain, and your faith is vain. In that case, too, we are found false witnesses for God, since we have testified that He raised up Christ, whom [upon that supposition] He did not raise up.[5] For if the dead rise not, neither has Christ risen. But if Christ be not risen, your faith is vain, since ye are yet in your sins. Therefore those who have fallen asleep in Christ have perished. If in this life only we have hope in Christ, we are more miserable than all men. But now Christ has risen from the dead, the first-fruits of those that sleep; for

---

word "Jesus," and in reading ἀεί as εἰ, which Harvey considers the true text.

[1] 2 Cor. iv. 10, etc.   [2] 2 Cor. iii. 3.   [3] Phil. iii. 11.

[4] The Syriac translation seems to take a literal meaning out of this passage: "If, as one of the sons of men, I have been cast forth to the wild beasts at Ephesus."

[5] This is in accordance with the Syriac, which omits the clause, εἴπερ ἄρα νεκροὶ οὐκ ἐγείρονται.

as by man [came] death, by man also [came] the resurrection of the dead."[1]

5. In all these passages, therefore, as I have already said, these men must either allege that the apostle expresses opinions contradicting himself, with respect to that statement, "Flesh and blood cannot inherit the kingdom of God;" or, on the other hand, they will be forced to make perverse and crooked interpretations of all the passages, so as to overturn and alter the sense of the words. For what sensible thing can they say, if they endeavour to interpret otherwise this which he writes: "For this corruptible must put on incorruption, and this mortal put on immortality;"[2] and, "That the life of Jesus may be made manifest in our mortal flesh;"[3] and all the other passages in which the apostle does manifestly and clearly declare the resurrection and incorruption of the flesh? And thus shall they be compelled to put a false interpretation upon passages such as these, they who do not choose to understand one correctly.

CHAP. XIV.—*Unless the flesh were to be saved, the Word would not have taken upon Him flesh of the same substance as ours: from this it would follow that neither should we have been reconciled by Him.*

1. And inasmuch as the apostle has not pronounced against the very substance of flesh and blood, that it cannot inherit the kingdom of God, the same apostle has everywhere adopted the term "flesh and blood" with regard to the Lord Jesus Christ, partly indeed to establish His human nature (for He did Himself speak of Himself as the Son of man), and partly that He might confirm the salvation of our flesh. For if the flesh were not in a position to be saved, the Word of God would in no wise have become flesh. And if the blood of the righteous were not to be inquired after, the Lord would certainly not have had blood [in His composition]. But inasmuch as blood cries out (*vocalis est*) from the beginning [of the world], God said to Cain, when he had slain his

---

[1] 1 Cor. xv. 13, etc.   [2] 1 Cor. xv. 53.   [3] 2 Cor. iv. 11.

brother, "The voice of thy brother's blood crieth to me."[1] And as their blood will be inquired after, he said to those with Noah, "For your blood of your souls will I require, [even] from the hand of all beasts;"[2] and again, "Whosoever will shed man's blood,[3] it shall be shed for his blood." In like manner, too, did the Lord say to those who should afterwards shed His blood, "All righteous blood shall be required which is shed upon the earth, from the blood of righteous Abel to the blood of Zacharias the son of Barachias, whom ye slew between the temple and the altar. Verily I say unto you, All these things shall come upon this generation."[4] He thus points out the recapitulation that should take place in His own person of the effusion of blood from the beginning, of all the righteous men and of the prophets, and that by means of Himself there should be a requisition of their blood. Now this [blood] could not be required unless it also had the capability of being saved; nor would the Lord have summed up these things in Himself, unless He had Himself been made flesh and blood after the way of the original formation [of man], saving in His own person at the end that which had in the beginning perished in Adam.

2. But if the Lord became incarnate for any other order of things, and took flesh of any other substance, He has not then summed up human nature in His own person, nor in that case can He be termed flesh. For flesh has been truly made [to consist in] a transmission of that thing moulded originally from the dust. But if it had been necessary for Him to draw the material [of his body] from another substance, the Father would at the beginning have moulded the material [of flesh] from a different substance [than from what He actually did]. But now the case stands thus, that the Word has saved that which really was [created, viz.] humanity which had perished, effecting by means of Himself that communion which should be held with it, and seeking

---

[1] Gen. iv. 10.   [2] Gen. ix. 5, 6, LXX.
[3] One of the MSS. reads here: Sanguis pro sanguine ejus effundetur.
[4] Matt. xxiii. 35, etc.; Luke xi. 50.

out its salvation. But the thing which had perished possessed flesh and blood. For the Lord, taking dust from the earth, moulded man; and it was upon his behalf that all the dispensation of the Lord's advent took place. He had Himself, therefore, flesh and blood, recapitulating in Himself not a certain other, but that original handiwork of the Father, seeking out that thing which had perished. And for this cause the apostle, in the Epistle to the Colossians, says, "And though ye were formerly alienated, and enemies to His knowledge by evil works, yet now ye have been reconciled in the body of His flesh, through His death, to present yourselves holy and chaste, and without fault in His sight."[1] He says, "Ye have been reconciled in the body of His flesh," because the righteous flesh has reconciled that flesh which was being kept under bondage in sin, and brought it into friendship with God.

3. If, then, any one allege that in this respect the flesh of the Lord was different from ours, because it indeed did not commit sin, neither was deceit found in His soul, while we, on the other hand, are sinners, he says what is the fact. But if he pretends that the Lord possessed another substance of flesh, the sayings respecting reconciliation will not agree with that man. For that thing is reconciled which had formerly been in enmity. Now, if the Lord had taken flesh from another substance, He would not, by so doing, have reconciled that one to God which had become inimical through transgression. But now, by means of communion with Himself, the Lord has reconciled man to God the Father, in reconciling us to Himself by the body of His own flesh, and redeeming us by His own blood, as the apostle says to the Ephesians, "In whom we have redemption through His blood, the remission of sins;"[2] and again to the same he says, "Ye who formerly were far off have been brought near in the blood of Christ;"[3] and again, "Abolishing in His flesh the enmities, [even] the law of commandments [contained] in ordinances."[4] And in every epistle the apostle plainly testifies, that through the flesh of our Lord, and through His blood, we have been saved.

[1] Col. i. 21, etc.   [2] Eph. i. 7.   [3] Eph. ii. 13.   [4] Eph. ii. 15.

4. If, therefore, flesh and blood are the things which procure for us life, it has not been declared of flesh and blood, in the literal meaning (*proprie*) of the terms, that they cannot inherit the kingdom of God; but [these words apply] to those carnal deeds already mentioned, which, perverting man to sin, deprive him of life. And for this reason he says, in the Epistle to the Romans: "Let not sin, therefore, reign in your mortal body, to be under its control: neither yield ye your members instruments of unrighteousness unto sin; but yield yourselves to God, as being alive from the dead, and your members as instruments of righteousness unto God."[1] In these same members, therefore, in which we used to serve sin, and bring forth fruit unto death, does He wish us to [be obedient] unto righteousness, that we may bring forth fruit unto life. Remember, therefore, my beloved friend, that thou hast been redeemed by the flesh of our Lord, re-established[2] by His blood; and "holding the Head, from which the whole body of the church, having been fitted together, takes increase"[3]—that is, acknowledging the advent in the flesh of the Son of God, and [His] divinity (*deum*), and looking forward with constancy to His human nature[4] (*hominem*), availing thyself also of these proofs drawn from Scripture—thou dost easily overthrow, as I have pointed out, all those notions of the heretics which were concocted afterwards.

CHAP. XV.—*Proofs of the resurrection from Isaiah and Ezekiel; the same God who created us will also raise us up.*

1. Now, that He who at the beginning created man, did promise him a second birth after his dissolution into earth,

---

[1] Rom. vi. 12, etc.

[2] "Et sanguine ejus redhibitus," corresponding to the Greek term ἀποκατασταθείς. "Redhibere" is properly a *forensic* term, meaning to cause any article to be restored to the vendor.

[3] Col. ii. 19.

[4] Harvey restores the Greek thus, καὶ τὸν αὐτοῦ ἄνθρωπον βεβαίως ἐκδεχόμενος, which he thinks has a reference to the patient waiting for "Christ's second advent to judge the world." The phrase might also be translated, "and receiving stedfastly His human nature."

Esaias thus declares: "The dead shall rise again, and they who are in the tombs shall arise, and they who are in the earth shall rejoice. For the dew which is from Thee is health to them."[1] And again: "I will comfort you, and ye shall be comforted in Jerusalem: and ye shall see, and your heart shall rejoice, and your bones shall flourish as the grass; and the hand of the Lord shall be known to those who worship Him."[2] And Ezekiel speaks as follows: "And the hand of the Lord came upon me, and the Lord led me forth in the Spirit, and set me down in the midst of the plain, and this place was full of bones. And He caused me to pass by them round about: and, behold, there were many upon the surface of the plain very dry. And He said unto me, Son of man, can these bones live? And I said, Lord, Thou who hast made them dost know. And He said unto me, Prophesy upon these bones, and thou shalt say to them, Ye dry bones, hear the word of the Lord. Thus saith the Lord to these bones, Behold, I will cause the spirit of life to come upon you, and I will lay sinews upon you, and bring up flesh again upon you, and I will stretch skin upon you, and will put my Spirit into you, and ye shall live; and ye shall know that I am the Lord. And I prophesied as the Lord had commanded me. And it came to pass, when I was prophesying, that, behold, an earthquake, and the bones were drawn together, each one to its own articulation: and I beheld, and, lo, the sinews and flesh were produced upon them, and the skins rose upon them round about, but there was no breath in them. And He said unto me, Prophesy to the breath, Son of man, and say to the breath, These things saith the Lord, Come from the four winds (*spiritibus*), and breathe upon these dead, that they may live. So I prophesied as the Lord had commanded me, and the breath entered into them; and they did live, and stood upon their feet, an exceeding great gathering."[3] And again he says, "Thus saith the Lord, Behold, I will set your graves open, and cause you to come out of your graves, and bring you into the land of Israel; and ye shall know that I am the Lord, when I shall open your sepulchres, that I may

---

[1] Isa. xxvi. 19.   [2] Isa. lxvi. 13.   [3] Ezek. xxvii. 1, etc.

bring my people again out of the sepulchres: and I will put my Spirit into you, and ye shall live; and I will place you in your land, and ye shall know that I am the Lord. I have said, and I will do, saith the Lord."[1] As we at once perceive that the Creator (*Demiurgo*) is in this passage represented as vivifying our dead bodies, and promising resurrection to them, and resuscitation from their sepulchres and tombs, conferring upon them immortality also (He says, "For as the tree of life, so shall their days be"[2]), He is shown to be the only God who accomplishes these things, and as Himself the good Father, benevolently conferring life upon those who have not life from themselves.

2. And for this reason did the Lord most plainly manifest Himself and the Father to His disciples, lest, forsooth, they might seek after another God besides Him who formed man, and who gave him the breath of life; and that men might not rise to such a pitch of madness as to feign another Father above the Creator. And thus also He healed by a word all the others who were in a weakly condition because of sin; to whom also He said, "Behold, thou art made whole, sin no more, lest a worse thing come upon thee:"[3] pointing out by this, that, because of the sin of disobedience, infirmities have come upon men. To that man, however, who had been blind from his birth, He gave sight, not by means of a word, but by an outward action; doing this not without a purpose, or because it so happened, but that He might show forth the hand of God, that which at the beginning had moulded man. And therefore, when His disciples asked Him for what cause the man had been born blind, whether for his own or his parents' fault, He replied, "Neither hath this man sinned, nor his parents, but that the works of God should be made manifest in him."[4] Now the work of God is the fashioning of man. For, as the Scripture says, He made [man] by a kind of process: "And the Lord took clay from the earth, and formed man."[5] Wherefore also the Lord spat on the ground and made clay, and

---

[1] Ezek. xxxvii. 12, etc. [2] Isa. lxv. 22. [3] John v. 14.
[4] John ix. 3. [5] Gen. ii. 7.

smeared it upon the eyes, pointing out the original fashioning [of man], how it was effected, and manifesting the hand of God to those who can understand by what [hand] man was formed out of the dust. For that which the artificer, the Word, had omitted to form in the womb, [viz. the blind man's eyes], He then supplied in public, that the works of God might be manifested in him, in order that we might not be seeking out another hand by which man was fashioned, nor another Father; knowing that this hand of God which formed us at the beginning, and which does form us in the womb, has in the last times sought us out who were lost, winning back His own, and taking up the lost sheep upon His shoulders, and with joy restoring it to the fold of life.

3. Now, that the Word of God forms us in the womb, He says to Jeremiah, "Before I formed thee in the womb, I knew thee; and before thou wentest forth from the belly, I sanctified thee, and appointed thee a prophet among the nations."[1] And Paul, too, says in like manner, "But when it pleased God, who separated me from my mother's womb, that I might declare Him among the nations."[2] As, therefore, we are by the Word formed in the womb, this very same Word formed the visual power in him who had been blind from his birth; showing openly who it is that fashions us in secret, since the Word Himself had been made manifest to men: and declaring the original formation of Adam, and the manner in which he was created, and by what hand he was fashioned, indicating the whole from a part. For the Lord who formed the visual powers is He who made the whole man, carrying out the will of the Father. And inasmuch as man, with respect to that formation which was after Adam, having fallen into transgression, needed the laver of regeneration, [the Lord] said to him [upon whom He had conferred sight], after He had smeared his eyes with the clay, "Go to Siloam, and wash;"[3] thus restoring to him both [his perfect] conformation, and that regeneration which takes place by means of the laver. And for this reason when he was washed he came seeing, that he might both

---

[1] Jer. i. 5.   [2] Gal. i. 15.   [3] John ix. 7.

know Him who had fashioned him, and that man might learn [to know] Him who has conferred upon him life.

4. All the followers of Valentinus, therefore, lose their case, when they say that man was not fashioned out of this earth, but from a fluid and diffused substance. For, from the earth out of which the Lord formed eyes for that man, from the same earth it is evident that man was also fashioned at the beginning. For it were incompatible that the eyes should indeed be formed from one source and the rest of the body from another; as neither would it be compatible that one [being] fashioned the body, and another the eyes. But He, the very same who formed Adam at the beginning, with whom also the Father spake, [saying], "Let us make man after our image and likeness,"[1] revealing Himself in these last times to men, formed visual organs (*visionem*) for him who had been blind [in that body which he had derived] from Adam. Wherefore also the Scripture, pointing out what should come to pass, says, that when Adam had hid himself because of his disobedience, the Lord came to him at eventide, called him forth, and said, "Where art thou?"[2] That means that in the last times the very same Word of God came to call man, reminding him of his doings, living in which he had been hidden from the Lord. For just as at that time God spake to Adam at eventide, searching him out; so in the last times, by means of the same voice, searching out his posterity, He has visited them.

CHAP. XVI.—*Since our bodies return to the earth, it follows that they have their substance from it; also, by the advent of the Word, the image of God in us appeared in a clearer light.*

1. And since Adam was moulded from this earth to which we belong, the Scripture tells us that God said to him, "In the sweat of thy face shalt thou eat thy bread, until thou turnest again to the dust from whence thou wert taken."[3] If then, after death, our bodies return to any other substance,

[1] Gen. i. 25.   [2] Gen. iii. 9.   [3] Gen. iii. 19.

it follows that from it also they have their substance. But if it be into this very [earth], it is manifest that it was also from it that man's frame was created; as also the Lord clearly showed, when from this very substance He formed eyes for the man [to whom He gave sight]. And thus was the hand of God plainly shown forth, by which Adam was fashioned, and we too have been formed; and since there is one and the same Father, whose voice from the beginning even to the end is present with His handiwork, and the substance from which we were formed is plainly declared through the Gospel, we should therefore not seek after another Father besides Him, nor [look for] another substance from which we have been formed, besides what was mentioned beforehand, and shown forth by the Lord; nor another hand of God besides that which, from the beginning even to the end, forms us and prepares us for life, and is present with His handiwork, and perfects it after the image and likeness of God.

2. And then, again, this Word was manifested when the Word of God was made man, assimilating Himself to man, and man to Himself, so that by means of his resemblance to the Son, man might become precious to the Father. For in times long past, it was *said* that man was created after the image of God, but it was not [actually] *shown*; for the Word was as yet invisible, after whose image man was created. Wherefore also he did easily lose the similitude. When, however, the Word of God became flesh, He confirmed both these: for He both showed forth the image truly, since He became Himself what was His image; and He re-established the similitude after a sure manner, by assimilating man to the invisible Father through means of the visible Word.

3. And not by the aforesaid things alone has the Lord manifested Himself, but [He has done this] also by means of His passion. For doing away with [the effects of] that disobedience of man which had taken place at the beginning by the occasion of a tree, "He became obedient unto death, even the death of the cross;"[1] rectifying that disobedience

[1] Phil. ii. 8.

which had occurred by reason of a tree, through that obedience which was [wrought out] upon the tree [of the cross]. Now He would not have come to do away, by means of that same [image], the disobedience which had been incurred towards our Maker if He proclaimed another Father. But inasmuch as it was by these things that we disobeyed God, and did not give credit to His word, so was it also by these same that He brought in obedience and consent as respects His Word; by which things He clearly shows forth God Himself, whom indeed we had offended in the first Adam, when he did not perform His commandment. In the second Adam, however, we are reconciled, being made obedient even unto death. For we were debtors to none other but to Him whose commandment we had transgressed at the beginning.

CHAP. XVII.—*There is but one Lord and one God, the Father and Creator of all things, who has loved us in Christ, given us commandments, and remitted our sins; whose Son and Word Christ proved Himself to be, when He forgave our sins.*

1. Now this being is the Creator (*Demiurgus*), who is, in respect of His love, the Father; but in respect of His power, He is Lord; and in respect of His wisdom, our Maker and Fashioner; by transgressing whose commandment we became His enemies. And therefore in the last times the Lord has restored us into friendship through His incarnation, having become "the Mediator between God and men;"[1] propitiating indeed for us the Father against whom we had sinned, and cancelling (*consolatus*) our disobedience by His own obedience; conferring also upon us the gift of communion with, and subjection to, our Maker. For this reason also He has taught us to say in prayer, "And forgive us our debts;"[2] since indeed He is our Father, whose debtors we were, having transgressed His commandments. But who is this Being? Is He some unknown one, and a Father who gives no com-

[1] 1 Tim. ii. 5.   [2] Matt. vi. 12.

mandment to any one? Or is He the God who is proclaimed in the Scriptures, to whom we were debtors, having transgressed His commandment? Now the commandment was given to man by the Word. For Adam, it is said, "heard the voice of the Lord God."[1] Rightly then does His Word say to man, "Thy sins are forgiven thee;"[2] He, the same against whom we had sinned in the beginning, grants forgiveness of sins in the end. But if indeed we had disobeyed the command of any other, while it was a different being who said, "Thy sins are forgiven thee;"[2] such an one is neither good, nor true, nor just. For how can he be good, who does not give from what belongs to himself? Or how can he be just, who snatches away the goods of another? And in what way can sins be truly remitted, unless that He against whom we have sinned has Himself granted remission "through the bowels of mercy of our God," in which "He has visited us"[3] through His Son?

2. And therefore, when He had healed the man sick of the palsy, [the evangelist] says: "The people upon seeing it glorified God, who gave such power unto men."[4] What God, then, did the bystanders glorify? Was it indeed that unknown Father invented by the heretics? And how could they glorify him who was altogether unknown to them? It is evident, therefore, that the Israelites glorified Him who has been proclaimed as God by the law and the prophets, who is also the Father of our Lord; and therefore He taught men, by the evidence of their senses through those signs which He accomplished, to give glory to God. If, however, He Himself had come from another Father, and men glorified a different Father when they beheld His miracles, He [in that case] rendered them ungrateful to that Father who had sent the gift of healing. But as the only-begotten Son had come for man's salvation from Him who is God, He did both stir up the incredulous by the miracles which He was in the habit of working, to give glory to the Father; and to the Pharisees, who did not admit the advent of His Son, and who

---

[1] Gen. iii. 8. [2] Matt. ix. 2; Luke v. 20.
[3] Luke i. 78. [4] Matt. ix. 8.

consequently did not believe in the remission [of sins] which was conferred by Him, He said, "That ye may know that the Son of man hath power to forgive sins."[1] And when He had said this, He commanded the paralytic man to take up the pallet upon which he was lying, and go into his house. By this work of His He confounded the unbelievers, and showed that He is Himself the voice of God, by which man received commandments, which he broke, and became a sinner; for the paralysis followed as a consequence of sins.

3. Therefore, by remitting sins, He did indeed heal man, while He also manifested Himself who He was. For if no one can forgive sins but God alone, while the Lord remitted them and healed men, it is plain that He was Himself the Word of God made the Son of man, receiving from the Father the power of remission of sins; since He was man, and since He was God, in order that since as man He suffered for us, so as God He might have compassion on us, and forgive us our debts, in which we were made debtors to God our Creator. And therefore David said beforehand, "Blessed are they whose iniquities are forgiven, and whose sins are covered. Blessed is the man to whom the Lord has not imputed sin;"[2] pointing out thus that remission of sins which follows upon His advent, by which "He has destroyed the handwriting" of our debt, and "fastened it to the cross;"[3] so that as by means of a tree we were made debtors to God, [so also] by means of a tree we may obtain the remission of our debt.

4. This fact has been strikingly set forth by many others, and especially through means of Elisha the prophet. For when his fellow-prophets were hewing wood for the construction of a tabernacle, and when the iron [head], shaken loose from the axe, had fallen into the Jordan and could not be found by them, upon Elisha's coming to the place, and learning what had happened, he threw some wood into the water. Then, when he had done this, the iron part of the axe floated up, and they took up from the surface of the water what they had previously lost.[4] By this action the prophet pointed out

---

[1] Matt. ix. 6.   [2] Ps. xxxii. 1, 2.
[3] Col. ii. 14.   [4] 2 Kings vi. 6.

that the sure word of God, which we had negligently lost by means of a tree, and were not in the way of finding again, we should receive anew by the dispensation of a tree, [viz. the cross of Christ]. For that the word of God is likened to an axe, John the Baptist declares [when he says] in reference to it, "But now also is the axe laid to the root of the trees."[1] Jeremiah also says to the same purport: "The word of God cleaveth the rock as an axe."[2] This word, then, what was hidden from us, did the dispensation of the tree make manifest, as I have already remarked. For as we lost it by means of a tree, by means of a tree again was it made manifest to all, showing the height, the length, the breadth, the depth in itself; and, as a certain man among our predecessors observed, "Through the extension of the hands of a divine person,[3] gathering together the two peoples to one God." For these were two hands, because there were two peoples scattered to the ends of the earth; but there was one head in the middle, as there is but one God, who is above all, and through all, and in us all.

CHAP. XVIII.—*God the Father and His Word have formed all created things (which they use) by their own power and wisdom, not out of defect or ignorance. The Son of God, who received all power from the Father, would otherwise never have taken flesh upon Him.*

1. And such or so important a dispensation He did not bring about by means of the creations of others, but by His own; neither by those things which were created out of ignorance and defect, but by those which had their substance from the wisdom and power of His Father. For He was neither unrighteous, so that He should covet the property of another; nor needy, that He could not by His own means impart life to His own, and make use of His own creation for

---

[1] Matt. iii. 10.   [2] Jer. xxxiii. 29.

[3] The Greek is preserved here, and reads, διὰ τῆς θείας ἐκτάσεως τῶν χειρῶν—literally, "through the divine extension of hands." The old Latin merely reads, "per extensionem manuum."

the salvation of man. For indeed the creation could not have sustained Him [on the cross], if He had sent forth [simply by commission] what was the fruit of ignorance and defect. Now we have repeatedly shown that the incarnate Word of God was suspended upon a tree, and even the very heretics do acknowledge that He was crucified. How, then, could the fruit of ignorance and defect sustain Him who contains the knowledge of all things, and is true and perfect? Or how could that creation which was concealed from the Father, and far removed from Him, have sustained His Word? And if this world were made by the angels (it matters not whether we suppose their ignorance or their cognizance of the Supreme God), when the Lord declared, "For I am in the Father, and the Father in me,"[1] how could this workmanship of the angels have borne to be burdened at once with the Father and the Son? How, again, could that creation which is beyond the Pleroma have contained Him who contains the entire Pleroma? Inasmuch, then, as all these things are impossible and incapable of proof, that preaching of the church is alone true [which proclaims] that His own creation bare Him, which subsists by the power, the skill, and the wisdom of God; which is sustained, indeed, after an invisible manner by the Father, but, on the contrary, after a visible manner it bore His Word: and this is the true [Word].

2. For the Father bears the creation and His own Word simultaneously, and the Word borne by the Father grants the Spirit to all as the Father wills.[2] To some He gives after the manner of creation what is made;[3] but to others [He gives] after the manner of adoption, that is, what is from God, namely generation. And thus one God the Father is declared, who is above all, and through all, and in all. The Father is indeed above all, and He is the Head of

---

[1] John xiv. 11.

[2] From this passage Harvey infers that Irenæus held the procession of the Holy Spirit from the Father and the Son,—a doctrine denied by the Oriental Church in after times.

[3] Grabe and Harvey insert the words, "quod est conditionis," but on slender authority.

Christ; but the Word is through all things, and is Himself the Head of the Church; while the Spirit is in us all, and He is the living water,[1] which the Lord grants to those who rightly believe in Him, and love Him, and who know that "there is one Father, who is above all, and through all, and in us all."[2] And to these things does John also, the disciple of the Lord, bear witness, when he speaks thus in the Gospel: "In the beginning was the Word, and the Word was with God, and the Word was God. This was in the beginning with God. All things were made by Him, and without Him was nothing made."[3] And then he said of the Word Himself: "He was in the world, and the world was made by Him, and the world knew Him not. To His own things He came, and His own people received Him not. However, as many as did receive Him, to these gave He power to become the sons of God, to those that believe in His name."[4] And again, showing the dispensation with regard to His human nature, John said: "And the Word was made flesh, and dwelt among us."[5] And in continuation he says, "And we beheld His glory, the glory as of the Only-begotten by the Father, full of grace and truth." He thus plainly points out to those willing to hear, that is, to those having ears, that there is one God, the Father over all, and one Word of God, who is through all, by whom all things have been made; and that this world belongs to Him, and was made by Him, according to the Father's will, and not by angels; nor by apostasy, defect, and ignorance; nor by any power of Prunicus, whom certain of them also call "the Mother;" nor by any other maker of the world ignorant of the Father.

3. For the Creator of the world is truly the Word of God: and this is our Lord, who in the last times was made man, existing in this world, and who in an invisible manner contains all things created, and is inherent in the entire creation, since the Word of God governs and arranges all things; and

---

[1] John vii. 39.
[2] Eph. iv. 6.
[3] John i. 1, etc.
[4] John i. 10, etc.
[5] John i. 14.

therefore He came to His own in a visible[1] manner, and was made flesh, and hung upon the tree, that He might sum up all things in Himself. "And His own peculiar people did not receive Him," as Moses declared this very thing among the people: "And thy life shall be hanging before thine eyes, and thou wilt not believe thy life."[2] Those therefore who did not receive Him did not receive life. "But to as many as received Him, to them gave He power to become the sons of God."[3] For it is He who has power from the Father over all things, since He is the Word of God, and very man, communicating with invisible beings after the manner of the intellect, and appointing a law observable to the outward senses, that all things should continue each in its own order; and He reigns manifestly over things visible and pertaining to men; and brings in just judgment and worthy upon all; as David also, clearly pointing to this, says, "Our God shall openly come, and will not keep silence."[4] Then he shows also the judgment which is brought in by Him, saying, "A fire shall burn in His sight, and a strong tempest shall rage round about Him. He shall call upon the heaven from above, and the earth, to judge His people."

CHAP. XIX.—*A comparison is instituted between the disobedient and sinning Eve and the Virgin Mary, her patroness. Various and discordant heresies are mentioned.*

1. That the Lord then was manifestly coming to His own things, and was sustaining them by means of that creation which is supported by Himself, and was making a recapitulation of that disobedience which had occurred in connection with a tree, through the obedience which was [exhibited by Himself when He hung] upon a tree, [the effects] also of that deception being done away with, by which that virgin Eve, who was already espoused to a man, was unhappily misled,— was happily announced, through means of the truth [spoken] by the angel to the Virgin Mary, who was [also espoused] to

---

[1] The text reads "invisibiliter," which seems clearly an error.
[2] Deut. xxviii. 66.   [3] John i. 13.   [4] Ps. l. 3, 4.

a man.¹ For just as the former was led astray by the word of an angel, so that she fled from God when she had transgressed His word; so did the latter, by an angelic communication, receive the glad tidings that she should sustain (*portaret*) God, being obedient to His word. And if the former did disobey God, yet the latter was persuaded to be obedient to God, in order that the Virgin Mary might become the patroness (*advocata*) of the virgin Eve. And thus, as the human race fell into bondage to death by means of a virgin, so is it rescued by a virgin; virginal disobedience having been balanced in the opposite scale by virginal obedience. For in the same way the sin of the first created man (*protoplasti*) receives amendment by the correction of the First-begotten, and the cunning of the serpent is conquered by the harmlessness of the dove, those bonds being unloosed by which we had been fast bound to death.

2. The heretics being all unlearned and ignorant of God's arrangements, and not acquainted with that dispensation by which He took upon Him human nature (*inscii ejus quæ est secundum hominem dispensationis*), inasmuch as they blind themselves with regard to the truth, do in fact speak against their own salvation. Some of them introduce another Father besides the Creator; some, again, say that the world and its substance was made by certain angels; certain others [maintain] that it was widely separated by Horos² from him whom they represent as being the Father—that it sprang forth (*floruisse*) of itself, and from itself was born. Then, again, others [of them assert] that it obtained substance in those things which are contained by the Father, from defect and ignorance; others still, despise the advent of the Lord manifest [to the senses], for they do not admit His incarnation; while others, ignoring the arrangement [that He should be born] of a virgin, maintain that He was begotten by Joseph. And still further, some affirm that neither their soul nor their body can receive eternal life, but merely the inner man.

¹ The text is here most uncertain and obscure.
² The text reads "porro," which makes no sense; so that Harvey looks upon it as a corruption of the reading "per Horum."

Moreover, they will have it that this [inner man] is that which is the understanding (*sensum*) in them, and which they decree as being the only thing to ascend to "the perfect." Others [maintain], as I have said in the first book, that while the soul is saved, their body does not participate in the salvation which comes from God; in which [book] I have also set forward the hypotheses of all these men, and in the second have pointed out their weakness and inconsistency.

CHAP. XX.—*Those pastors are to be heard to whom the apostles committed the churches, possessing one and the same doctrine of salvation; the heretics, on the other hand, are to be avoided. We must think soberly with regard to the mysteries of the faith.*

1. Now all these [heretics] are of much later date than the bishops to whom the apostles committed the churches; which fact I have in the third book taken all pains to demonstrate. It follows, then, as a matter of course, that these heretics aforementioned, since they are blind to the truth, and deviate from the [right] way, will walk in various roads; and therefore the footsteps of their doctrine are scattered here and there without agreement or connection. But the path of those belonging to the church circumscribes the whole world, as possessing the sure tradition from the apostles, and gives unto us to see that the faith of all is one and the same, since all receive one and the same God the Father, and believe in the same dispensation regarding the incarnation of the Son of God, and are cognizant of the same gift of the Spirit, and are conversant with the same commandments, and preserve the same form of ecclesiastical constitution,[1] and expect the same advent of the Lord, and await the same salvation of the complete man, that is, of the soul and body. And undoubtedly the preaching of the church is true and

---

[1] "Et eandem figuram ejus quæ est erga ecclesiam ordinationis custodientibus." Grabe supposes this refers to the ordained ministry of the church, but Harvey thinks it refers more probably to its general constitution.

stedfast, in which one and the same way of salvation is shown throughout the whole world. For to her is entrusted the light of God; and therefore the "wisdom" of God, by means of which she saves all men, "is declared in [its] going forth; it uttereth [its voice] faithfully in the streets, is preached on the tops of the walls, and speaks continually in the gates of the city."[1] For the church preaches the truth everywhere, and she is the seven-branched candlestick which bears the light of Christ.

2. Those, therefore, who desert the preaching of the church, call in question the knowledge of the holy presbyters, not taking into consideration of how much greater consequence is a religious man, even in a private station, than a blasphemous and impudent sophist.[2] Now, such are all the heretics, and those who imagine that they have hit upon something more beyond the truth, so that by following those things already mentioned, proceeding on their way variously, inharmoniously, and foolishly, not keeping always to the same opinions with regard to the same things, as blind men are led by the blind, they shall deservedly fall into the ditch of ignorance lying in their path, ever seeking and never finding out the truth.[3] It behoves us, therefore, to avoid their doctrines, and to take careful heed lest we suffer any injury from them; but to flee to the church, and be brought up in her bosom, and be nourished with the Lord's Scriptures. For the church has been planted as a garden (*paradisus*) in this world; therefore says the Spirit of God, "Thou mayest freely eat from every tree of the garden,"[4] that is, Eat ye from every Scripture of the Lord; but ye shall not eat with an uplifted mind, nor touch any heretical discord. For these men do profess that they have themselves the knowledge of good and evil; and they set their own impious minds above the God who made them. They therefore form opinions on what is beyond the limits of the understanding. For this cause also

---

[1] Prov. i. 20, 21.

[2] That is, the private Christian as contrasted with the sophist of the schools.

[3] 2 Tim. iii. 7. [4] Gen. ii. 16.

the apostle says, "Be not wise beyond what it is fitting to be wise, but be wise prudently,"[1] that we be not cast forth by eating of the "knowledge" of these men (that knowledge which knows more than it should do) from the paradise of life. Into this paradise the Lord has introduced those who obey His call, "summing up in Himself all things which are in heaven, and which are on earth;"[2] but the things in heaven are spiritual, while those on earth constitute the dispensation in human nature (*secundum hominem est dispositio*). These things, therefore, He recapitulated in Himself: by uniting man to the Spirit, and causing the Spirit to dwell in man, He is Himself made the head of the Spirit, and gives the Spirit to be the head of man: for through Him (the Spirit) we see, and hear, and speak.

CHAP. XXI.—*Christ is the Head of all things already mentioned. It was fitting that He should be sent by the Father, the Creator of all things, to assume human nature, and should be tempted by Satan, that He might fulfil the promises, and carry off a glorious and perfect victory.*

1. He has therefore, in His work of recapitulation, summed up all things, both waging war against our enemy, and crushing him who had at the beginning led us away captives in Adam, and trampling upon his head, as thou canst perceive in Genesis that God said to the serpent, "And I will put enmity between thee and the woman, and between thy seed and her seed; He shall be on the watch for (*observabit*[3]) thy head, and thou on the watch for His heel."[4] For from that time, He who should be born of a woman, [namely] from the Virgin, after the likeness of Adam, was preached as keeping watch for the head of the serpent. This is the seed of which the apostle says in the Epistle to the Galatians, "that the law of works was established until the seed should come to whom the promise was made."[5] This fact is exhibited in

---

[1] Rom. xii. 3.   [2] Eph. i. 10.
[3] $τηρήσει$ and $τερίσει$ have probably been confounded.
[4] Gen. iii. 15.   [5] Gal. iii. 19.

a still clearer light in the same epistle, where he thus speaks: "But when the fulness of time was come, God sent forth His Son, made of a woman."[1] For indeed the enemy would not have been fairly vanquished, unless it had been a man [born] of woman who conquered him. For it was by means of a woman that he got the advantage over man at first, setting himself up as man's opponent. And therefore does the Lord profess Himself to be the Son of man, comprising in Himself that original man out of whom the woman was fashioned (*ex quo ea quæ secundum mulierem est plasmatio facta est*), in order that, as our species went down to death through a vanquished man, so we may ascend to life again through a victorious one; and as through a man death received the palm [of victory] against us, so again by a man we may receive the palm against death.

2. Now the Lord would not have recapitulated in Himself that ancient and primary enmity against the serpent, fulfilling the promise of the Creator (*Demiurgi*), and performing His command, if He had come from another Father. But as He is one and the same, who formed us at the beginning, and sent His Son at the end, the Lord did perform His command, being made of a woman, by both destroying our adversary, and perfecting man after the image and likeness of God. And for this reason He did not draw the means of confounding him from any other source than from the words of the law, and made use of the Father's commandment as a help towards the destruction and confusion of the apostate angel. Fasting forty days, like Moses and Elias, He afterwards hungered, first, in order that we may perceive that He was a real and substantial man—for it belongs to a man to suffer hunger when fasting; and secondly, that His opponent might have an opportunity of attacking Him. For as at the beginning it was by means of food that [the enemy] persuaded man, although not suffering hunger, to transgress God's commandments, so in the end he did not succeed in persuading Him that was an hungered to take that food which proceeded from God. For, when tempting

[1] Gal. iv. 4.

Him, he said, "If thou be the Son of God, command that these stones be made bread."[1] But the Lord repulsed him by the commandment of the law, saying, "It is written, Man doth not live by bread alone."[2] As to those words [of His enemy,] "If thou be the Son of God," [the Lord] made no remark; but by thus acknowledging His human nature He baffled His adversary, and exhausted the force of his first attack by means of His Father's word. The corruption of man, therefore, which occurred in paradise by both [of our first parents] eating, was done away with by [the Lord's] want of food in this world.[3] But he, being thus vanquished by the law, endeavoured again to make an assault by himself quoting a commandment of the law. For, bringing Him to the highest pinnacle of the temple, he said to Him, "If thou art the Son of God, cast thyself down. For it is written, That God shall give His angels charge concerning thee, and in their hands they shall bear thee up, lest perchance thou dash thy foot against a stone;"[4] thus concealing a falsehood under the guise of Scripture, as is done by all the heretics. For that was indeed written, [namely], "That He hath given His angels charge concerning Him;" but "cast thyself down from hence" no Scripture said in reference to Him: this kind of persuasion the devil produced from himself. The Lord therefore confuted him out of the law, when He said, "It is written again, Thou shalt not tempt the Lord thy God;"[5] pointing out by the word contained in the law that which is the duty of man, that he should not tempt God; and in regard to Himself, since He appeared in human form, [declaring] that He would not tempt the Lord his God.[6] The pride of reason, therefore, which was in the serpent, was put to nought by the humility

---

[1] Matt. iv. 3.   [2] Deut. viii. 3.

[3] The Latin of this obscure sentence is: Quæ ergo fuit in Paradiso repletio hominis per duplicem gustationem, dissoluta est per eam, quæ fuit in hoc mundo, indigentiam. Harvey thinks that *repletio* is an error of the translation reading ἀναπλήρωσις for ἀναπήρωσις. This conjecture is adopted above.

[4] Ps. lxxxix. 11.   [5] Deut. vi. 16.

[6] This sentence is one of great obscurity.

found in the man [Christ]; and now twice was the devil conquered from Scripture, when he was detected as advising things contrary to God's commandment, and was shown to be the enemy of God by [the expression of] his thoughts. He then, having been thus signally defeated, and then, as it were, concentrating his forces, drawing up in order all his available power for falsehood, in the third place ".showed Him all the kingdoms of the world, and the glory of them,"[1] saying, as Luke relates, "All these will I give thee,—for they are delivered to me; and to whom I will, I give them,—if thou wilt fall down and worship me." The Lord then, exposing him in his true character, says, "Depart, Satan; for it is written, Thou shalt worship the Lord thy God, and Him only shalt thou serve."[2] He both revealed him by this name, and showed [at the same time] who He Himself was. For the Hebrew word "Satan" signifies an apostate. And thus, vanquishing him for the third time, He spurned him from Him finally as being conquered out of the law; and there was done away with that infringement of God's commandment which had occurred in Adam, by means of the precept of the law, which the Son of man observed, who did not transgress the commandment of God.

3. Who, then, is this Lord God to whom Christ bears witness, whom no man shall tempt, whom all should worship, and serve Him alone? It is, beyond all manner of doubt, that God who also gave the law. For these things had been predicted in the law, and by the words (*sententiam*) of the law the Lord showed that the law does indeed declare the Word of God from the Father; and the apostate angel of God is destroyed by its voice, being exposed in his true colours, and vanquished by the Son of man keeping the commandment of God. For as in the beginning he enticed man to transgress his Maker's law, and thereby got him into his power; yet his power consists in transgression and apostasy, and with these he bound man [to himself]; so again, on the other hand, it was necessary that through man himself he should, when conquered, be bound with the same chains with which

[1] Luke iv. 6, 7.   [2] Matt. iv. 10.

he had bound man, in order that man, being set free, might return to his Lord, leaving to him (Satan) those bonds by which he himself had been fettered, that is, sin. For when Satan is bound, man is set free; since "none can enter a strong man's house and spoil his goods, unless he first bind the strong man himself."[1] The Lord therefore exposes him as speaking contrary to the word of that God who made all things, and subdues him by means of the commandment. Now the law is the commandment of God. The Man proves him to be a fugitive from and a transgressor of the law, an apostate also from God. After [the Man had done this], the Word bound him securely as a fugitive from Himself, and made spoil of his goods,—namely, those men whom he held in bondage, and whom he unjustly used for his own purposes. And justly indeed is he led captive, who had led men unjustly into bondage; while man, who had been led captive in times past, was rescued from the grasp of his possessor, according to the tender mercy of God the Father, who had compassion on His own handiwork, and gave to it salvation, restoring it by means of the Word—that is, by Christ—in order that men might learn by actual proof that he receives incorruptibility not of himself, but by the free gift of God.

CHAP. XXII.—*The true Lord and the one God is declared by the law, and manifested by Christ his Son in the Gospel; whom alone we should adore, and from Him we must look for all good things, not from Satan.*

1. Thus then does the Lord plainly show that it was the true Lord and the one God who had been set forth by the law; for Him whom the law proclaimed as God, the same did Christ point out as the Father, whom also it behoves the disciples of Christ alone to serve. By means of the statements of the law, He put our adversary to utter confusion; and the law directs us to praise God the Creator (*Demiurgum*), and to serve Him alone. Since this is the case, we must not seek for another Father besides Him, or above Him, since

[1] Matt. xii. 29 and Mark iii. 27.

there is one God who justifies the circumcision by faith, and the uncircumcision through faith.[1] For if there were any other perfect Father above Him, He (Christ) would by no means have overthrown Satan by means of His words and commandments. For one ignorance cannot be done away with by means of another ignorance, any more than one defect by another defect. If, therefore, the law is due to ignorance and defect, how could the statements contained therein bring to nought the ignorance of the devil, and conquer the strong man? For a strong man can be conquered neither by an inferior nor by an equal, but by one possessed of greater power. But the Word of God is the superior above all, He who is loudly proclaimed in the law: "Hear, O Israel, the Lord thy God is one God;" and, "Thou shalt love the Lord thy God with all thy heart;" and, "Him shalt thou adore, and Him alone shalt thou serve."[2] Then in the Gospel, casting down the apostasy by means of these expressions, He did both overcome the strong man by His Father's voice, and He acknowledges the commandment of the law to express His own sentiments, when He says, "Thou shalt not tempt the Lord thy God."[3] For He did not confound the adversary by the saying of any other, but by that belonging to His own Father, and thus overcame the strong man.

2. He taught by His commandment that we who have been set free should, when hungry, take that food which is given by God; and that, when placed in the exalted position of every grace [that can be received], we should not, either by trusting to works of righteousness, or when adorned with supereminent [gifts of] ministration, by any means be lifted up with pride, nor should we tempt God, but should feel humility in all things, and have ready to hand [this saying], "Thou shalt not tempt the Lord thy God."[4] As also the apostle taught, saying, "Minding not high things, but consenting to things of low estate;"[5] that we should neither be ensnared with riches, nor mundane glory, nor present fancy,

---

[1] Rom. iii. 30.   [2] Deut. vi. 4, 5, 13.   [3] Matt. iv. 7.
[4] Deut. vi. 16.   [5] Rom. xii. 16.

but should know that we must "worship the Lord thy God, and serve Him alone," and give no heed to him who falsely promised things not his own, when he said, "All these will I give thee, if, falling down, thou wilt worship me." For he himself confesses that to adore him, and to do his will, is to fall from the glory of God. And in what thing either pleasant or good can that man who has fallen participate? Or what else can such a person hope for or expect, except death? For death is next neighbour to him who has fallen. Hence also it follows that he will not give what he has promised. For how can he make grants to him who has fallen? Moreover, since God rules over men and him too, and without the will of our Father in heaven not even a sparrow falls to the ground,[1] it follows that his declaration, "All these things are delivered unto me, and to whomsoever I will I give them," proceeds from him when puffed up with pride. For the creation is not subjected to his power, since indeed he is himself but one among created things. Nor shall he give away the rule over men to men; but both all other things, and all human affairs, are arranged according to God the Father's disposal. Besides, the Lord declares that "the devil is a liar from the beginning, and the truth is not in him."[2] If then he be a liar, and the truth be not in him, he certainly did not speak truth, but a lie, when he said, "For all these things are delivered to me, and to whomsoever I will I give them."[3]

CHAP. XXIII.—*The devil is well practised in falsehood, by which Adam having been led astray, sinned on the sixth day of the creation, in which day also he has been renewed by Christ.*

1. He had indeed been already accustomed to lie against God, for the purpose of leading men astray. For at the beginning, when God had given to man a variety of things for food, while He commanded him not to eat of one tree only, as the Scripture tells us that God said to Adam:

[1] Matt. x. 29.   [2] John viii. 44.   [3] Luke iv. 6.

"From every tree which is in the garden thou shalt eat food; but from the tree of knowledge of good and evil, from this ye shall not eat: for in the day that ye shall eat of it, ye shall die by death;"[1] he then, lying against the Lord, tempted man, as the Scripture says that the serpent said to the woman: "Has God indeed said this, Ye shall not eat from every tree of the garden?"[2] And when she had exposed the falsehood, and simply related the command, as He had said, "From every tree of the garden we shall eat; but of the fruit of the tree which is in the midst of the garden, God hath said, Ye shall not eat of it, neither shall ye touch it, lest ye die:"[3] when he had [thus] learned from the woman the command of God, having brought his cunning into play, he finally deceived her by a falsehood, saying, "Ye shall not die by death; for God knew that in the day ye shall eat of it your eyes shall be opened, and ye shall be as gods, knowing good and evil."[4] In the first place, then, in the garden of God he disputed about God, as if God was not there, for he was ignorant of the greatness of God; and then, in the next place, after he had learned from the woman that God had said that they should die if they tasted the aforesaid tree, opening his mouth, he uttered the third falsehood, "Ye shall not die by death." But that God was true, and the serpent a liar, was proved by the result, death having passed upon them who had eaten. For along with the fruit they did also fall under the power of death, because they did eat in disobedience; and disobedience to God entails death. Wherefore, as they became forfeit to death, from that [moment] they were handed over to it.

2. Thus, then, in the day that they did eat, in the same did they die, and became death's debtors, since it was one day of the creation. For it is said, "There was made in the evening, and there was made in the morning, one day." Now in this same day that they did eat, in that also did they die. But according to the cycle and progress of the days, after which one is termed first, another second, and another third, if anybody seeks diligently to learn upon what day out of the

[1] Gen. ii. 16, 17.   [2] Gen. iii. 1.   [3] Gen. iii. 2, 3.   [4] Gen. iii. 4.

seven it was that Adam died, he will find it by examining the dispensation of the Lord. For by summing up in Himself the whole human race from the beginning to the end, He has also summed up its death. From this it is clear that the Lord suffered death, in obedience to His Father, upon that day on which Adam died while he disobeyed God. Now he died on the same day in which he did eat. For God said, "In that day on which ye shall eat of it, ye shall die by death." The Lord, therefore, recapitulating in Himself this day, underwent His sufferings upon the day preceding the Sabbath, that is, the sixth day of the creation, on which day man was created; thus granting him a second creation by means of His passion, which is that [creation] out of death. And there are some, again, who relegate the death of Adam to the thousandth year; for since "a day of the Lord is as a thousand years,"[1] he did not overstep the thousand years, but died within them, thus bearing out the sentence of his sin. Whether, therefore, with respect to disobedience, which is death; whether [we consider] that, on account of that, they were delivered over to death, and made debtors to it; whether with respect to [the fact that on] one and the same day on which they ate they also died (for it is one day of the creation); whether [we regard this point], that, with respect to this cycle of days, they died on the day in which they did also eat, that is, the day of the preparation, which is termed "the pure supper," that is, the sixth day of the feast, which the Lord also exhibited when He suffered on that day; or whether [we reflect] that he (Adam) did not overstep the thousand years, but died within their limit,—it follows that, in regard to all these significations, God is indeed true. For they died who tasted of the tree; and the serpent is proved a liar and a murderer, as the Lord said of him: "For he is a murderer from the beginning, and the truth is not in him."[2]

[1] 2 Pet. iii. 8.   [2] John viii. 44.

CHAP. XXIV.—*Of the constant falsehood of the devil, and of the powers and governments of the world, which we ought to obey, inasmuch as they are appointed of God, not of the devil.*

1. As therefore the devil lied at the beginning, so did he also in the end, when he said, "All these are delivered unto me, and to whomsoever I will I give them."[1] For it is not he who has appointed the kingdoms of this world, but God; for "the heart of the king is in the hand of God."[2] And the Word also says by Solomon, "By me kings do reign, and princes administer justice. By me chiefs are raised up, and by me kings rule the earth."[3] Paul the apostle also says upon this same subject: "Be ye subject to all the higher powers; for there is no power but of God: now those which are have been ordained of God."[4] And again, in reference to them he says, "For he beareth not the sword in vain; for he is the minister of God, the avenger for wrath to him who does evil."[5] Now, that he spake these words, not in regard to angelical powers, nor of invisible rulers—as some venture to expound the passage—but of those of actual human authorities, [he shows when] he says, "For this cause pay ye tribute also: for they are God's ministers, doing service for this very thing."[6] This also the Lord confirmed, when He did not do what He was tempted to by the devil; but He gave directions that tribute should be paid to the tax-gatherers for Himself and Peter;[7] because "they are the ministers of God, serving for this very thing."

2. For since man, by departing from God, reached such a pitch of fury as even to look upon his brother as his enemy, and engaged without fear in every kind of restless conduct, and murder, and avarice; God imposed upon mankind the fear of man, as they did not acknowledge the fear of God, in order that, being subjected to the authority of men, and kept under restraint by their laws, they might attain

---

[1] Matt. iv. 9; Luke iv. 6.   [2] Prov. xxi. 1.   [3] Prov. viii. 15.
[4] Rom. xiii. 1.   [5] Rom. xiii. 4.   [6] Rom. xiii. 6.   [7] Matt. xvii. 27.

to some degree of justice, and exercise mutual forbearance through dread of the sword suspended full in their view, as the apostle says: "For he beareth not the sword in vain; for he is the minister of God, the avenger for wrath upon him who does evil." And for this reason too, magistrates themselves, having laws as a clothing of righteousness whenever they act in a just and legitimate manner, shall not be called in question for their conduct, nor be liable to punishment. But whatsoever they do to the subversion of justice, iniquitously, and impiously, and illegally, and tyrannically, in these things shall they also perish; for the just judgment of God comes equally upon all, and in no case is defective. Earthly rule, therefore, has been appointed by God for the benefit of nations, and not by the devil, who is never at rest at all, nay, who does not love to see even nations conducting themselves after a quiet manner, so that under the fear of human rule, men may not eat each other up like fishes; but that, by means of the establishment of laws, they may keep down an excess of wickedness among the nations. And considered from this point of view, those who exact tribute from us are "God's ministers, serving for this very purpose."

3. As, then, "the powers that be are ordained of God," it is clear that the devil lied when he said, "These are delivered unto me; and to whomsoever I will, I give them." For by the law of the same Being as calls men into existence are kings also appointed, adapted for those men who are at the time placed under their government. Some of these [rulers] are given for the correction and the benefit of their subjects, and for the preservation of justice; but others, for the purposes of fear and punishment and rebuke: others, as [the subjects] deserve it, are for deception, disgrace, and pride; while the just judgment of God, as I have observed already, passes equally upon all. The devil, however, as he is the apostate angel, can only go to this length, as he did at the beginning, [namely] to deceive and lead astray the mind of man into disobeying the commandments of God, and gradually to darken the hearts of those who would endeavour to

serve him, to the forgetting of the true God, but to the adoration of himself as God.

4. Just as if any one, being an apostate, and seizing in a hostile manner another man's territory, should harass the inhabitants of it, in order that he might claim for himself the glory of a king among those ignorant of his apostasy and robbery; so likewise also the devil, being one among those angels who are placed over the spirit of the air, as the Apostle Paul has declared in his Epistle to the Ephesians,[1] becoming envious of man, was rendered an apostate from the divine law: for envy is a thing foreign to God. And as his apostasy was exposed by man, and man became the [means of] searching out his thoughts (*et examinatio sententiæ ejus, homo factus est*), he has set himself to this with greater and greater determination, in opposition to man, envying his life, and wishing to involve him in his own apostate power. The Word of God, however, the Maker of all things, conquering him by means of human nature, and showing him to be an apostate, has, on the contrary, put him under the power of man. For He says, "Behold, I confer upon you the power of treading upon serpents and scorpions, and upon all the power of the enemy,"[2] in order that, as he obtained dominion over man by apostasy, so again his apostasy might be deprived of power by means of man turning back again to God.

CHAP. XXV.—*The fraud, pride, and tyrannical kingdom of Antichrist, as described by Daniel and Paul.*

1. And not only by the particulars already mentioned, but also by means of the events which shall occur in the time of Antichrist is it shown that he, being an apostate and a robber, is anxious to be adored as God; and that, although a mere slave, he wishes himself to be proclaimed as a king. For he (Antichrist) being endued with all the power of the devil, shall come, not as a righteous king, nor as a legitimate king, [*i.e.* one] in subjection to God, but an impious, unjust, and lawless one; as an apostate, iniquitous and

[1] Eph. ii. 2.   [2] Luke x. 19.

murderous; as a robber, concentrating in himself [all] satanic apostasy, and setting aside idols to persuade [men] that he himself is God, raising up himself as the only idol, having in himself the multifarious errors of the other idols. This he does, in order that they who do [now] worship the devil by means of many abominations, may serve himself by this one idol, of whom the apostle thus speaks in the second Epistle to the Thessalonians: "Unless there shall come a falling away first, and the man of sin shall be revealed, the son of perdition, who opposeth and exalteth himself above all that is called God, or that is worshipped; so that he sitteth in the temple of God, showing himself as if he were God." The apostle therefore clearly points out his apostasy, and that he is lifted up above all that is called God, or that is worshipped—that is, above every idol—for these are indeed so called by men, but are not [really] gods; and that he will endeavour in a tyrannical manner to set himself forth as God.

2. Moreover, he (the apostle) has also pointed out this which I have shown in many ways, that the temple in Jerusalem was made by the direction of the true God. For the apostle himself, speaking in his own person, distinctly called it the temple of God. Now I have shown in the third book, that no one is termed God by the apostles when speaking for themselves, except Him who truly is God, the Father of our Lord, by whose directions the temple which is at Jerusalem was constructed for those purposes which I have already mentioned; in which [temple] the enemy shall sit, endeavouring to show himself as Christ, as the Lord also declares: "But when ye shall see the abomination of desolation, which has been spoken of by Daniel the prophet, standing in the holy place (let him that readeth understand), then let those who are in Judea flee into the mountains; and he who is upon the house-top, let him not come down to take anything out of his house: for there shall then be great hardship, such as has not been from the beginning of the world until now, nor ever shall be."[1]

3. Daniel too, looking forward to the end of the last king-

[1] Matt. xxiv. 15, 21.

dom, *i.e.* the ten last kings, amongst whom the kingdom of those men shall be partitioned, and upon whom the son of perdition shall come, declares that ten horns shall spring from the beast, and that another little horn shall arise in the midst of them, and that three of the former shall be rooted up before his face. He says: "And, behold, eyes were in this horn as the eyes of a man, and a mouth speaking great things, and his look was more stout than his fellows. I was looking, and this horn made war against the saints, and prevailed against them, until the Ancient of days came and gave judgment to the saints of the most high God, and the time came, and the saints obtained the kingdom."[1] Then, further on, in the interpretation of the vision, there was said to him: "The fourth beast shall be the fourth kingdom upon earth, which shall excel all other kingdoms, and devour the whole earth, and tread it down, and cut it in pieces. And its ten horns are ten kings which shall arise; and after them shall arise another, who shall surpass in evil deeds all that were before him, and shall overthrow three kings; and he shall speak words against the most high God, and wear out the saints of the most high God, and shall purpose to change times and laws; and [everything] shall be given into his hand until a time of times and a half time,"[2] that is, for three years and six months, during which time, when he comes, he shall reign over the earth. Of whom also the Apostle Paul again, speaking in the second [Epistle] to the Thessalonians, and at the same time proclaiming the cause of his advent, thus says: "And then shall the wicked one be revealed, whom the Lord Jesus shall slay with the spirit of His mouth, and destroy by the presence of His coming; whose coming [*i.e.* the wicked one's] is after the working of Satan, in all power, and signs, and portents of lies, and with all deceivableness of wickedness for those who perish; because they did not receive the love of the truth, that they might be saved. And therefore God will send them the working of error, that they may believe a lie; that they all may be judged who did not believe the truth, but gave consent to iniquity."[3]

[1] Dan. vii. 8, etc.   [2] Dan. vii. 23, etc.   [3] 2 Thess. ii. 8.

4. The Lord also spoke as follows to those who did not believe in Him: "I have come in my Father's name, and ye have not received me: when another shall come in his own name, him ye will receive,"[1] calling Antichrist "the other," because he is alienated from the Lord. This is also the unjust judge, whom the Lord mentioned as one "who feared not God, neither regarded man,"[2] to whom the widow fled in her forgetfulness of God,—that is, the earthly Jerusalem,—to be avenged of her adversary. Which also he shall do in the time of his kingdom: he shall remove his kingdom into that [city], and shall sit in the temple of God, leading astray those who worship him, as if he were Christ. To this purpose Daniel says again: "And he shall desolate the holy place; and sin has been given for a sacrifice,[3] and righteousness been cast away in the earth, and he has been active (*fecit*), and gone on prosperously."[4] And the angel Gabriel, when explaining his vision, states with regard to this person: "And towards the end of their kingdom a king of a most fierce countenance shall arise, one understanding [dark] questions, and exceedingly powerful, full of wonders; and he shall corrupt, direct, influence (*faciet*), and put strong men down, the holy people likewise; and his yoke shall be directed as a wreath [round their neck]; deceit shall be in his hand, and he shall be lifted up in his heart: he shall also ruin many by deceit, and lead many to perdition, bruising them in his hand like eggs."[5] And then he points out the time that his tyranny shall last, during which the saints shall be put to flight, they who offer a pure sacrifice unto God: "And in the midst of the week," he says, "the sacrifice and the libation shall be taken away, and the abomination of desolation [shall be brought] into the temple: even unto the consummation of

---

[1] John v. 43.   [2] Luke xviii. 2, etc.

[3] This may refer to Antiochus Epiphanes, Antichrist's prototype, who offered swine upon the altar in the temple at Jerusalem. The LXX. version has, ἐδόθη ἐπὶ τὴν θυσίαν ἁμαρτία, *i.e.* sin has been given against (or, *upon*) the sacrifice.

[4] Dan. viii. 12.

[5] Dan. viii. 23, etc.

the time shall the desolation be complete."¹   Now three years and six months constitute the half-week.

5. From all these passages are revealed to us, not merely the particulars of the apostasy, and [the doings] of him who concentrates in himself every satanic error, but also that there is one and the same God the Father, who was declared by the prophets, but made manifest by Christ. For if what Daniel prophesied concerning the end has been confirmed by the Lord, when He said, " When ye shall see the abomination of desolation, which has been spoken of by Daniel the prophet"² (and the angel Gabriel gave the interpretation of the visions to Daniel, and he is the archangel of the Creator (*Demiurgi*), who also proclaimed to Mary the visible coming and the incarnation of Christ), then one and the same God is most manifestly pointed out, who sent the prophets, and made promise³ of the Son, and called us into His knowledge.

CHAP. XXVI.—*John and Daniel have predicted the dissolution and desolation of the Roman Empire, which shall precede the end of the world and the eternal kingdom of Christ. The Gnostics are refuted, those tools of Satan, who invent another Father different from the Creator.*

1. In a still clearer light has John, in the Apocalypse, indicated to the Lord's disciples what shall happen in the last times, and concerning the ten kings who shall then arise, among whom the empire which now rules [the earth] shall be partitioned. He teaches us what the ten horns shall be which were seen by Daniel, telling us that thus it had been said to him: " And the ten horns which thou sawest are ten kings, who have received no kingdom as yet, but shall receive power as if kings one hour with the beast. These have one mind, and give their strength and power to the beast. These shall make war with the Lamb, and the Lamb shall overcome them, because He is the Lord of lords and the King of kings."⁴

---

¹ Dan. ix. 27.   ² Matt. xxiv. 15.
³ The MSS. have " præmisit," but Harvey suggests " promisit," which we have adopted.
⁴ Rev. xvii. 12, etc.

It is manifest, therefore, that of these [potentates], he who is to come shall slay three, and subject the remainder to his power, and that he shall be himself the eighth among them. And they shall lay Babylon waste, and burn her with fire, and shall give their kingdom to the beast, and put the church to flight. After that they shall be destroyed by the coming of our Lord. For that the kingdom must be divided, and thus come to ruin, the Lord [declares when He] says: "Every kingdom divided against itself is brought to desolation, and every city or house divided against itself shall not stand."[1] It must be, therefore, that the kingdom, the city, and the house be divided into ten; and for this reason He has already foreshadowed the partition and division [which shall take place]. Daniel also says particularly, that the end of the fourth kingdom consists in the toes of the image seen by Nebuchadnezzar, upon which came the stone cut out without hands; and as he does himself say: "The feet were indeed the one part iron, the other part clay, until the stone was cut out without hands, and struck the image upon the iron and clay feet, and dashed them into pieces, even to the end."[2] Then afterwards, when interpreting this, he says: "And as thou sawest the feet and the toes, partly indeed of clay, and partly of iron, the kingdom shall be divided, and there shall be in it a root of iron, as thou sawest iron mixed with baked clay. And the toes were indeed the one part iron, but the other part clay."[3] The ten toes, therefore, are these ten kings, among whom the kingdom shall be partitioned, of whom some indeed shall be strong and active, or energetic; others, again, shall be sluggish and useless, and shall not agree; as also Daniel says: "Some part of the kingdom shall be strong, and part shall be broken from it. As thou sawest the iron mixed with the baked clay, there shall be minglings among the human race, but no cohesion one with the other, just as iron cannot be welded on to pottery ware."[4] And since an end shall take place, he says: "And in the days of these kings shall the God of heaven raise up a kingdom which shall never decay, and His king-

---

[1] Matt. xii. 25.   [2] Dan. ii. 33, 34.
[3] Dan. ii. 41, 42.   [4] Dan. ii. 42, 43.

dom shall not be left to another people. It shall break in pieces and shatter all kingdoms, and shall itself be exalted for ever. As thou sawest that the stone was cut without hands from the mountain, and brake in pieces the baked clay, the iron, the brass, the silver, and the gold, God has pointed out to the king what shall come to pass after these things; and the dream is true, and the interpretation trustworthy."[1]

2. If therefore the great God showed future things by Daniel, and confirmed them by His Son; and if Christ is the stone which is cut out without hands, who shall destroy temporal kingdoms, and introduce an eternal one, which is the resurrection of the just; as he declares, "The God of heaven shall raise up a kingdom which shall never be destroyed,"—let those thus confuted come to their senses, who reject the Creator (*Demiurgum*), and do not agree that the prophets were sent beforehand from the same Father from whom also the Lord came, but who assert that prophecies originated from diverse powers. For those things which have been predicted by the Creator alike through all the prophets has Christ fulfilled in the end, ministering to His Father's will, and completing His dispensations with regard to the human race. Let those persons, therefore, who blaspheme the Creator, either by openly expressed words, such as the disciples of Marcion, or by a perversion of the sense [of Scripture], as those of Valentinus and all the Gnostics falsely so called, be recognised as agents of Satan by all those who worship God; through whose agency Satan now, and not before, has been seen to speak against God, even Him who has prepared eternal fire for every kind of apostasy. For he did not venture to blaspheme his Lord openly of himself; as also in the beginning he led man astray through the instrumentality of the serpent, concealing himself as it were from God. Truly has Justin remarked:[2]

---

[1] Dan. ii. 44, 45.

[2] The Greek text is here preserved by Eusebius, *Hist. Eccl.* iv. 18; but we are not told from what work of Justin Martyr it is extracted. The work is now lost. An ancient catena continues the Greek for several lines further.

That before the Lord's appearance Satan never dared to blaspheme God, inasmuch as he did not yet know his own sentence, because it was contained in parables and allegories; but that after the Lord's appearance, when he had clearly ascertained from the words of Christ and His apostles that eternal fire has been prepared for him as he apostatized from God of his own free-will, and likewise for all who unrepentant continue in the apostasy, he now blasphemes, by means of such men, the Lord who brings judgment [upon him] as being already condemned, and imputes the guilt of his apostasy to his Maker, not to his own voluntary disposition. Just as it is with those who break the laws, when punishment overtakes them: they throw the blame upon those who frame the laws, but not upon themselves. In like manner do those men, filled with a satanic spirit, bring innumerable accusations against our Creator, who has both given to us the spirit of life, and established a law adapted for all; and they will not admit that the judgment of God is just. Wherefore also they set about imagining some other Father who neither cares about nor exercises a providence over our affairs, nay, one who even approves of all sins.

CHAP. XXVII.—*The future judgment by Christ. Communion with and separation from the Divine Being. The eternal punishment of unbelievers.*

1. If the Father, then, does not exercise judgment, [it follows] that judgment does not belong to Him, or that He consents to all those actions which take place; and if He does not judge, all persons will be equal, and accounted in the same condition. The advent of Christ will therefore be without an object, yea, absurd, inasmuch as [in that case] He exercises no judicial power. For "He came to divide a man against his father, and the daughter against the mother, and the daughter-in-law against the mother-in-law;"[1] and when two are in one bed, to take the one, and to leave the other; and of two women grinding at the mill, to take one

---
[1] Matt. x. 25.

and leave the other:[1] [also] at the time of the end, to order the reapers to collect first the tares together, and bind them in bundles, and burn them with unquenchable fire, but to gather up the wheat into the barn;[2] and to call the lambs into the kingdom prepared for them, but to send the goats into everlasting fire, which has been prepared by His Father for the devil and his angels.[3] And why is this? Has the Word come for the ruin and for the resurrection of many? For the ruin, certainly, of those who do not believe Him, to whom also He has threatened a greater damnation in the judgment-day than that of Sodom and Gomorrah;[4] but for the resurrection of believers, and those who do the will of His Father in heaven. If then the advent of the Son comes indeed alike to all, but is for the purpose of judging, and separating the believing from the unbelieving, since, as those who believe do His will agreeably to their own choice, and as, [also] agreeably to their own choice, the disobedient do not consent to His doctrine; it is manifest that His Father has made all in a like condition, each person having a choice of his own, and a free understanding; and that He has regard to all things, and exercises a providence over all, " making His sun to rise upon the evil and on the good, and sending rain upon the just and unjust."[5]

2. And to as many as continue in their love towards God, does He grant communion with Him. But communion with God is life and light, and the enjoyment of all the benefits which He has in store. But on as many as, according to their own choice, depart from God, He inflicts that separation from Himself which they have chosen of their own accord. But separation from God is death, and separation from light is darkness; and separation from God consists in the loss of all the benefits which He has in store. Those, therefore, who cast away by apostasy these forementioned things, being in fact destitute of all good, do experience every kind of punishment. God, however, does not punish them immediately of Himself, but that punishment falls upon them because they

---

[1] Luke xvii. 34. [2] Matt. xiii. 30. [3] Matt. xxv. 33, etc.
[4] Luke x. 12. [5] Matt. v. 45.

are destitute of all that is good. Now, good things are eternal and without end with God, and therefore the loss of these is also eternal and never-ending. It is in this matter just as occurs in the case of a flood of light: those who have blinded themselves, or have been blinded by others, are for ever deprived of the enjoyment of light. It is not, [however], that the light has inflicted upon them the penalty of blindness, but it is that the blindness itself has brought calamity upon them: and therefore the Lord declared, "He that believeth in me is not condemned,"[1] that is, is not separated from God, for he is united to God through faith. On the other hand, He says, "He that believeth not is condemned already, because he has not believed in the name of the only-begotten Son of God;" that is, he separated himself from God of his own accord. "For this is the condemnation, that light is come into this world, and men have loved darkness rather than light. For every one who doeth evil hateth the light, and cometh not to the light, lest his deeds should be reproved. But he that doeth truth cometh to the light, that his deeds may be made manifest, that he has wrought them in God."

CHAP. XXVIII.—*The distinction to be made between the righteous and the wicked. The future apostasy in the time of Antichrist, and the end of the world.*

1. Inasmuch, then, as in this world (αἰῶνι) some persons betake themselves to the light, and by faith unite themselves with God, but others shun the light, and separate themselves from God, the Word of God comes preparing a fit habitation for both. For those indeed who are in the light, that they may derive enjoyment from it, and from the good things contained in it; but for those in darkness, that they may partake in its calamities. And on this account He says, that those upon the right hand are called into the kingdom of heaven, but that those on the left He will send into eternal fire; for they have deprived themselves of all good.

2. And for this reason the apostle says: "Because they

[1] John iii. 18, 21.

received not the love of God, that they might be saved, therefore God shall also send them the operation of error, that they may believe a lie, that they all may be judged who have not believed the truth, but consented to unrighteousness."[1] For when he (Antichrist) is come, and of his own accord concentrates in his own person the apostasy, and accomplishes whatever he shall do according to his own will and choice, sitting also in the temple of God, so that his dupes may adore him as the Christ; wherefore also shall he deservedly "be cast into the lake of fire:"[2] [this will happen according to divine appointment], God by His prescience foreseeing all this, and at the proper time sending such a man, "that they may believe a lie, that they all may be judged who did not believe the truth, but consented to unrighteousness;" whose coming John has thus described in the Apocalypse: "And the beast which I had seen was like unto a leopard, and his feet as of a bear, and his mouth as the mouth of a lion; and the dragon conferred his own power upon him, and his throne, and great might. And one of his heads was as it were slain unto death; and his deadly wound was healed, and all the world wondered after the beast. And they worshipped the dragon because he gave power to the beast; and they worshipped the beast, saying, Who is like unto this beast, and who is able to make war with him? And there was given unto him a mouth speaking great things, and blasphemy and power was given to him during forty and two months. And he opened his mouth for blasphemy against God, to blaspheme His name and His tabernacle, and those who dwell in heaven. And power was given him over every tribe, and people, and tongue, and nation. And all who dwell upon the earth worshipped him, [every one] whose name was not written in the book of the Lamb slain from the foundation of the world. If any one have ears, let him hear. If any one shall lead into captivity, he shall go into captivity. If any shall slay with the sword, he must be slain with the sword. Here is the endurance and the faith of the saints."[3] After this he likewise describes his armour-bearer, whom he

---

[1] 2 Thess. ii. 10–12.   [2] Rev. xix. 20.   [3] Rev. xiii. 2, etc.

also terms a false prophet: "He spake as a dragon, and exercised all the power of the first beast in his sight, and caused the earth, and those that dwell therein, to adore the first beast, whose deadly wound was healed. And he shall perform great wonders, so that he can even cause fire to descend from heaven upon the earth in the sight of men, and he shall lead the inhabitants of the earth astray."[1] Let no one imagine that he performs these wonders by divine power, but by the working of magic. And we must not be surprised if, since the demons and apostate spirits are at his service, he through their means performs wonders, by which he leads the inhabitants of the earth astray. John says further: "And he shall order an image of the beast to be made, and he shall give breath to the image, so that the image shall speak; and he shall cause those to be slain who will not adore it." He says also: "And he will cause a mark [to be put] in the forehead and in the right hand, that no one may be able to buy or sell, unless he who has the mark of the name of the beast or the number of his name; and the number is six hundred and sixty-six,"[2] that is, six times a hundred, six times ten, and six units. [He gives this] as a summing up of the whole of that apostasy which has taken place during six thousand years.

3. For in as many days as this world was made, in so many thousand years shall it be concluded. And for this reason the Scripture says: "Thus the heaven and the earth were finished, and all their adornment. And God brought to a conclusion upon the sixth day the works that He had made; and God rested upon the seventh day from all His works."[3] This is an account of the things formerly created, as also it is a prophecy of what is to come. For the day of the Lord is as a thousand years;[4] and in six days created things were completed: it is evident, therefore, that they will come to an end at the sixth thousand year.

4. And therefore throughout all time, man, having been moulded at the beginning by the hands of God, that is, of

---

[1] Rev. xiii. 11, etc.
[2] Rev. xiii. 14, etc.
[3] Gen. ii. 2.
[4] 2 Pet. iii. 8.

the Son and of the Spirit, is made after the image and likeness of God: the chaff, indeed, which is the apostasy, being cast away; but the wheat, that is, those who bring forth fruit to God in faith, being gathered into the barn. And for this cause tribulation is necessary for those who are saved, that having been after a manner broken up, and rendered fine, and sprinkled over by the patience of the Word of God, and set on fire [for purification], they may be fitted for the royal banquet. As a certain man of ours said, when he was condemned to the wild beasts because of his testimony with respect to God: "I am the wheat of Christ, and am ground by the teeth of the wild beasts, that I may be found the pure bread of God."[1]

CHAP. XXIX.—*All things have been created for the service of man. The deceits, wickedness, and apostate power of Antichrist. This was prefigured at the deluge, as afterwards by the persecution of Shadrach, Meshach, and Abednego.*

1. In the previous books I have set forth the causes for which God permitted these things to be made, and have pointed out that all such have been created for the benefit of that human nature which is saved, ripening for immortality that which is [possessed] of its own free will and its own power, and preparing and rendering it more adapted for eternal subjection to God. And therefore the creation is suited to [the wants of] man; for man was not made for its sake, but creation for the sake of man. Those nations, however, who did not of themselves raise up their eyes unto heaven, nor returned thanks to their Maker, nor wished to behold the light of truth, but who were like blind mice concealed in the depths of ignorance, the word justly reckons

---

[1] This is quoted from the Epistle of Ignatius to the Romans, ch. iv. It is found in the two Greek recensions of his works, and also in the Syriac. See vol. i. pp. 212 and 282 of this series. The Latin translation is here followed: the Greek of Ignatius would give "the wheat of God," and omits "of God" towards the end, as quoted by Eusebius.

"as waste water from a sink, and as the turning-weight of a balance—in fact, as nothing;"[1] so far useful and serviceable to the just, as stubble conduces towards the growth of the wheat, and its straw, by means of combustion, serves for working gold. And therefore, when in the end the church shall be suddenly caught up from this, it is said, "There shall be tribulation such as has not been since the beginning, neither shall be."[2] For this is the last contest of the righteous, in which, when they overcome, they are crowned with incorruption.

2. And there is therefore in this beast, when he comes, a recapitulation made of all sorts of iniquity and of every deceit, in order that all apostate power, flowing into and being shut up in him, may be sent into the furnace of fire. Fittingly, therefore, shall his name possess the number six hundred and sixty-six, since he sums up in his own person all the commixture of wickedness which took place previous to the deluge, due to the apostasy of the angels. For Noah was six hundred years old when the deluge came upon the earth, sweeping away the rebellious world, for the sake of that most infamous generation which lived in the times of Noah. And [Antichrist] also sums up every error of devised idols since the flood, together with the slaying of the prophets and the cutting off of the just. For that image which was set up by Nebuchadnezzar had indeed a height of sixty cubits, while the breadth was six cubits; on account of which Ananias, Azarias, and Misaël, when they did not worship it, were cast into a furnace of fire, pointing out prophetically, by what happened to them, the wrath against the righteous which shall arise towards the [time of the] end. For that image, taken as a whole, was a prefiguring of this man's coming, decreeing that he should undoubtedly himself alone be worshipped by all men. Thus, then, the six hundred years of Noah, in whose time the deluge occurred because of the apostasy, and the number of the cubits of the image for which these just men were sent into the fiery furnace, do indicate the number of the name of that man in whom is concen-

[1] Isa. xl. 15. [2] Matt. xxiv. 21.

trated the whole apostasy of six thousand years, and unrighteousness, and wickedness, and false prophecy, and deception; for which things' sake a cataclysm of fire shall also come [upon the earth].

CHAP. XXX.—*Although certain as to the number of the name of Antichrist, yet we should come to no rash conclusions as to the name itself, because this number is capable of being fitted to many names. Reasons for this point being reserved by the Holy Spirit. Antichrist's reign and death.*

1. Such, then, being the state of the case, and this number being found in all the most approved and ancient copies[1] [of the Apocalypse], and those men who saw John face to face bearing their testimony [to it]; while reason also leads us to conclude that the number of the name of the beast, [if reckoned] according to the Greek mode of calculation by the [value of] the letters contained in it, will amount to six hundred and sixty and six; that is, the number of tens shall be equal to that of the hundreds, and the number of hundreds equal to that of the units (for that number which [expresses] the digit six being adhered to throughout, indicates the recapitulations of that apostasy, taken in its full extent, which occurred at the beginning, during the intermediate periods, and which shall take place at the end),—I do not know how it is that some have erred following the ordinary mode of speech, and have vitiated the middle number in the name, deducting the amount of fifty from it, so that instead of six decads they will have it that there is but one. [I am inclined to think that this occurred through the fault of the copyists, as is wont to happen, since numbers also are expressed by letters; so that the Greek letter which expresses the number sixty was easily expanded into the letter Iota of the

---

[1] ἐν πᾶσι τοῖς σπουδαίοις καὶ ἀρχαίοις ἀντιγράφοις. This passage is interesting, as showing how very soon the autographs of the New Testament must have perished, and various readings crept into the MSS. of the canonical books.

Greeks.]¹ Others then received this reading without examination; some in their simplicity, and upon their own responsibility, making use of this number expressing one decad; while some, in their inexperience, have ventured to seek out a name which should contain the erroneous and spurious number. Now, as regards those who have done this in simplicity, and without evil intent, we are at liberty to assume that pardon will be granted them by God. But as for those who, for the sake of vainglory, lay it down for certain that names containing the spurious number are to be accepted, and affirm that this name, hit upon by themselves, is that of him who is to come; such persons shall not come forth without loss, because they have led into error both themselves and those who confided in them. Now, in the first place, it is loss to wander from the truth, and to imagine that as being the case which is not; then again, as there shall be no light punishment [inflicted] upon him who either adds or subtracts anything from the Scripture,² under that such a person must necessarily fall. Moreover, another danger, by no means trifling, shall overtake those who falsely presume that they know the name of Antichrist. For if these men assume one [number], when this [Antichrist] shall come having another, they will be easily led away by him, as supposing him not to be the expected one, who must be guarded against.

2. These men, therefore, ought to learn [what really is the state of the case], and go back to the true number of the name, that they be not reckoned among false prophets. But, knowing the sure number declared by Scripture, that is, six hundred sixty and six, let them await, in the first place, the division of the kingdom into ten; then, in the next place, when these kings are reigning, and beginning to set their affairs in order, and advance their kingdom, [let them learn] to acknowledge that he who shall come claiming the kingdom for himself, and shall terrify those men of whom we

---

¹ That is, Ξ into EI, according to Harvey, who considers the whole of this clause as an evident interpolation. It does not occur in the Greek here preserved by Eusebius (*Hist. Eccl.* v. 8).

² Rev. xxii. 19.

have been speaking, having a name containing the aforesaid number, is truly the abomination of desolation. This, too, the apostle affirms: "When they shall say, Peace and safety, then sudden destruction shall come upon them."[1] And Jeremiah does not merely point out his sudden coming, but he even indicates the tribe from which he shall come, where he says, "We shall hear the voice of his swift horses from Dan; the whole earth shall be moved by the voice of the neighing of his galloping horses: he shall also come and devour the earth, and the fulness thereof, the city also, and they that dwell therein."[2] This, too, is the reason that this tribe is not reckoned in the Apocalypse along with those which are saved.[3]

3. It is therefore more certain, and less hazardous, to await the fulfilment of the prophecy, than to be making surmises, and casting about for any names that may present themselves, inasmuch as many names can be found possessing the number mentioned; and the same question will, after all, remain unsolved. For if there are many names found possessing this number, it will be asked which among them shall the coming man bear. It is not through a want of names containing the number of that name that I say this, but on account of the fear of God, and zeal for the truth: for the name *Evanthas* (ΕΥΑΝΘΑΣ) contains the required number, but I make no allegation regarding it. Then also *Lateinos* (ΛΑΤΕΙΝΟΣ) has the number six hundred and sixty-six; and it is a very probable [solution], this being the name of the last kingdom [of the four seen by Daniel]. For the Latins are they who at present bear rule: I will not, however, make any boast over this [coincidence]. *Teitan* too, (ΤΕΙΤΑΝ, the first syllable being written with the two Greek vowels ε and ι), among all the names which are found among us, is rather worthy of credit. For it has in itself the predicted number, and is composed of six letters, each syllable containing three letters; and [the word itself] is ancient, and removed from ordinary use; for among our kings we find none bearing this name Titan, nor have any of the idols which are worshipped in public among the Greeks and bar-

---
[1] 1 Thess. v. 3.   [2] Jer. viii. 16.   [3] Rev. vii. 5-7.

barians this appellation. Among many persons, too, this name is accounted divine, so that even the sun is termed "Titan" by those who do now possess [the rule]. This word, too, contains a certain outward appearance of vengeance, and of one inflicting merited punishment because he (Antichrist) pretends that he vindicates the oppressed.[1] And besides this, it is an ancient name, one worthy of credit, of royal dignity, and still further, a name belonging to a tyrant. Inasmuch, then, as this name "Titan" has so much to recommend it, there is a strong degree of probability, that from among the many [names suggested], we infer, that perchance he who is to come shall be called "Titan." We will not, however, incur the risk of pronouncing positively as to the name of Antichrist; for if it were necessary that his name should be distinctly revealed in this present time, it would have been announced by him who beheld the apocalyptic vision. For that was seen no very long time since, but almost in our day, towards the end of Domitian's reign.

4. But he indicates the number of the name now, that when this man comes we may avoid him, being aware who he is: the name, however, is suppressed, because it is not worthy of being proclaimed by the Holy Spirit. For if it had been declared by Him, he (Antichrist) might perhaps continue for a long period. But now as "he was, and is not, and shall ascend out of the abyss, and goes into perdition,"[2] as one who has no existence; so neither has his name been declared, for the name of that which does not exist is not proclaimed. But when this Antichrist shall have devastated all things in this world, he will reign for three years and six months, and sit in the temple at Jerusalem; and then the Lord will come from heaven in the clouds, in the glory of the Father, sending this man and those who follow him into the lake of fire; but bringing in for the righteous the times of the kingdom, that is, the rest, the hallowed seventh day;

[1] Massuet here quotes Cicero and Ovid in proof of the sun being termed *Titan*. The Titans waged war against the gods, to avenge themselves upon Saturn.
[2] Rev. xvii. 8.

and restoring to Abraham the promised inheritance, in which kingdom the Lord declared, that "many coming from the east and from the west should sit down with Abraham, Isaac, and Jacob."[1]

CHAP. XXXI.—*The preservation of our bodies is confirmed by the resurrection and ascension of Christ: the souls of the saints during the intermediate period are in a state of expectation of that time when they shall receive their perfect and consummated glory.*

1. Since, again, some who are reckoned among the orthodox go beyond the pre-arranged plan for the exaltation of the just, and are ignorant of the methods by which they are disciplined beforehand for incorruption, they thus entertain heretical opinions. For the heretics, despising the handiwork of God, and not admitting the salvation of their flesh, while they also treat the promise of God contemptuously, and pass beyond God altogether in the sentiments they form, affirm that immediately upon their death they shall pass above the heavens and the Demiurge, and go to the Mother (Achamoth) or to that Father whom they have feigned. Those persons, therefore, who disallow a resurrection affecting the whole man (*universam reprobant resurrectionem*), and as far as in them lies remove it from the midst [of the Christian scheme], how can they be wondered at, if again they know nothing as to the plan of the resurrection? For they do not choose to understand, that if these things are as they say, the Lord Himself, in whom they profess to believe, did not rise again upon the third day; but immediately upon His expiring on the cross, undoubtedly departed on high, leaving His body to the earth. But the case was, that for three days He dwelt in the place where the dead were, as the prophet says concerning Him: "And the Lord remembered His dead saints who slept formerly in the land of sepulture; and He descended to them, to rescue and save them."[2] And the Lord Himself says, "As Jonas re-

[1] Matt. viii. 11.   [2] See Book iii. 20, 4.

mained three days and three nights in the whale's belly, so shall the Son of man be in the heart of the earth."[1] Then also the apostle says, "But when He ascended, what is it but that He also descended into the lower parts of the earth?"[2] This, too, David says when prophesying of Him, "And Thou hast delivered my soul from the nethermost hell;"[3] and on His rising again the third day, He said to Mary, who was the first to see and to worship Him, "Touch me not, for I have not yet ascended to the Father; but go to the disciples, and say unto them, I ascend unto my Father, and unto your Father."[4]

2. If, then, the Lord observed the law of the dead, that He might become the first-begotten from the dead, and tarried until the third day "in the lower parts of the earth;"[5] then afterwards rising in the flesh, so that He even showed the print of the nails to His disciples,[6] He thus ascended to the Father;—[if all these things occurred, I say], how must these men not be put to confusion, who allege that "the lower parts" refer to this world of ours, but that their inner man, leaving the body here, ascends into the super-celestial place? For as the Lord "went away in the midst of the shadow of death,"[7] where the souls of the dead were, yet afterwards arose in the body, and after the resurrection was taken up [into heaven], it is manifest that the souls of His disciples also, upon whose account the Lord underwent these things, shall go away into the invisible place allotted to them by God, and there remain until the resurrection, awaiting that event; then receiving their bodies, and rising in their entirety, that is bodily, just as the Lord arose, they shall come thus into the presence of God. "For no disciple is above the Master, but every one that is perfect shall be as his Master."[8] As our Master, therefore, did not at once depart, taking flight [to heaven], but awaited the time of His resurrection prescribed by the Father, which had been also shown forth through Jonas, and rising again after three days

---

[1] Matt. xi. 40.   [2] Eph. iv. 9.   [3] Ps. lxxxvi. 23.
[4] John xx. 17.   [5] Eph. iv. 9.   [6] John xx. 20, 27.
[7] Ps. xxiii. 4.   [8] Luke vi. 40.

was taken up [to heaven]; so ought we also to await the time of our resurrection prescribed by God and foretold by the prophets, and so, rising, be taken up, as many as the Lord shall account worthy of this [privilege].[1]

CHAP. XXXII.—*In that flesh in which the saints have suffered so many afflictions, they shall receive the fruits of their labours; especially since all creation waits for this, and God promises it to Abraham and his seed.*

Inasmuch, therefore, as the opinions of certain [orthodox persons] are derived from heretical discourses, they are both ignorant of God's dispensations, and of the mystery of the resurrection of the just, and of the [earthly] kingdom which is the commencement of incorruption, by means of which kingdom those who shall be worthy are accustomed gradually to partake of the divine nature (*capere Deum*[2]); and it is necessary to tell them respecting those things, that it behoves the righteous first to receive the promise of the inheritance which God promised to the fathers, and to reign in it, when they rise again to behold God in this creation which is renovated, and that the judgment should take place afterwards. For it is just that in that very creation in which they toiled or were afflicted, being proved in every way by suffering, they should receive the reward of their suffering; and that in the creation in which they were slain because of their love to God, in that they should be revived again; and that in the creation in which they endured servitude, in that they should reign. For God is rich in all things, and all things are His. It is fitting, therefore, that the creation itself, being restored to its primeval condition, should without restraint be

---

[1] The five following chapters were omitted in the earlier editions, but added by Feuardentius. Most MSS., too, did not contain them. It is probable that the scribes of the middle ages rejected them on account of their inculcating millenarian notions, which had been long extinct in the church. Quotations from these five chapters have been collected by Harvey from Syriac and Armenian MSS. lately come to light.

[2] Or, "gradually to comprehend God."

under the dominion of the righteous; and the apostle has made this plain in the Epistle to the Romans, when he thus speaks: "For the expectation of the creature waiteth for the manifestation of the sons of God. For the creature has been subjected to vanity, not willingly, but by reason of him who hath subjected the same in hope; since the creature itself shall also be delivered from the bondage of corruption into the glorious liberty of the sons of God."[1]

2. Thus, then, the promise of God, which He gave to Abraham, remains stedfast. For thus He said: "Lift up thine eyes, and look from this place where now thou art, towards the north and south, and east and west. For all the earth which thou seest, I will give to thee and to thy seed, even for ever."[2] And again He says, "Arise, and go through the length and breadth of the land, since I will give it unto thee;"[3] and [yet] he did not receive an inheritance in it, not even a footstep, but was always a stranger and a pilgrim therein.[4] And upon the death of Sarah his wife, when the Hittites were willing to bestow upon him a place where he might bury her, he declined it as a gift, but bought the burying-place (giving for it four hundred talents of silver) from Ephron the son of Zohar the Hittite.[5] Thus did he await patiently the promise of God, and was unwilling to appear to receive from men, what God had promised to give him, when He said again to him as follows: "I will give this land to thy seed, from the river of Egypt even unto the great river Euphrates."[6] If, then, God promised him the inheritance of the land, yet he did not receive it during all the time of his sojourn there, it must be, that together with his seed, that is, those who fear God and believe in Him, he shall receive it at the resurrection of the just. For his seed is the church, which receives the adoption to God through the Lord, as John the Baptist said: "For God is able from the stones to raise up children to Abraham."[7] Thus also the apostle says in the Epistle to the Galatians: "But ye,

---

[1] Rom. viii. 19, etc.   [2] Gen. xiii. 13, 14.   [3] Gen. xiii. 17.
[4] Acts vii. 5; Heb. xi. 13.   [5] Gen. xxiii. 11.   [6] Gen. xv. 13.
[7] Luke iii. 8.

brethren, as Isaac was, are the children of the promise."[1] And again, in the same epistle, he plainly declares that they who have believed in Christ do receive Christ, the promise to Abraham thus saying, "The promises were spoken to Abraham, and to his seed. Now He does not say, And of seeds, as if [He spake] of many, but as of one, And to thy seed, which is Christ."[2] And again, confirming his former words, he says, "Even as Abraham believed God, and it was accounted to him for righteousness. Know ye therefore, that they which are of faith are the children of Abraham. But the Scripture, foreseeing that God would justify the heathen through faith, declared to Abraham beforehand, That in thee shall all nations be blessed. So then they which are of faith shall be blessed with faithful Abraham."[3] Thus, then, they who are of faith shall be blessed with faithful Abraham, and these are the children of Abraham. Now God made promise of the earth to Abraham and his seed; yet neither Abraham nor his seed, that is, those who are justified by faith, do now receive any inheritance in it; but they shall receive it at the resurrection of the just. For God is true and faithful; and on this account He said, " Blessed are the meek, for they shall inherit the earth."[4]

CHAP. XXXIII.—*Further proofs of the same proposition, drawn from the promises made by Christ, when He declared that He would drink of the fruit of the vine with His disciples in His Father's kingdom, while at the same time He promised to reward them an hundred-fold, and to make them partake of banquets. The blessing pronounced by Jacob had pointed out this already, as Papias and the elders have interpreted it.*

1. For this reason, when about to undergo His sufferings, that He might declare to Abraham and those with him the glad tidings of the inheritance being thrown open, [Christ], after He had given thanks while holding the cup, and had

[1] Gal. iv. 28.   [2] Gal. iii. 16.
[3] Gal. iii. 6, etc.   [4] Matt. v. 5.

drunk of it, and given it to the disciples, said to them: "Drink ye all of it: this is my blood of the new covenant, which shall be shed for many for the remission of sins. But I say unto you, I will not drink henceforth of the fruit of this vine, until that day when I will drink it new with you in my Father's kingdom."[1] Thus, then, He will Himself renew the inheritance of the earth, and will re-organize the mystery of the glory of [His] sons; as David says, "He who hath renewed the face of the earth."[2] He promised to drink of the fruit of the vine with His disciples, thus indicating both these points: the inheritance of the earth in which the new fruit of the vine is drunk, and the resurrection of His disciples in the flesh. For the new flesh which rises again is the same which also received the new cup. And He cannot by any means be understood as drinking of the fruit of the vine when settled down with His [disciples] above in a super-celestial place; nor, again, are they who drink it devoid of flesh, for to drink of that which flows from the vine pertains to flesh, and not spirit.

2. And for this reason the Lord declared, "When thou makest a dinner or a supper, do not call thy friends, nor thy neighbours, nor thy kinsfolk, lest they ask thee in return, and so repay thee. But call the lame, the blind, and the poor, and thou shalt be blessed, since they cannot recompense thee, but a recompense shall be made thee at the resurrection of the just."[3] And again He says, "Whosoever shall have left lands, or houses, or parents, or brethren, or children because of me, he shall receive in this world an hundred-fold, and in that to come he shall inherit eternal life."[4] For what are the hundred-fold [rewards] in this world, the entertainments given to the poor, and the suppers for which a return is made? These are [to take place] in the times of the kingdom, that is, upon the seventh day, which has been sanctified, in which God rested from all the works which He created, which is the true Sabbath of the righteous, in which they shall not be engaged in any earthly occupation; but

[1] Matt. xxvi. 27. [2] Ps. civ. 30.
[3] Luke xiv. 12, 13. [4] Matt. xix. 29; Luke xviii. 29, 30.

shall have a table at hand prepared for them by God, supplying them with all sorts of dishes.

3. The blessing of Isaac with which he blessed his younger son Jacob has the same meaning, when he says, "Behold, the smell of my son is as the smell of a full field which the Lord has blessed."[1] But "the field is the world."[2] And therefore he added, "God give to thee of the dew of heaven, and of the fatness of the earth, plenty of corn and wine. And let the nations serve thee, and kings bow down to thee; and be thou lord over thy brother, and thy father's sons shall bow down to thee: cursed shall be he who shall curse thee, and blessed shall be he who shall bless thee."[3] If any one, then, does not accept these things as referring to the appointed kingdom, he must fall into much contradiction and contrariety, as is the case with the Jews, who are involved in absolute perplexity. For not only did not the nations in this life serve this Jacob; but even after he had received the blessing, he himself going forth [from his home], served his uncle Laban the Syrian for twenty years;[4] and not only was he not made lord of his brother, but he did himself bow down before his brother Esau, upon his return from Mesopotamia to his father, and offered many gifts to him.[5] Moreover, in what way did he inherit much corn and wine here, he who emigrated to Egypt because of the famine which possessed the land in which he was dwelling, and became subject to Pharaoh, who was then ruling over Egypt? The predicted blessing, therefore, belongs unquestionably to the times of the kingdom, when the righteous shall bear rule upon their rising from the dead;[6] when also the creation, having been renovated and set free, shall fructify with an abundance of all kinds of food, from the dew of heaven, and from the fertility of the earth: as the elders who saw John,

---

[1] Gen. xxvii. 27, etc. [2] Matt. xiii. 38. [3] Gen. xxvii. 28, 29.
[4] Gen. xxxi. 41. [5] Gen. xxxiii. 3.
[6] From this to the end of the section there is an Armenian version extant, to be found in the *Spicil. Solesm.* i. p. 1, edited by M. Pitra, Paris 1852, and which was taken by him from an Armenian MS. in the Mechitarist Library at Venice, described as being of the twelfth century.

the disciple of the Lord, related that they had heard from him how the Lord used to teach in regard to these times, and say: The days will come, in which vines shall grow, each having ten thousand branches, and in each branch ten thousand twigs, and in each true[1] twig ten thousand shoots, and in each one of the shoots ten thousand clusters, and on every one of the clusters ten thousand grapes, and every grape when pressed will give five and twenty metretes of wine. And when any one of the saints shall lay hold of a cluster,[2] another shall cry out, "I am a better cluster, take me; bless the Lord through me." In like manner [the Lord declared] that a grain of wheat would produce ten thousand ears, and that every ear should have ten thousand grains, and every grain would yield ten pounds (*quinque bilibres*) of clear, pure, fine flour; and that all other fruit-bearing trees,[3] and seeds and grass, would produce in similar proportions (*secundum congruentiam iis consequentem*); and that all animals feeding [only] on the productions of the earth, should [in those days] become peaceful and harmonious among each other, and be in perfect subjection to man.

4. And these things are borne witness to in writing by Papias, the hearer of John, and a companion of Polycarp, in his fourth book; for there were five books compiled (συντεταγμένα) by him. And he says in addition, "Now these things are credible to believers." And he says that, "when the traitor Judas did not give credit to them, and put the question, 'How then can things about to bring forth so abundantly be wrought by the Lord?' the Lord declared, 'They who shall come to these [times] shall see.'" When prophesying of these times, therefore, Esaias says: "The wolf also shall feed with the lamb, and the leopard shall take his rest with the kid; the calf also, and the bull, and the lion shall eat together; and a little boy shall lead them. The ox

---

[1] This word "true" is not found in the Armenian.

[2] Or, following Arm. vers., "But if any one shall lay hold of an holy cluster."

[3] The Arm. vers. is here followed; the old Latin reads, "Et reliqua autem poma."

and the bear shall feed together, and their young ones shall agree together; and the lion shall eat straw as well as the ox. And the infant boy shall thrust his hand into the asp's den, into the nest also of the adder's brood; and they shall do no harm, nor have power to hurt anything in my holy mountain." And again he says, in recapitulation, "Wolves and lambs shall then browse together, and the lion shall eat straw like the ox, and the serpent earth as if it were bread; and they shall neither hurt nor annoy anything in my holy mountain, saith the Lord."[1] I am quite aware that some persons endeavour to refer these words to the case of savage men, both of different nations and various habits, who come to believe, and when they have believed, act in harmony with the righteous. But although this is [true] now with regard to some men coming from various nations to the harmony of the faith, nevertheless in the resurrection of the just [the words shall also apply] to those animals mentioned. For God is rich in all things. And it is right that when the creation is restored, all the animals should obey and be in subjection to man, and revert to the food originally given by God (for they had been originally subjected in obedience to Adam), that is, the productions of the earth. But some other occasion, and not the present, is [to be sought] for showing that the lion shall [then] feed on straw. And this indicates the large size and rich quality of the fruits. For if that animal, the lion, feeds upon straw [at that period], of what a quality must the wheat itself be whose straw shall serve as suitable food for lions?

CHAP. XXXIV.—*He fortifies his opinions with regard to the temporal and earthly kingdom of the saints after their resurrection, by the various testimonies of Isaiah, Ezekiel, Jeremiah, and Daniel; also by the parable of the servants watching, to whom the Lord promised that He would minister.*

1. Then, too, Isaiah himself has plainly declared that there

[1] Isa. xl. 6, etc.

shall be joy of this nature at the resurrection of the just, when he says: "The dead shall rise again; those, too, who are in the tombs shall arise, and those who are in the earth shall rejoice. For the dew from Thee is health to them."[1] And this again Ezekiel also says: "Behold, I will open your tombs, and will bring you forth out of your graves; when I will draw my people from the sepulchres, and I will put breath in you, and ye shall live; and I will place you on your own land, and ye shall know that I am the Lord."[2] And again the same speaks thus: "These things, saith the Lord, I will gather Israel from all nations whither they have been driven, and I shall be sanctified in them in the sight of the sons of the nations: and they shall dwell in their own land, which I gave to my servant Jacob. And they shall dwell in it in peace; and they shall build houses, and plant vineyards, and dwell in hope, when I shall cause judgment to fall among all who have dishonoured them, among those who encircle them round about; and they shall know that I am the Lord their God, and the God of their fathers."[3] Now I have shown a short time ago that the church is the seed of Abraham; and for this reason, that we may know that He who in the New Testament "raises up from the stones children unto Abraham,"[4] is He who will gather, according to the Old Testament, those that shall be saved from all the nations, Jeremiah says: "Behold, the days come, saith the Lord, that they shall no more say, The Lord liveth, who led the children of Israel from the north, and from every region whither they had been driven; He will restore them to their own land which He gave to their fathers."[5]

2. That the whole creation shall, according to God's will, obtain a vast increase, that it may bring forth and sustain fruits such [as we have mentioned], Isaiah declares: "And there shall be upon every high mountain, and upon every prominent hill, water running everywhere in that day, when many shall perish, when walls shall fall. And the light of

[1] Isa. xxvi. 19.   [2] Ezek. xxxvii. 12, etc.   [3] Ezek. xxviii. 25, 26.
[4] Matt. iii. 9.   [5] Jer. xxiii. 7, 6.

the moon shall be as the light of the sun, seven times that of the day, when He shall heal the anguish of His people, and do away with the pain of His stroke."[1] Now "the pain of the stroke" means that inflicted at the beginning upon disobedient man in Adam, that is, death; which [stroke] the Lord will heal when He raises us from the dead, and restores the inheritance of the fathers, as Isaiah again says: "And thou shalt be confident in the Lord, and He will cause thee to pass over the whole earth, and feed thee with the inheritance of Jacob thy father."[2] This is what the Lord declared: "Happy are those servants whom the Lord when He cometh shall find watching. Verily I say unto you, that He shall gird Himself, and make them to sit down [to meat], and will come forth and serve them. And if He shall come in the evening watch, and find them so, blessed are they, because He shall make them sit down, and minister to them; or if this be in the second, or it be in the third, blessed are they."[3] Again John also says the very same in the Apocalypse: "Blessed and holy is he who has part in the first resurrection."[4] Then, too, Isaiah has declared the time when these events shall occur; he says: "And I said, Lord, how long? Until the cities be wasted without inhabitant, and the houses be without men, and the earth be left a desert. And after these things the Lord shall remove us men far away (*longe nos faciet Deus homines*), and those who shall remain shall multiply upon the earth."[5] Then Daniel also says this very thing: "And the kingdom and dominion, and the greatness of those under the heaven, is given to the saints of the Most High God, whose kingdom is everlasting, and all dominions shall serve and obey Him."[6] And lest the promise named should be understood as referring to this time, it was declared to the prophet: "And come thou, and stand in thy lot at the consummation of the days."[7]

3. Now, that the promises were not announced to the prophets and the fathers alone, but to the churches united

---

[1] Isa. xxx. 25, 26.   [2] Isa. lviii. 14.   [3] Luke xii. 37, 38.
[4] Rev. xx. 6.   [5] Isa. vi. 11.   [6] Dan. vii. 27.
[7] Dan. xii. 13.

to these from the nations, whom also the Spirit terms "the islands" (both because they are established in the midst of turbulence, suffer the storm of blasphemies, exist as a harbour of safety to those in peril, and are the refuge of those who love the height [of heaven], and strive to avoid Bythus, that is, the depth of error), Jeremiah thus declares: "Hear the word of the Lord, ye nations, and declare it to the isles afar off; say ye, that the Lord will scatter Israel, He will gather him, and keep him, as one feeding his flock of sheep. For the Lord hath redeemed Jacob, and rescued him from the hand of one stronger than he. And they shall come and rejoice in Mount Zion, and shall come to what is good, and into a land of wheat, and wine, and fruits, of animals and of sheep; and their soul shall be as a tree bearing fruit, and they shall hunger no more. At that time also shall the virgins rejoice in the company of the young men: the old men, too, shall be glad, and I will turn their sorrow into joy; and I will make them exult, and will magnify them, and satiate the souls of the priests the sons of Levi; and my people shall be satiated with my goodness."[1] Now, in the preceding book[2] I have shown that all the disciples of the Lord are Levites and priests, they who used in the temple to profane the Sabbath, but are blameless.[3] Promises of such a nature, therefore, do indicate in the clearest manner the feasting of that creation in the kingdom of the righteous, which God promises that He will Himself serve.

4. Then again, speaking of Jerusalem, and of Him reigning there, Isaiah declares, "Thus saith the Lord, Happy is he who hath seed in Zion, and servants in Jerusalem. Behold, a righteous king shall reign, and princes shall rule with judgment."[4] And with regard to the foundation on which it shall be rebuilt, he says: "Behold, I will lay in order for thee a carbuncle stone, and sapphire for thy foundations; and I will lay thy ramparts with jasper, and thy gates with crystal, and thy wall with choice stones: and all thy children shall be taught of God, and great shall be the peace of thy

---

[1] Jer. xxxi. 10, etc. [2] See iv. 8, 3.
[3] Matt. xii. 5. [4] Isa. xxxi. 9, xxxii. 1.

children; and in righteousness shalt thou be built up."[1] And yet again does he say the same thing: "Behold, I make Jerusalem a rejoicing, and my people [a joy]; for the voice of weeping shall be no more heard in her, nor the voice of crying. Also there shall not be there any immature [one], nor an old man who does not fulfil his time: for the youth shall be of a hundred years; and the sinner shall die a hundred years old, yet shall be accursed. And they shall build houses, and inhabit them themselves; and shall plant vineyards, and eat the fruit of them themselves, and shall drink wine. And they shall not build, and others inhabit; neither shall they prepare the vineyard, and others eat. For as the days of the tree of life shall be the days of the people in thee; for the works of their hands shall endure."[2]

CHAP. XXXV.—*He contends that these testimonies already alleged cannot be understood allegorically of celestial blessings, but that they shall have their fulfilment after the coming of Antichrist, and the resurrection, in the terrestrial Jerusalem. To the former prophecies he subjoins others drawn from Isaiah, Jeremiah, and the Apocalypse of John.*

1. If, however, any shall endeavour to allegorize [prophecies] of this kind, they shall not be found consistent with themselves in all points, and shall be confuted by the teaching of the very expressions [in question]. For example: "When the cities" of the Gentiles "shall be desolate, so that they be not inhabited, and the houses so that there shall be no men in them, and the land shall be left desolate."[3] "For, behold," says Isaiah, "the day of the Lord cometh past remedy, full of fury and wrath, to lay waste the city of the earth, and to root sinners out of it."[4] And again he says, "Let him be taken away, that he behold not the glory of God."[5] And when these things are done, he says, "God will remove men far away, and those that are left shall multiply

---

[1] Isa. liv. 11–14. [2] Isa. lxv. 18. [3] Isa. vi. 11.
[4] Isa. xiii. 9. [5] Isa. xxvi. 10.

in the earth."¹ "And they shall build houses, and shall inhabit them themselves: and plant vineyards, and eat of them themselves."² For all these and other words were unquestionably spoken in reference to the resurrection of the just, which takes place after the coming of Antichrist, and the destruction of all nations under his rule; in [the times of] which [resurrection] the righteous shall reign in the earth, waxing stronger by the sight of the Lord: and through Him they shall become accustomed to partake in the glory of God the Father, and shall enjoy in the kingdom intercourse and communion with the holy angels, and union with spiritual beings; and [with respect to] those whom the Lord shall find in the flesh, awaiting Him from heaven, and who have suffered tribulation, as well as escaped the hands of the Wicked one. For it is in reference to them that the prophet says: "And those that are left shall multiply upon the earth." And Jeremiah³ the prophet has pointed out, that as many believers as God has prepared for this purpose, to multiply those left upon earth, should both be under the rule of the saints to minister to this Jerusalem, and that [His] kingdom shall be in it, saying, "Look around Jerusalem towards the east, and behold the joy which comes to thee from God Himself. Behold, thy sons shall come whom thou hast sent forth: they shall come in a band from the east even unto the west, by the word of that Holy One, rejoicing in that splendour which is from thy God. O Jerusalem, put off thy robe of mourning and of affliction, and put on that beauty of eternal splendour from thy God. Gird thyself with the double garment of that righteousness proceeding from thy God; place the mitre of eternal glory upon thine head. For God will show thy glory to the whole earth under heaven. For thy name shall for ever be called by God Himself, the peace of righteousness and glory to him that worships God. Arise, Jerusalem, stand on high, and look towards the east, and behold thy sons from the

---

¹ Isa. vi. 12.   ² Isa. lxv. 21

³ The long quotation following is not found in Jeremiah, but in the apocryphal book of Baruch, chap. iv. 36, etc., and the whole of chap. v.

rising of the sun, even to the west, by the word of that Holy One, rejoicing in the very remembrance of God. For the footmen have gone forth from thee, while they were drawn away by the enemy. God shall bring them in to thee, being borne with glory as the throne of a kingdom. For God has decreed that every high mountain shall be brought low, and the eternal hills, and that the valleys be filled, so that the surface of the earth be rendered smooth, that Israel, the glory of God, may walk in safety. The woods, too, shall make shady places, and every sweet-smelling tree shall be for Israel itself by the command of God. For God shall go before with joy in the light of His splendour, with the pity and righteousness which proceeds from Him."

2. Now all these things being such as they are, cannot be understood in reference to super-celestial matters; "for God," it is said, "will show to the whole earth that is under heaven thy glory." But in the times of the kingdom, the earth has been called again by Christ [to its pristine condition], and Jerusalem rebuilt after the pattern of the Jerusalem above, of which the prophet Isaiah says, "Behold, I have depicted thy walls upon my hands, and thou art always in my sight."[1] And the apostle, too, writing to the Galatians, says in like manner, "But the Jerusalem which is above is free, which is the mother of us all."[2] He does not say this with any thought of an erratic Æon, or of any other power which departed from the Pleroma, or of Prunicus, but of the Jerusalem which has been delineated on [God's] hands. And in the Apocalypse John saw this new [Jerusalem] descending upon the new earth.[3] For after the times of the kingdom, he says, "I saw a great white throne, and Him who sat upon it, from whose face the earth fled away, and the heaven; and there was no more place for them."[4] And he sets forth, too, the things connected with the general resurrection and the judgment, mentioning "the dead, great and small." "The sea," he says, "gave up the dead which it had in it, and death and hell delivered up the dead that they contained; and the books were opened. Moreover," he

[1] Isa. xlix. 16.   [2] Gal. iv. 26.   [3] Rev. xxi. 2.   [4] Rev. xx. 11.

says, "the book of life was opened, and the dead were judged out of those things that were written in the books, according to their works; and death and hell were sent into the lake of fire, the second death."[1] Now this is what is called Gehenna, which the Lord styled eternal fire.[2] "And if any one," it is said, "was not found written in the book of life, he was sent into the lake of fire."[3] And after this, he says, "I saw a new heaven and a new earth, for the first heaven and earth have passed away; also there was no more sea. And I saw the holy city, new Jerusalem, coming down from heaven, as a bride adorned for her husband." "And I heard," it is said, "a great voice from the throne, saying, Behold, the tabernacle of God is with men, and He will dwell with them; and they shall be His people, and God Himself shall be with them as their God. And He will wipe away every tear from their eyes; and death shall be no more, neither sorrow, nor crying, neither shall there be any more pain, because the former things have passed away."[4] Isaiah also declares the very same: "For there shall be a new heaven and a new earth; and there shall be no remembrance of the former, neither shall the heart think about them, but they shall find in it joy and exultation."[5] Now this is what has been said by the apostle: "For the fashion of this world passeth away."[6] To the same purpose did the Lord also declare, "Heaven and earth shall pass away."[7] When these things, therefore, pass away above the earth, John, the Lord's disciple, says that the new Jerusalem above shall [then] descend, as a bride adorned for her husband; and that this is the tabernacle of God, in which God will dwell with men. Of this Jerusalem the former one is an image—that Jerusalem of the former earth in which the righteous are disciplined beforehand for incorruption and prepared for salvation. And of this tabernacle Moses received the pattern in the mount;[8] and nothing is capable of being allegorized, but all things are stedfast, and true, and substantial, having

[1] Rev. xx. 12-14.   [2] Matt. xxv. 41.   [3] Rev. xx. 15.
[4] Rev. xxi. 1-4.   [5] Isa. lxv. 17, 18.   [6] 1 Cor. vii. 31.
[7] Matt. xxvi. 35.   [8] Ex. xxv. 40.

been made by God for righteous men's enjoyment. For as it is God truly who raises up man, so also does man truly rise from the dead, and not allegorically, as I have shown repeatedly. And as he rises actually, so also shall he be actually disciplined beforehand for incorruption, and shall go forwards and flourish in the times of the kingdom, in order that he may be capable of receiving the glory of the Father. Then, when all things are made new, he shall truly dwell in the city of God. For it is said, " He that sitteth on the throne said, Behold, I make all things new. And the Lord says, Write all this; for these words are faithful and true. And He said to me, They are done."[1] And this is the truth of the matter.

CHAP. XXXVI.—*Men shall be actually raised: the world shall not be annihilated; but there shall be various mansions for the saints, according to the rank allotted to each individual. All things shall be subject to God the Father, and so shall He be all in all.*

1. For since there are real men, so must there also be a real establishment (*plantationem*), that they vanish not away among non-existent things, but progress among those which have an actual existence. For neither is the substance nor the essence of the creation annihilated (for faithful and true is He who has established it), but " the *fashion* of the world passeth away;"[2] that is, those things among which transgression has occurred, since man has grown old in them. And therefore this [present] fashion has been formed temporary, God foreknowing all things; as I have pointed out in the preceding book,[3] and have also shown, as far as was possible, the cause of the creation of this world of temporal things. But when this [present] fashion [of things] passes away, and man has been renewed, and flourishes in an incorruptible state, so as to preclude the possibility of becoming old, [then] there shall be the new heaven and the new earth, in which the new man shall remain [continually],

[1] Rev. xxi. 5, 6.   [2] 1 Cor. vii. 31.   [3] Lib. iv. 5, 6.

always holding fresh converse with God. And since (*or, that*) these things shall ever continue without end, Isaiah declares, "For as the new heavens and the new earth which I do make, continue in my sight, saith the Lord, so shall your seed and your name remain."[1] And as the presbyters say, Then those who are deemed worthy of an abode in heaven shall go there, others shall enjoy the delights of paradise, and others shall possess the splendour of the city; for everywhere the Saviour[2] shall be seen according as they who see Him shall be worthy.

2. [They say, moreover], that there is this distinction between the habitation of those who produce an hundred-fold, and that of those who produce sixty-fold, and that of those who produce thirty-fold: for the first will be taken up into the heavens, the second will dwell in paradise, the last will inhabit the city; and that it was on this account the Lord declared, "In my Father's house are many mansions."[3] For all things belong to God, who supplies all with a suitable dwelling-place; even as His Word says, that a share is allotted to all by the Father, according as each person is or shall be worthy. And this is the couch on which the guests shall recline, having been invited to the wedding.[4] The presbyters, the disciples of the apostles, affirm that this is the gradation and arrangement of those who are saved, and that they advance through steps of this nature; also that they ascend through the Spirit to the Son, and through the Son to the Father, and that in due time the Son will yield up His work to the Father, even as it is said by the apostle, "For He must reign till He hath put all enemies under His feet. The last enemy that shall be destroyed is death."[5] For in the times of the kingdom, the righteous man who is upon the earth shall then forget to die. "But when He saith, All things shall be subdued unto Him, it is manifest that He is excepted who did put all things under Him. And when all things shall be subdued unto Him, then shall the

---

[1] Isa. lxvi. 22.
[2] Thus in a Greek fragment; in the Old Latin, *Deus*.
[3] John xiv. 2.   [4] Matt. xxii. 10.   [5] 1 Cor. xx. 25, 26.

Son also Himself be subject unto Him who put all things under Him, that God may be all in all."¹

3. John, therefore, did distinctly foresee the first "resurrection of the just,"² and the inheritance in the kingdom of the earth; and what the prophets have prophesied concerning it harmonize [with his vision]. For the Lord also taught these things, when He promised that He would have the mixed cup new with His disciples in the kingdom. The apostle, too, has confessed that the creation shall be free from the bondage of corruption, [so as to pass] into the liberty of the sons of God.³ And in all these things, and by them all, the same God the Father is manifested, who fashioned man, and gave promise of the inheritance of the earth to the fathers, who brought it (the creature) forth [from bondage] at the resurrection of the just, and fulfils the promises for the kingdom of His Son; subsequently bestowing in a paternal manner those things which neither the eye has seen, nor the ear has heard, nor has [thought concerning them] arisen within the heart of man.⁴ For there is the one Son, who accomplished His Father's will; and one human race also in which the mysteries of God are wrought, " which the angels desire to look into;"⁵ and they are not able to search out the wisdom of God, by means of which His handiwork, confirmed and incorporated with His Son, is brought to perfection; that His offspring, the First-begotten Word, should descend to the creature (*facturam*), that is, to what had been moulded (*plasma*), and that it should be contained by Him; and, on the other hand, the creature should contain the Word, and ascend to Him, passing beyond the angels, and be made after the image and likeness of God.⁶

---

¹ 1 Cor. xv. 27, 28.   ² Luke xiv. 14.   ³ Rom. viii. 21.
⁴ 1 Cor. ii. 9; Isa. lxiv. 4.   ⁵ 1 Pet. i. 12.
⁶ Grabe and others suppose that some part of the work has been lost, so that the above was not its original conclusion.

FRAGMENTS FROM THE LOST WRITINGS OF IRENÆUS.

I.

ADJURE thee, who shalt transcribe this book,[1] by our Lord Jesus Christ, and by His glorious appearing, when He comes to judge the living and the dead, that thou compare what thou hast transcribed, and be careful to set it right according to this copy from which thou hast transcribed; also, that thou in like manner copy down this adjuration, and insert it in the transcript.

II.

These[2] opinions, Florinus, that I may speak in mild terms, are not of sound doctrine; these opinions are not consonant to the church, and involve their votaries in the utmost impiety; these opinions, even the heretics beyond the church's pale have never ventured to broach; these opinions, those presbyters who preceded us, and who were conversant with the apostles, did not hand down to thee. For, while I was yet a boy, I saw thee in Lower Asia with Polycarp, distinguishing thyself in the royal court,[3] and endeavouring to gain his approbation. For I have a more vivid recollection of what occurred at that time than of recent events (inas-

---

[1] This fragment is quoted by Eusebius, *Hist. Eccl.* v. 20. It occurred at the close of the lost treatise of Irenæus entitled *De Ogdoade*.

[2] This interesting extract we also owe to Eusebius, who (*ut sup.*) took it from the work *De Ogdoade*, written after this former friend of Irenæus had lapsed to Valentinianism. Florinus had previously held that God was the author of evil, which sentiment Irenæus opposed in a treatise, now lost, called περὶ μοναρχίας.

[3] Comp. vol. i. p. 476, and Phil. iv. 22.

much as the experiences of childhood, keeping pace with the growth of the soul, become incorporated with it); so that I can even describe the place where the blessed Polycarp used to sit and discourse—his going out, too, and his coming in—his general mode of life and personal appearance, together with the discourses which he delivered to the people; also how he would speak of his familiar intercourse with John, and with the rest of those who had seen the Lord; and how he would call their words to remembrance. Whatsoever things he had heard from them respecting the Lord, both with regard to His miracles and His teaching, Polycarp having thus received [information] from the eye-witnesses of the Word of life, would recount them all in harmony with the Scriptures. These things, through God's mercy which was upon me, I then listened to attentively, and treasured them up not on paper, but in my heart; and I am continually, by God's grace, revolving these things accurately in my mind. And I can bear witness before God, that if that blessed and apostolical presbyter had heard any such thing, he would have cried out, and stopped his ears, exclaiming as he was wont to do: "O good God, for what times hast Thou reserved me, that I should endure these things?" And he would have fled from the very spot where, sitting or standing, he had heard such words. This fact, too, can be made clear, from his epistles which he despatched, whether to the neighbouring churches to confirm them, or to certain of the brethren, admonishing and exhorting them.

III.

For[1] the controversy is not merely as regards the day, but

---

[1] See preface to vol. i. p. xviii. We are indebted again to Eusebius for this valuable fragment from the Epistle of Irenæus to Victor Bishop of Rome (*Hist. Eccl.* v. 24; copied also by Nicephorus, iv. 39). It appears to have been a synodical epistle to the head of the Roman church, the historian saying that it was written by Irenæus, "in the name of (ἐκ προσώπου) those brethren over whom he ruled throughout Gaul." Neither are these expressions to be limited to the church at Lyons, for the same authority records (v. 23) that it was the testimony "of the dioceses throughout Gaul, which Irenæus superintended" (Harvey).

also as regards the form itself of the fast.[1] For some consider themselves bound to fast one day, others two days, others still more, while others [do so during] forty: the diurnal and the nocturnal hours they measure out together as their [fasting] day.[2] And this variety among the observers [of the fasts] had not its origin in our time, but long before in that of our predecessors, some of whom probably, being not very accurate in their observance of it, handed down to posterity the custom as it had, through simplicity or private fancy, been [introduced among them]. And yet nevertheless all these lived in peace one with another, and we also keep peace together. Thus, in fact, the difference [in observing] the fast establishes the harmony of [our common] faith.[3] And the presbyters preceding Soter in the government of the church which thou dost now rule—I mean, Anicetus and Pius, Hyginus and Telesphorus, and Sixtus—did neither themselves observe it [after that fashion], nor permit those with them[4] to do so. Notwithstanding this, those who did not keep [the feast in this way] were peacefully disposed towards those who came to them from other dioceses in which it was [so] observed, although such observance was [felt] in more decided contrariety [as presented] to those who did not fall in with it; and none were ever cast out [of the church] for this matter. On the contrary, those presbyters who preceded thee, and who did not observe [this custom], sent the Eucharist to those of other dioceses who did observe it.[5] And when the blessed Polycarp was sojourning

---

[1] According to Harvey, the early paschal controversy resolved itself into two particulars: (*a*) as regards the precise day on which our Lord's resurrection should be celebrated; (*b*) as regards the custom of the fast preceding it.

[2] Both reading and punctuation are here subjects of controversy. We have followed Massuet and Harvey.

[3] "The observance of *a* day, though not everywhere the same, showed unity, so far as faith in the Lord's resurrection was concerned."—HARVEY.

[4] Following the reading of Rufinus, the ordinary text has μετ' αὐτούς, *i.e.* after them.

[5] This practice was afterwards forbidden by the Council of Laodicea, A.D. 320.

in Rome in the time of Anicetus, although a slight controversy had arisen among them as to certain other points, they were at once well inclined towards each other [with regard to the matter in hand], not willing that any quarrel should arise between them upon this head. For neither could Anicetus persuade Polycarp to forego the observance [in his own way], inasmuch as these things had been always [so] observed by John the disciple of our Lord, and by other apostles with whom he had been conversant; nor, on the other hand, could Polycarp succeed in persuading Anicetus to keep [the observance in his way], for he maintained that he was bound to adhere to the usage of the presbyters who preceded him. And in this state of affairs they held fellowship with each other; and Anicetus conceded to Polycarp in the church the celebration of the Eucharist, by way of showing him respect; so that they parted in peace one from the other, maintaining peace with the whole church, both those who did observe [this custom] and those who did not.[1]

IV.

As[2] long as any one has the means of doing good to his neighbours, and does not do so, he shall be reckoned a stranger to the love of the Lord.[3]

V.

The[4] will and the energy of God is the effective and foreseeing cause of every time and place and age, and of every

---

[1] It was perhaps in reference to this pleasing episode in the annals of the church, that the Council of Arles, A.D. 314, decreed that the holy Eucharist should be consecrated by any foreign bishop present at its celebration.

[2] Quoted by Maximus Bishop of Turin, A.D. 422, *Serm.* vii. *de Eleemos.*, as from the Epistle to Pope Victor. It is also found in some other ancient writers.

[3] One of the MSS. reads here τοῦ Θεοῦ, of God.

[4] Also quoted by Maximus Turinensis, *Op.* ii. 152, who refers it to Irenæus' *Sermo de Fide*, which work, not being referred to by Eusebius or Jerome, causes Massuet to doubt the authenticity of the fragment. Harvey, however, accepts it.

nature. The will is the reason (λόγος) of the intellectual soul, which [reason] is within us, inasmuch as it is the faculty belonging to it which is endowed with freedom of action. The will is the mind desiring [some object], and an appetite possessed of intelligence, yearning after that thing which is desired.

VI.

Since[1] God is vast, and the Architect of the world, and omnipotent, He created things that reach to immensity both by the Architect of the world and by an omnipotent will, and with a new effect, potently and efficaciously, in order that the entire fulness of those things which have been produced might come into being, although they had no previous existence— that is, whatever does not fall under [our] observation, and also what lies before our eyes. And so does He contain all things in particular, and leads them on to their own proper result, on account of which they were called into being and produced, in no way changed into anything else than what it (the end) had originally been by nature. For this is the property of the working of God, not merely to proceed to the infinitude of the understanding, or even to overpass [our] powers of mind, reason and speech, time and place, and every age; but also to go beyond substance, and fulness or perfection.

VII.

This[2] [custom], of not bending the knee upon Sunday,

[1] We owe this fragment also to Maximus, who quoted it from the same work, *de Fide*, written by Irenæus to Demetrius, a deacon of Vienne. This and the last fragment were first printed by Feuardentius, who obtained them from Faber; no reference, however, being given as to the source from whence the Latin version was derived. The Greek of this Fragment vi. is not extant.

[2] Taken from a work (*Quæs. et Resp. ad Othod.*) ascribed to Justin Martyr, but certainly written after the Nicene Council. It is evident that this is not an exact quotation from Irenæus, but a summary of his words. The "Sunday" here referred to must be Easter Sunday. Massuet's emendation of the text has been adopted, ἐπ' αὐτοῦ for ἐπ' αὐτῶν.

is a symbol of the resurrection, through which we have been set free, by the grace of Christ, from sins, and from death, which has been put to death under Him. Now this custom took its rise from apostolic times, as the blessed Irenæus, the martyr and bishop of Lyons, declares in his treatise *On Easter*, in which he makes mention of Pentecost also; upon which [feast] we do not bend the knee, because it is of equal significance with the Lord's day, for the reason already alleged concerning it.

VIII.

For[1] as the ark [of the covenant] was gilded within and without with pure gold, so was also the body of Christ pure and resplendent; for it was adorned within by the Word, and shielded without by the Spirit, in order that from both [materials] the splendour of the natures might be clearly shown forth.

IX.

Ever,[2] indeed, speaking well of the deserving, but never ill of the undeserving, we also shall attain to the glory and kingdom of God.

X.

It is indeed proper to God, and befitting His character, to show mercy and pity, and to bring salvation to His creatures, even though they be brought under danger of destruction. " For with Him," says the Scripture, " is propitiation."[3]

---

[1] Cited by Leontius of Byzantium, who flourished about the year A.D. 600; but he does not mention the writing of Irenæus from which it is extracted. Massuet conjectures that it is from the *De Ogdoade*, addressed to the apostate Florinus.

[2] This fragment and the next three are from the *Parallela* of John of Damascus. Frag. ix. x. xii. seem to be quotations from the treatise of Irenæus on the resurrection. No. xi. is extracted from his *Miscellaneous Dissertations*, a work mentioned by Eusebius, βιβλίον τι διαλεξέων διαφόρων.

[3] Ps. cxxx. 7.

XI.

The business of the Christian is nothing else than to be ever preparing for death (μελετᾷν ἀποθνήσκειν).

XII.

We therefore have formed the belief that [our] bodies also do rise again. For although they go to corruption, yet they do not perish; for the earth, receiving the remains, preserves them, even like fertile seed mixed with more fertile ground. Again, as a bare grain is sown, and, germinating by the command of God its Creator, rises again, clothed upon and glorious, but not before it has died and suffered decomposition, and become mingled with the earth; so [it is seen from this, that] we have not entertained a vain belief in the resurrection of the body. But although it is dissolved at the appointed time, because of the primeval disobedience, it is placed, as it were, in the crucible of the earth, to be re-cast again; not then as this corruptible [body], but pure, and no longer subject to decay: so that to each body its own soul shall be restored; and when it is clothed upon with this, it shall not experience sorrow, but shall rejoice, continuing permanently in a state of purity, having for its companion a just consort, not an insidious one, possessing in every respect the things pertaining to it, it shall receive these with perfect accuracy;[1] it shall not receive bodies diverse from what they had been, nor delivered from suffering or disease, nor as [rendered] glorious, but as they departed this life, in sins or in righteous actions: and such as they were, such shall they be clothed with upon resuming life; and such as they were in unbelief, such shall they be faithfully judged.

XIII.

For[2] when the Greeks, having arrested the slaves of

---

[1] This sentence in the original seems incomplete; we have followed the conjectural restoration of Harvey.

[2] "This extract is found in Œcumenius upon 1 Pet. c. iii. p. 198;

Christian catechumens, then used force against them, in order to learn from them some secret thing [practised] among Christians, these slaves, having nothing to say that would meet the wishes of their tormentors, except that they had heard from their masters that the divine communion was the body and blood of Christ, and imagining that it was actually flesh and blood, gave their inquisitors answer to that effect. Then these latter, assuming such to be the case with regard to the practices of Christians, gave information regarding it to other Greeks, and sought to compel the martyrs Sanctus and Blandina to confess, under the influence of torture, [that the allegation was correct]. To these men Blandina replied very admirably in these words: "How should those persons endure such [accusations], who, for the sake of the practice [of piety], did not avail themselves even of the flesh that was permitted [them to eat]?"

XIV.

How[1] is it possible to say that the serpent, created by God dumb and irrational, was endowed with reason and speech? For if it had the power of itself to speak, to discern, to understand, and to reply to what was spoken by the woman, there would have been nothing to prevent every serpent from doing this also. If, however, they say again that it was according to the divine will and dispensation that this [serpent] spake with a human voice to Eve, they render God the author of sin. Neither was it possible for the evil demon to impart speech to a speechless nature, and thus from that which is not to produce that which is; for if that were the case, he never would have ceased (with the view of leading men astray) from conferring with and deceiving them by means of serpents, and beasts, and birds. From what quarter, too, did it, being a beast, obtain infor-

and the words used by him indicate, as Grabe has justly observed, that he only condensed a longer passage."—HARVEY.

[1] From the *Contemplations* of Anastasius Sinaita, who flourished A.D. 685. Harvey doubts as to this fragment being a genuine production of Irenæus; and its whole style of reasoning confirms the suspicion.

mation regarding the injunction of God to the man given to him alone, and in secret, not even the woman herself being aware of it? Why also did it not prefer to make its attack upon the man instead of the woman? And if thou sayest that it attacked her as being the weaker of the two, [I reply that], on the contrary, she was the stronger, since she appears to have been the helper of the man in the transgression of the commandment. For she did by herself alone resist the serpent, and it was after holding out for a while and making opposition that she ate of the tree, being circumvented by craft; whereas Adam, making no fight whatever, nor refusal, partook of the fruit handed to him by the woman, which is an indication of the utmost imbecility and effeminacy of mind. And the woman indeed, having been vanquished in the contest by a demon, is deserving of pardon; but Adam shall deserve none, for he was worsted by a woman,—he who, in his own person, had received the command from God. But the woman, having heard of the command from Adam, treated it with contempt, either because she deemed it unworthy of God to speak by means of it, or because she had her doubts, perhaps even held the opinion that the command was given to her by Adam of his own accord. The serpent found her working alone, so that he was enabled to confer with her apart. Observing her then either eating or not eating from the trees, he put before her the fruit of the [forbidden] tree. And if he saw her eating, it is manifest that she was partaker of a body subject to corruption. "For everything going in at the mouth, is cast out into the draught."[1] If then corruptible, it is obvious that she was also mortal. But if mortal, then there was certainly no curse; nor was that a [condemnatory] sentence, when the voice of God spake to the man, "For earth thou art, and unto earth shalt thou return,"[2] as the true course of things proceeds [now and always]. Then again, if the serpent observed the woman not eating, how did he induce her to eat who never had eaten? And who pointed out to this accursed man-slaying serpent that the sentence of death pronounced against

[1] Matt. xv. 17.   [2] Gen. iii. 19.

them by God would not take [immediate] effect, when He said, "For in the day that ye eat thereof, ye shall surely die?" And not this merely, but that along with the impunity[1] [attending their sin] the eyes of those should be opened who had not seen until then? But with the opening [of their eyes] referred to, they made entrance upon the path of death.

XV.

When,[2] in times of old, Balaam spake these things in parables, he was not acknowledged; and now, when Christ has appeared and fulfilled them, He was not believed. Wherefore [Balaam], foreseeing this, and wondering at it, exclaimed, "Alas! alas! who shall live when God brings these things to pass?"[3]

XVI.

Expounding again the law to that generation which followed those who were slain in the wilderness, he published Deuteronomy; not as giving to them a different law from that which had been appointed for their fathers, but as recapitulating this latter, in order that they, by hearing what had happened to their fathers, might fear God with their whole heart.

XVII.

By these Christ was typified, and acknowledged, and brought into the world; for He was prefigured in Joseph: then from Levi and Judah He was descended according to the flesh, as King and Priest; and He was acknowledged by

---

[1] The Greek reads the barbarous word ἀθριξίᾳ, which Massuet thinks is a corruption of ἀθανασίᾳ, immortality. We have, however, followed the conjecture of Harvey, who would substitute ἀπληξίᾳ, which seems to agree better with the context.

[2] This and the eight following fragments may be referred to the *Miscellaneous Dissertations* of our author; see note on Frag. ix. They are found in three MSS. in the Imperial Collection at Paris, on the Pentateuch, Joshua, Judges, and Ruth.

[3] Num. xxiv. 23.

Simeon in the temple: through Zebulon He was believed in among the Gentiles, as says the prophet, "the land of Zabulon;"[1] and through Benjamin [that is, Paul] He was glorified, by being preached throughout all the world.[2]

XVIII.

And this was not without meaning; but that by means of the number of the ten men,[3] he (Gideon) might appear as having Jesus for a helper, as [is indicated] by the compact entered into with them. And when he did not choose to partake with them in their idol-worship, they threw the blame upon him: for "Jerubbaal" signifies the judgment-seat of Baal.

XIX.

"Take unto thee Joshua ($'I\eta\sigma o\hat{v}\nu$) the son of Nun."[4] For it was proper that Moses should lead the people out of Egypt, but that Jesus (*Joshua*) should lead them into the inheritance. Also that Moses, as was the case with the law, should cease to be, but that Joshua ($'I\eta\sigma o\hat{v}\nu$), as the word, and no untrue type of the Word made flesh ($\dot{\epsilon}\nu\upsilon\pi o\sigma\tau\acute{a}\tau o\nu$), should be a preacher to the people. Then again, [it was fit] that Moses should give manna as food to the fathers, but Joshua wheat;[5] as the first-fruits of life, a type of the body of Christ, as also the Scripture declares that the manna of the Lord ceased when the people had eaten wheat from the land.[6]

---

[1] Isa. ix. 1.

[2] Compare the statement of Clemens Romanus, vol. i. p. 11 of this series, where, speaking of St. Paul, he says: "After preaching both in the east and west . . . . having taught righteousness to the whole world, and come to the extreme limit of the west."

[3] See Judg. vi. 27. It is not very clear how Irenæus makes out this allegory, but it is thought that he refers to the initial letter in the name $'I\eta\sigma o\hat{v}\varsigma$, which stands for *ten* in the Greek enumeration. Compare the *Epistle of Barnabas*, vol. i. p. 117 of this series.

[4] Num. xxvii. 18.

[5] Harvey conceives the reading here (which is doubtful) to have been $\tau\grave{o}\nu$ $\nu\acute{\epsilon}o\nu$ $\sigma\hat{\iota}\tau o\nu$, the new wheat; and sees an allusion to the wave-sheaf of the new corn offered in the temple on the morning of our Lord's resurrection.

[6] Josh. v. 12.

XX.

"And[1] he laid his hands upon him."[2] The countenance of Joshua was also glorified by the imposition of the hands of Moses, but not to the same degree [as that of Moses]. Inasmuch, then, as he had obtained a certain degree of grace, [the Lord] said, "And thou shalt confer upon him of thy glory."[3] For [in this case] the thing given does not cease to belong to the giver.

XXI.

But he does not give, as Christ did, by means of breathing, because he is not the fount of the Spirit.

XXII.

"Thou shalt not go with them, neither shalt thou curse the people."[4] He does not hint at anything with regard to the people, for they all lay before his view, but [he refers] to the mystery of Christ pointed out beforehand. For as He was to be born of the fathers according to the flesh, the Spirit gives instructions to the man (Balaam) beforehand, lest, going forth in ignorance, he might pronounce a curse upon the people.[5] Not, indeed, that [his curse] could take any effect contrary to the will of God; but [this was done] as an exhibition of the providence of God which He exercised towards them on account of their forefathers.

XXIII.

"And he mounted upon his ass."[6] The ass was the type of the body of Christ, upon whom all men, resting from their labours, are borne as in a chariot. For the Saviour has taken

---

[1] Massuet seems to more than doubt the genuineness of this fragment and the next, and would ascribe them to the pen of Apollinaris, bishop of Hierapolis in Phrygia, a contemporary of Irenæus. Harvey passes over these two fragments.

[2] Num. xxvii. 23. [3] Num. xxvii. 20. [4] Num. xxii. 12.

[5] The conjectural emendation of Harvey has been adopted here, but the text is very corrupt and uncertain.

[6] Num. xxii. 22, 23.

up the burden of our sins.[1] Now the angel who appeared to Balaam was the Word Himself; and in His hand He held a sword, to indicate the power which He had from above.

XXIV.

"God is not as a man."[2] He thus shows that all men are indeed guilty of falsehood, inasmuch as they change from one thing to another (μεταφερόμενοι); but such is not the case with God, for He always continues true, perfecting whatever He wishes.

XXV.

"To inflict vengeance from the Lord on Midian."[3] For this man (Balaam), when he speaks no longer in the Spirit of God, but contrary to God's law, by setting up a different law with regard to fornication,[4] is certainly not then to be counted as a prophet, but as a soothsayer. For he who did not keep to the commandment of God, received the just recompense of his own evil devices.[5]

XXVI.

Know[6] thou that every man is either empty or full. For if he has not the Holy Spirit, he has no knowledge of the Creator; he has not received Jesus Christ the Life; he knows not the Father who is in heaven; if he does not live after the dictates of reason, after the heavenly law, he is not a sober-minded person, nor does he act uprightly: such an one is empty. If, on the other hand, he receives God, who says, "I will dwell with them, and walk in them, and I will be their God,"[7] such an one is not empty, but full.

---

[1] From one of the MSS. Stieren would insert ἐν τῷ ἰδίῳ σώματι, in His own body; see 1 Pet. ii. 24.

[2] Num. xxiii. 19. [3] Num. xxxi. 3.
[4] Num. xxxi. 16. [5] Num. xxxi. 8.

[6] It is not certain from what work of Irenæus this extract is derived; Harvey thinks it to be from his work περὶ ἐπιστήμης, i.e. concerning Knowledge.

[7] Lev. xxvi. 12.

XXVII.

The little boy, therefore, who guided Samson by the hand,[1] pre-typified John the Baptist, who showed to the people the faith in Christ. And the house in which they were assembled signifies the world, in which dwell the various heathen and unbelieving nations, offering sacrifice to their idols. Moreover, the two pillars are the two covenants. The fact, then, of Samson leaning himself upon the pillars, [indicates] this, that the people, when instructed, recognised the mystery of Christ.

XXVIII.

"And the man of God said, Where did it fall? And he showed him the place. And he cut down a tree, and cast it in there, and the iron floated."[2] This was a sign that souls should be borne aloft ($\dot{a}\nu a\gamma\omega\gamma\hat{\eta}s$ $\psi v\chi\hat{\omega}\nu$) through the instrumentality of wood, upon which He suffered who can lead those souls aloft that follow His ascension. This event was also an indication of the fact, that when the holy soul of Christ descended [to Hades], many souls ascended and were seen in their bodies.[3] For just as the wood, which is the lighter body, was submerged in the water; but the iron, the heavier one, floated: so, when the Word of God became one with flesh, by a physical and hypostatic union, the heavy and terrestrial [part], having been rendered immortal, was borne up into heaven, by the divine nature, after the resurrection.

XXIX.

The[4] Gospel according to Matthew was written to the Jews. For they laid particular stress upon the fact that Christ [should be] of the seed of David. Matthew also, who had a still greater desire [to establish this point], took par-

---

[1] Judg. xvi. 26.   [2] 2 Kings vi. 6. Comp. book v. chap. xvii. 4.
[3] Matt. xxvii. 52.
[4] Edited by P. Possin, in a *Catena Patrum* on St. Matthew. See book iii. chap. xi. 8.

ticular pains to afford them convincing proof that Christ is of the seed of David; and therefore he commences with [an account of] His genealogy.

XXX.[1]

"The axe unto the root,"[2] he says, urging us to the knowledge of the truth, and purifying us by means of fear, as well as preparing [us] to bring forth fruit in due season.

XXXI.

Observe[3] that, by means of the grain of mustard seed in the parable, the heavenly doctrine is denoted which is sown like seed in the world, as in a field, [seed] which has an inherent force, fiery and powerful. For the Judge of the whole world is thus proclaimed, who, having been hidden in the heart of the earth in a tomb for three days, and having become a great tree, has stretched forth His branches to the ends of the earth. Sprouting out from Him, the twelve apostles, having become fair and fruitful boughs, were made a shelter for the nations as for the fowls of heaven, under which boughs, all having taken refuge, as birds flocking to a nest, have been made partakers of that wholesome and celestial food which is derived from them.

XXXII.[4]

Josephus says, that when Moses had been brought up in the royal palaces, he was chosen as general against the Ethiopians; and having proved victorious, obtained in marriage the daughter of that king, since indeed, out of her affection for him, she delivered the city up to him.[5]

---

[1] From the same *Catena*. Compare book v. chap. xvii. 4.
[2] Matt. iii. 10.
[3] First edited in Latin by Corderius, afterwards in Greek by Grabe, and also by Dr Cramer in his *Catena* on St. Luke.
[4] Massuet's Fragment xxxii. is here passed over; it is found in book iii. chap. xviii. 7.
[5] See Josephus' *Antiquities*, book ii. chap. x., where we read that this king's daughter was called Tharbis. Immediately upon the sur-

Why was it, that when these two (Aaron and Miriam) had both acted with despite towards him (Moses), the latter alone was adjudged punishment?[1] First, because the woman was the more culpable, since both nature and the law place the woman in a subordinate condition to the man. Or perhaps it was that Aaron was to a certain degree excusable, in consideration of his being the elder [brother], and adorned with the dignity of high priest. Then again, inasmuch as the leper was accounted by the law unclean, while at the same time the origin and foundation of the priesthood lay in Aaron, [the Lord] did not award a similar punishment to him, lest this stigma should attach itself to the entire [sacerdotal] race; but by means of his sister's [example] He awoke his fears, and taught him the same lesson. For Miriam's punishment affected him to such an extent, that no sooner did she experience it, than he entreated [Moses], who had been injured, that he would by his intercession do away with the affliction. And he did not neglect to do so, but at once poured forth his supplication. Upon this the Lord, who loves mankind, made him understand how He had not chastened her as a judge, but as a father; for He said, "If her father had spit in her face, should she not be ashamed? Let her be shut out from the camp seven days, and after that let her come in again."[2]

XXXIII.

Inasmuch[3] as certain men, impelled by what considerations I know not, remove from God the half of His creative power,

---

render of this city (Saba, afterwards called Meroë) Moses married her, and returned to Egypt. Whiston, in the notes to his translation of Josephus, says, "Nor, perhaps, did St. Stephen refer to anything else when he said of Moses, before he was sent by God to the Israelites, that he was not only learned in all the wisdom of the Egyptians, but was also mighty in words and in deeds" (Acts vii. 22).

[1] Num. xii. 1, etc.   [2] Num. xii. 14.

[3] Harvey considers this fragment to be a part of the work of Irenæus referred to by Photius under the title *De Universo*, or *de Substantiâ Mundi*. It is to be found in Codex 3011 of the Bodleian Library, Oxford.

by asserting that He is merely the cause of quality resident in matter, and by maintaining that matter itself is uncreated, come now let us put the question, What is at any time ... is immutable. Matter, then, is immutable. But if matter be immutable, and the immutable suffers no change in regard to quality, it does not form the substance of the world. For which reason it seems to them superfluous, that God has annexed qualities to matter, since indeed matter admits of no possible alteration, it being in itself an uncreated thing. But further, if matter be uncreated, it has been made altogether according to a certain quality, and this immutable, so that it cannot be receptive of more qualities, nor can it be the thing of which the world is made. But if the world be not made from it, [this theory] entirely excludes God from exercising power on the creation [of the world].

XXXIV.

"And[1] dipped himself," says [the Scripture], "seven times in Jordan."[2] It was not for nothing that Naaman of old, when suffering from leprosy, was purified upon his being baptized, but [it served] as an indication to us. For as we are lepers in sin, we are made clean, by means of the sacred water and the invocation of the Lord, from our old transgressions; being spiritually regenerated as new-born babes, even as the Lord has declared: "Except a man be born again through water and the Spirit, he shall not enter into the kingdom of heaven."[4]

XXXV.

If the corpse of Elisha raised a dead man,[1] how much more shall God, when He has quickened men's dead bodies, bring them up for judgment?

---

[1] This and the next fragment first appeared in the Benedictine edition reprinted at Venice, 1734. They were taken from a MS. *Catena* on the books of Kings in the Coislin Collection.

[2] 2 Kings v. 14.   [3] John iii. 5.   [4] 2 Kings xiii. 21.

XXXVI.

True[1] knowledge, then, consists in the understanding of Christ, which Paul terms the wisdom of God hidden in a mystery, which "the natural man receiveth not,"[2] the doctrine of the cross; of which if any man "taste,"[3] he will not accede to the disputations and quibbles of proud and puffed-up men,[4] who go into matters of which they have no perception.[5] For the truth is unsophisticated ($\dot{\alpha}\sigma\chi\eta\mu\acute{\alpha}\tau\iota\sigma\tau\sigma\varsigma$); and "the word is nigh thee, in thy mouth and in thy heart,"[6] as the same apostle declares, being easy of comprehension to those who are obedient. For it renders us like to Christ, if we experience "the power of His resurrection and the fellowship of His sufferings."[7] For this is the affinity[8] of the apostolical teaching and the most holy "faith delivered unto us,"[9] which the unlearned receive, and those of slender knowledge have taught, not "giving heed to endless genealogies,"[10] but studying rather [to observe] a straightforward course of life; lest, having been deprived of the Divine Spirit, they fail to attain to the kingdom of heaven. For truly the first thing is to deny one's self and to follow Christ; and those who do this are borne onward to perfection, having fulfilled all their Teacher's will, becoming sons of God by spiritual regeneration, and heirs of the kingdom of heaven; those who seek which first shall not be forsaken.

---

[1] This extract and the next three were discovered in the year 1715 by Pfaff, a learned Lutheran, in the Royal Library at Turin. The MSS. from which they were taken were neither catalogued nor classified, and have now disappeared from the collection. It is impossible to say with any degree of probability from what treatises of our author these four fragments have been culled. For a full account of their history, see Stieren's edition of Irenæus, vol. ii. p. 381.

[2] 1 Cor. ii. 14.   [3] 1 Pet. ii. 3.
[4] 1 Tim. vi. 4, 5.   [5] Col. ii. 18.
[6] Rom. x. 8; Deut. xxx. 14.   [7] Phil. iii. 10.

[8] Harvey's conjectural emendation, $\dot{\epsilon}\pi\iota\pi\lambda\sigma\kappa\acute{\eta}$ for $\dot{\epsilon}\pi\iota\lambda\sigma\gamma\acute{\eta}$, has been adopted here.

[9] Jude 3.   [10] 1 Tim. i. 4.

XXXVII.

Those who have become acquainted with the secondary (*i.e.* under Christ) constitutions of the apostles,[1] are aware that the Lord instituted a new oblation in the new covenant, according to [the declaration of] Malachi the prophet. For, "from the rising of the sun even to the setting my name has been glorified among the Gentiles, and in every place incense is offered to my name, and a pure sacrifice;"[2] as John also declares in the Apocalypse: "The incense is the prayers of the saints."[3] Then again, Paul exhorts us "to present our bodies a living sacrifice, holy, acceptable unto God, which is your reasonable service."[4] And again, "Let us offer the sacrifice of praise, that is, the fruit of the lips."[5] Now those oblations are not according to the law, the handwriting of which the Lord took away from the midst by cancelling it;[6] but they are according to the Spirit, for we must worship God "in spirit and in truth."[7] And therefore the oblation of the Eucharist is not a carnal one, but a spiritual; and in this respect it is pure. For we make an oblation to God of the bread and the cup of blessing, giving Him thanks in that He has commanded the earth to bring forth these fruits for our nourishment. And then, when we have perfected the oblation, we invoke the Holy Spirit, that He may exhibit this sacrifice, both the bread the body of Christ, and the cup the blood of Christ, in order that the receivers of these antitypes[8] may obtain remission of sins and life eternal. Those

---

[1] ταῖς δευτέραις τῶν ἀποστόλων διατάξεσι. Harvey thinks that these words imply, "the formal constitution, which the apostles, acting under the impulse of the Spirit, though still in a secondary capacity, gave to the church."

[2] Mal. i. 11.

[3] Rev. v. 8. The same view of the eucharistic oblation, etc., is found in book iv. chap. xvii.: as also in Justin Martyr; see p. 139 of his works in this series.

[4] Rom. xii. 1.   [5] Heb. xiii. 15.   [6] Col. ii. 14.   [7] John iv. 24.

[8] Harvey explains this word ἀντιτύπων as meaning an "exact counterpart." He refers to the word where it occurs in *Contra Hæreses*, lib. i. chap. xxiv., as confirmatory of his view. See vol. i. p. 24, line 20, where

persons, then, who perform these oblations in remembrance of the Lord, do not fall in with Jewish views, but, performing the service after a spiritual manner, they shall be called sons of wisdom.

XXXVIII.

The[1] apostles ordained, that "we should not judge any one in respect to meat or drink, or in regard to a feast day, or the new moons, or the sabbaths."[2] Whence then these contentions? whence these schisms? We keep the feast, but in the leaven of malice and wickedness, cutting in pieces the church of God; and we preserve what belongs to its exterior, that we may cast away these better things, faith and love. We have heard from the prophetic words that these feasts and fasts are displeasing to the Lord.[3]

XXXIX.

Christ,[4] who was called the Son of God before the ages, was manifested in the fulness of time, in order that He might cleanse us through His blood, who were under the power of sin, presenting us as pure sons to His Father, if we yield ourselves obediently to the chastisement of the Spirit. And in the end of time He shall come to do away with all evil, and to reconcile all things, in order that there may be an end of all impurities.

---

this word is translated "emblem" by him. Towards the end of his long note he says: "ἀντίτυπος here conveys the idea of identity between the body of Christ and the consecrated bread. The two are not co-existent as distinct substances, *consubstantially;* but the bread, through the energy of the word, IS the Lord's body."

[1] Taken apparently from the *Epistle to Blastus, de Schismate.* Compare a similar passage, lib. iv. chap. xxxiii. 7.

[2] Col. ii. 16.   [3] Isa. i. 14.

[4] "From the same collection at Turin. The passage seems to be of cognate matter with the treatise *De Resurrec.* Pfaff referred it either to the διαλέξεις διάφοροι or to the ἐπιδειξις ἀποστολικοῦ κηρύγματος."—HARVEY.

XL.

"And[1] he found the jaw-bone of an ass."[2] It is to be observed that, after [Samson had committed] fornication, the holy Scripture no longer speaks of the things happily accomplished by him in connection with the formula, "The Spirit of the Lord came upon him."[3] For thus, according to the holy apostle, the sin of fornication is perpetrated against the body, as involving also sin against the temple of God.[4]

XLI.

This[5] indicates the persecution against the church set on foot by the nations who still continue in unbelief. But he (Samson) who suffered those things, trusted that there would be a retaliation against those waging this war. But retaliation through what means? First of all, by his betaking himself to the Rock[6] not cognizable to the senses;[7] secondly, by the finding of the jaw-bone of an ass. Now the type of the jaw-bone is the body of Christ.

XLII.

Speaking always well of the worthy, but never ill of the unworthy, we also shall attain to the glory and kingdom of God.

XLIII.

In[8] these things there was signified by prophecy that the

---

[1] This and the four following fragments are taken from MSS. in the Vatican Library at Rome. They are apparently quoted from the homiletical expositions of the historical books already referred to.

[2] Judg. xv. 15.   [3] Judg. xiv. 6–19.   [4] 1 Cor. iii. 16, 17.

[5] These words were evidently written during a season of persecution in Gaul; but what that persecution was, it is useless to conjecture.

[6] Judg. xv. 11.

[7] That is, when he fled to the rock Etam, he typified the true believer taking refuge in the spiritual Rock, Christ.

[8] Most probably from a homily upon the third and fourth chapters of Ezekiel. It is found repeated in Stieren's and Migne's edition as Fragment xlviii. extracted from a *Catena* on the Book of Judges.

people, having become transgressors, shall be bound by the chains of their own sins. But the breaking of the bonds of their own accord indicates that, upon repentance, they shall be again loosed from the shackles of sin.

XLIV.

It[1] is not an easy thing for a soul, under the influence of error, to be persuaded of the contrary opinion.

XLV.

"And[2] Balaam the son of Beor they slew with the sword."[3] For, speaking no longer by the Spirit of God, but setting up another law of fornication contrary to the law of God,[4] this man shall no longer be reckoned as a prophet, but as a soothsayer. For, as he did not continue in the commandment of God, he received the just reward of his evil devices.

XLVI.

"The[5] god of the world;"[6] that is, Satan, who was designated God to those who believe not.

XLVII.

The[7] birth of John [the Baptist] brought the dumbness of Zacharias to an end. For he did not burden his father, when

---

[1] We give this brief fragment as it appears in the editions of Stieren, Migne, and Harvey, who speculate as to its origin. They seem to have overlooked the fact that it is the Greek original of the old Latin, *non facile est ab errore apprehensam resipiscere animam,*—a sentence found towards the end of book iii. chap. ii.; see vol. i. p. 260, lines 23, 24, of our translation.

[2] With the exception of the initial text, this fragment is almost identical with No. xxv.

[3] Num. xxxi. 8. [4] Rev. ii. 14.

[5] From the *Catena* on St. Paul's Epistles to the Corinthians, edited by Dr. Cramer, and reprinted by Stieren.

[6] 2 Cor. iv. 4.

[7] Extracted from a MS. of Greek theology in the Palatine Library at Vienna. The succeeding fragment in the editions of Harvey, Migne, and Stieren, is omitted, as it is merely a transcript of lib. iii. ch. x. 4; see vol. i. p. 285, lines 8–12.

the voice issued forth from silence; but as when not believed it rendered him tongue-tied, so did the voice sounding out clearly set his father free, to whom he had both been announced and born. Now the voice and the burning light[1] were a precursor of the Word and the Light.

XLVIII.

As[2] therefore seventy tongues are indicated by number, and from[3] dispersion the tongues are gathered into one by means of their interpretation; so is that ark declared a type of the body of Christ, which is both pure and immaculate. For[4] as that ark was gilded with pure gold both within and without, so also is the body of Christ pure and resplendent, being adorned within by the Word, and shielded on the outside by the Spirit, in order that from both [materials] the splendour of the natures might be exhibited together.

XLIX.

Now[5] therefore, by means of this which has been already brought forth a long time since, the Word has assigned an interpretation. We are convinced that there exist [so to speak] two men in each one of us. The one is confessedly a hidden thing, while the other stands apparent; one is corporeal, the other spiritual; although the generation of both may be compared to that of twins. For both are revealed to the world as but one, for the soul was not anterior to the body in its essence; nor, in regard to its formation, did the body precede the soul: but both these were produced at one time; and their nourishment consists in purity and sweetness.

[1] John v. 35.
[2] This fragment commences a series derived from the Nitrian Collection of Syriac MSS. in the British Museum.
[3] The Syriac text is here corrupt and obscure.
[4] See No. viii., which is the same as the remainder of this fragment.
[5] The Syriac MS. introduces this quotation as follows: "From the holy Irenæus Bp. of Lyons, from the first section of his interpretation of the Song of Songs."

L.

For[1] then there shall in truth be a common joy consummated to all those who believe unto life, and in each individual shall be confirmed the mystery of the Resurrection, and the hope of incorruption, and the commencement of the eternal kingdom, when God shall have destroyed death and the devil. For that human nature and flesh which has risen again from the dead shall die no more; but after it had been changed to incorruption, and made like to spirit, when the heaven was opened, [our Lord] full of glory offered it (the flesh) to the Father.

LI.

Now,[2] however, inasmuch as the books of these men may possibly have escaped your observation, but have come under our notice, I call your attention to them, that for the sake of your reputation you may expel these writings from among you, as bringing disgrace upon you, since their author boasts himself as being one of your company. For they constitute a stumbling-block to many, who simply and unreservedly receive, as coming from a presbyter, the blasphemy which they utter against God. Just [consider] the writer of these things, how by means of them he does not injure assistants [in divine service] only, who happen to be prepared in mind for blasphemies against God, but also damages those among us, since by his books he imbues their minds with false doctrines concerning God.

---

[1] This extract is introduced as follows: "For Irenæus Bishop of Lyons, who was a contemporary of the disciple of the apostle, Polycarp Bishop of Smyrna, and martyr, and for this reason is held in just estimation, wrote to an Alexandrian to the effect that it is right, with respect to the feast of the Resurrection, that we should celebrate it upon the first day of the week." This shows us that the extract must have been taken from the work *Against Schism* addressed to Blastus.

[2] From the same MS. as the preceding fragment. It is thus introduced: "And Irenæus Bp. of Lyons, to Victor Bp. of Rome, concerning Florinus, a presbyter, who was a partisan of the error of Valentinus, and published an abominable book, thus wrote."

LII.

The[1] sacred books acknowledge with regard to Christ, that as He is the Son of man, so is the same Being not a [mere] man; and as He is flesh, so is He also spirit, and the Word of God, and God. And as He was born of Mary in the last times, so did He also proceed from God as the First-begotten of every creature; and as He hungered, so did He satisfy [others]; and as He thirsted, so did He of old cause the Jews to drink, for the "Rock was Christ"[2] Himself: thus does Jesus now give to His believing people power to drink spiritual waters, which spring up to life eternal.[3] And as He was the son of David, so was He also the Lord of David. And as He was from Abraham, so did He also exist before Abraham.[4] And as He was the servant of God, so is He the Son of God, and Lord of the universe. And as He was spit upon ignominiously, so also did He breathe the Holy Spirit into His disciples.[5] And as He was saddened, so also did He give joy to His people. And as He was capable of being handled and touched, so again did He, in a non-apprehensible form, pass through the midst of those who sought to injure Him,[6] and entered without impediment through closed doors.[7] And as He slept, so did He also rule the sea, the winds, and the storms. And as He suffered, so also is He alive, and life-giving, and healing all our infirmity. And as He died, so is He also the Resurrection of the dead. He suffered shame on earth, while He is higher than all glory and praise in heaven; who, "though He was crucified through weakness, yet He liveth by divine power;"[8] who "descended into the lower parts of the earth," and who "ascended up above the heavens;"[9] for whom a manger sufficed, yet who filled all things; who was dead, yet who liveth for ever and ever. Amen.

[1] This extract had already been printed by M. Petra in his *Spicilegium Solesmense*, p. 6.
[2] 1 Cor. x. 4.
[3] John iv. 14.
[4] John viii. 58.
[5] John xx. 22.
[6] John viii. 59.
[7] John xx. 26.
[8] 2 Cor. xiii. 4.
[9] Eph. iv. 9, 10.

LIII.

With[1] regard to Christ, the law and the prophets and the evangelists have proclaimed that He was born of a virgin, that He suffered upon a beam of wood, and that He appeared from the dead; that He also ascended to the heavens, and was glorified by the Father, and is the Eternal King; that He is the perfect Intelligence, the Word of God, who was begotten before the light; that He was the Founder of the universe, along with it (light), and the Maker of man; that He is All in all: Patriarch among the patriarchs; Law in the laws; Chief Priest among priests; Ruler among kings; the Prophet among prophets; the Angel among angels; the Man among men; Son in the Father; God in God; King to all eternity. For it is He who sailed [in the ark] along with Noah, and who guided Abraham; who was bound along with Isaac, and was a Wanderer with Jacob; the Shepherd of those who are saved, and the Bridegroom of the church; the Chief also of the cherubim, the Prince of the angelic powers; God of God; Son of the Father; Jesus Christ; King for ever and ever. Amen.

LIV.

The[2] law and the prophets and evangelists have declared that Christ was born of a virgin, and suffered on the cross; was raised also from the dead, and taken up to heaven; that He was glorified, and reigns for ever. He is Himself termed the Perfect Intellect, the Word of God. He is the First-begotten,[3] after a transcendent manner, the Creator of man; All in all; Patriarch among the patriarchs; Law in the law; the Priest among priests; among kings Prime Leader;

---

[1] This extract from the Syriac is a shorter form of the next fragment, which seems to be interpolated in some places. The latter is from an Armenian MS. in the Mechitarist Library at Venice.

[2] This fragment is thus introduced in the Armenian copy: "From St. Irenæus, bishop, follower of the apostles, on the Lord's resurrection."

[3] The Armenian text is confused here; we have adopted the conjectural emendation of Quatremere.

the Prophet among the prophets; the Angel among angels; the Man among men; Son in the Father; God in God; King to all eternity. He was sold with Joseph, and He guided Abraham; was bound along with Isaac, and wandered with Jacob; with Moses He was Leader, and, respecting the people, Legislator. He preached in the prophets; was incarnate of a virgin; born in Bethlehem; received by John, and baptized in Jordan; was tempted in the desert, and proved to be the Lord. He gathered the apostles together, and preached the kingdom of heaven; gave light to the blind, and raised the dead; was seen in the temple, but was not held by the people as worthy of credit; was arrested by the priests, conducted before Herod, and condemned in the presence of Pilate; He manifested Himself in the body, was suspended upon a beam of wood, and raised from the dead; shown to the apostles, and, having been carried up to heaven, sitteth on the right hand of the Father, and has been glorified by Him as the Resurrection of the dead. Moreover, He is the Salvation of the lost, the Light to those dwelling in darkness, and Redemption to those who have been born; the Shepherd of the saved, and the Bridegroom of the church; the Charioteer of the cherubim, the Leader of the angelic host; God of God; Jesus Christ our Saviour.

LV.

"Then[1] drew near unto Him the mother of Zebedee's children, with her sons, worshipping, and seeking a certain thing from Him."[2] These people are certainly not void of understanding, nor are the words set forth in that passage of no signification: being stated beforehand like a preface, they have some agreement with those points formerly expounded.

"Then drew near." Sometimes virtue excites our ad-

---

[1] From an Armenian MS. in the Library of the Mechitarist Convent at Vienna, edited by M. Pitra, who considers this fragment as of very doubtful authority. It commences with this heading: "From the second series of Homilies of Saint Irenæus, follower of the Apostles; a Homily upon the Sons of Zebedee."

[2] Matt. xx. 20.

miration, not merely on account of the display which is given of it, but also of the occasion when it was manifested. I may refer, for example, to the premature fruit of the grape, or of the fig, or to any fruit whatsoever, from which, during its process [of growth], no man expects maturity or full development; yet, although any one may perceive that it is still somewhat imperfect, he does not for that reason despise as useless the immature grape when plucked, but he gathers it with pleasure as appearing early in the season; nor does he consider whether the grape is possessed of perfect sweetness; nay, he at once experiences satisfaction from the thought that this one has appeared before the rest. Just in the same way does God also, when He perceives the faithful possessing wisdom though still imperfect, and but a small degree of faith, overlook their defect in this respect, and therefore does not reject them; nay, but on the contrary, He kindly welcomes and accepts them as premature fruits, and honours the mind, whatsoever it may be, which is stamped with virtue, although not yet perfect. He makes allowance for it, as being among the harbingers of the vintage,[1] and esteems it highly, inasmuch as, being of a readier disposition than the rest, it has forestalled, as it were, the blessing to itself.

Abraham therefore, Isaac, and Jacob, our fathers, are to be esteemed before all, since they did indeed afford us such early examples of virtue. How many martyrs can be compared to Daniel? How many martyrs, I ask, can rival the three youths in Babylon, although the memory of the former has not been brought before us so conspicuously as that of the latter? These were truly first-fruits, and indications of the [succeeding] fructification. Hence God has directed their life to be recorded, as a model for those who should come after.

And that their virtue was thus accepted by God, as the first-fruits of the produce, hear what He has Himself declared: "As a grape," He says, "I have found Israel in the wilderness, and as first-ripe figs your fathers."[2] Call

---

[1] That is, the wine which flows from the grapes before they are trodden out.

[2] Hos. ix. 10.

not therefore the faith of Abraham merely blessed because he believed. Do you wish to look upon Abraham with admiration? Then behold how that one man alone professed piety when in the world six hundred had been contaminated with error. Dost thou wish Daniel to carry thee away to amazement? Behold that [city] Babylon, haughty in the flower and pride of impiousness, and its inhabitants completely given over to sin of every description. But he, emerging from the depth, spat out the brine of sins, and rejoiced to plunge into the sweet waters of piety. And now, in like manner, with regard to that mother of Zebedee's children, do not admire merely what she said, but also the time at which she uttered these words. For when was it that she drew near to the Redeemer? Not after the resurrection, nor after the preaching of His name, nor after the establishment of His kingdom; but it was when the Lord said, "Behold, we go up to Jerusalem, and the Son of man shall be delivered to the chief priests and the scribes; and they shall kill Him, and on the third day He shall rise again."[1]

These things the Saviour told in reference to His sufferings and cross; to these persons He predicted His passion. Nor did He conceal the fact that it should be of a most ignominious kind, at the hands of the chief priests. This woman, however, had attached another meaning to the dispensation of His sufferings. The Saviour was foretelling death; and she asked for the glory of immortality. The Lord was asserting that He must stand arraigned before impious judges; but she, taking no note of that judgment, requested as of the judge: "Grant," she said, "that these my two sons may sit, one on the right hand, and the other on the left, in Thy glory." In the one case the passion is referred to, in the other the kingdom is understood. The Saviour was speaking of the cross, while she had in view the glory which admits no suffering. This woman, therefore, as I have already said, is worthy of our admiration, not merely for what she sought, but also for the occasion of her making the request.

She did indeed suffer, not merely as a pious person, but

[1] Matt. xx. 18.

also as a woman. For, having been instructed by His words, she considered and believed that it would come to pass, that the kingdom of Christ should flourish in glory, and walk in its vastness throughout the world, and be increased by the preaching of piety. She understood, as was [in fact] the case, that He who appeared in a lowly guise had delivered and received every promise. I will inquire upon another occasion, when I come to treat upon this humility, whether the Lord rejected her petition concerning His kingdom. But she thought that the same confidence would not be possessed by her, when, at the appearance of the angels, He should be ministered to by the angels, and receive service from the entire heavenly host. Taking the Saviour, therefore, apart in a retired place, she earnestly desired of Him those things which transcend every human nature.

INDEXES.

I.—INDEX OF TEXTS.

	VOL. PAGE		VOL. PAGE
Gen. i. 1,	i. 123	Gen. xxiii. 11,	i. 142
i. 2,	i. 74	xxiv. 22, 25,	i. 76
i. 3,	ii. 5	xxv. 23,	i. 452
i. 25,	ii. 98	xxv. 26,	i. 452
i. 26,	i. 89, 107, 363, 377, 439	xxvii. 27, 28, 29,	ii. 145
i. 28,	i. 406	xxxi. 2,	i. 67
ii. 2,	ii. 132	xxxi. 11,	i. 404
ii. 5,	i. 358	xxxi. 41,	ii. 145
ii. 7,	i. 253, 439, ii. 96	xxxiii. 3,	ii. 145
ii. 8,	ii. 66	xxxv. 22,	i. 77
ii. 16,	ii. 109	xxxviii.	i. 459
ii. 16, 17,	ii. 117	xlii.	i. 77
ii. 25,	i. 361	xlix. 10-12,	i. 404
iii. 3, 4,	ii. 117	xlix. 18,	i. 284
iii. 9,	ii. 98	xlix. 28,	i. 77
iii. 13,	i. 366	Ex. i. 13, 14,	i. 477
iii. 14,	i. 364	iii. 4,	i. 404
iii. 15,	ii. 50, 110	iii. 6,	i. 387
iii. 16,	i. 364	iii. 7, 8,	i. 396, 411
iii. 19,	ii. 98, 166	iii. 8,	i. 270
iv. 7,	i. 305, 432, 433	iii. 14,	i. 270
iv. 10,	ii. 92	iii. 19,	i. 475
vi. 15,	i. 77	vii. 1,	i. 272
vi. 18,	i. 76	vii. 9,	i. 357
ix. 5, 6,	ii. 92	viii. 19,	i. 357
ix. 27,	i. 268	ix. 35,	i. 474
xii. 3,	i. 451	xi. 2,	i. 476
xiii. 13, 14, 15, 17,	ii. 142	xiii. 2,	i. 14
xv. 5,	i. 278, 395	xvii. 11,	ii. 11
xv. 13,	ii. 142	xvii. 16,	i. 328
xv. 19,	i. 76	xx. 5,	i. 103
xvii. 9-11,	i. 422	xx. 12,	i. 403
xvii. 12,	i. 76	xxi. 13,	i. 422
xvii. 17,	i. 394	xxiv. 4,	i. 77
xviii. 1,	i. 396	xxv. 10,	i. 207
xviii. 30,	i. 404	xxv. 17,	i. 207
xix. 22,	i. 388	xxv. 23,	i. 207
xix. 24,	i. 269	xxv. 31,	i. 207
xix. 31, 32,	ii. 2	xxv. 32,	i. 207
xix. 33,	ii. 2	xxv. 40,	i. 418, ii. 154
xix. 35,	ii. 2	xxvi. 1,	i. 75, 76, 208
xxii. 6,	i. 388	xxvi. 2,	i. 208

INDEX OF TEXTS.

Reference	Vol. Page	Reference	Vol. Page
Ex. xxvi. 7,	i. 208	Deut. xviii. 1,	i. 399
xxvi. 8,	i. 77	xxi. 23,	i. 339
xxvi. 16,	i. 208	xxviii. 66,	i. 405, ii. 106
xxvi. 26,	i. 208	xxx. 14,	ii. 175
xxvi. 37,	i. 210	xxx. 19, 20,	i. 424
xxvii. 1,	i. 210	xxxii. 1,	i. 379
xxviii. 1,	i. 210	xxxii. 4,	i. 344
xxviii. 2,	i. 77	xxxii. 6,	i. 405, ii. 2
xxviii. 5,	i. 210	xxxii. 8, LXX.,	i. 307
xxviii. 17,	i. 76	xxxii. 9,	i. 307
xxx. 23,	i. 208	xxxiii. 9,	i. 398
xxx. 34,	i. 208	Josh. iii. 12,	i. 77
xxxii. 6,	i. 469	iv. 3,	i. 77
xxxiii. 2, 3,	i. 420	v. 12,	ii. 168
xxxiii. 7,	i. 463	x. 17,	i. 210
xxxiii. 20,	i. 78, 442	Judg. vi. 27,	ii. 168
xxxiii. 20-22,	i. 446	vi. 37,	i. 335
xxxiv. 6, 7,	i. 445	xiv. 6-19,	ii. 178
xxxvi. 8,	i. 76	xv. 11,	ii. 178
xxxvi. 21,	i. 76	xv. 15,	ii. 178
Lev. x. 1, 2,	i. 462	xvi. 26,	ii. 171
xi. 2,	ii. 74	1 Sam. ix. 22,	i. 76
xxvi. 12,	ii. 170	xi. 27,	i. 465
Num. xii. 1,	ii. 173	xii. 1,	i. 466
xii. 7,	i. 272	xii. 3,	i. 464
xii. 8,	i. 406	xv. 22,	i. 426
xii. 14,	ii. 173	xvi. 10,	i. 76
xiv. 30,	i. 474	xviii.	i. 465
xv. 32,	i. 398	xx. 5,	i. 76
xvi. 15,	i. 464	2 Sam. v. 7,	i. 384
xvi. 33,	i. 463	1 Kings iv. 34,	i. 467
xviii. 20,	i. 399	viii. 27,	i. 467
xxi. 8,	i. 382	x. 1,	i. 467
xxii. 12, 22, 23,	ii. 169	xi. 1,	i. 467
xxiii. 19,	ii. 170	xi. 31,	i. 76
xxiv. 17,	i. 279	xiv. 10,	i. 463
xxiv. 23,	ii. 167	xviii. 21,	i. 271
xxvii. 18,	ii. 168	xviii. 36,	i. 271
xxvii. 20, 23,	ii. 169	xix. 11, 12,	i. 446
xxxi. 3,	ii. 170	2 Kings v. 14,	ii. 174
xxxi. 8,	ii. 170	vi. 6,	ii. 102, 174
xxxi. 16,	ii. 170	xiii. 21,	ii. 174
xxxviii. 8,	ii. 179	Ps. ii. 8,	i. 453
Deut. iv. 14,	i. 424	iii. 5,	ii. 16
iv. 19,	i. 272	iii. 6,	ii. 3
iv. 24,	i. 445	viii. 1,	i. 63
v. 2,	i. 423	viii. 3,	i. 407
v. 8,	i. 272	ix. 12,	i. 341
v. 22,	i. 419, 424	xiv. 3,	i. 78
v. 24,	i. 443	xviii. 45,	ii. 51
vi. 4, 6, 13,	i. 379	xix. 1,	i. 63
vi. 16,	ii. 112, 115	xix. 6,	ii. 16
viii. 3,	i. 424, ii. 112	xxi. 4,	i. 252
x. 12,	i. 424	xxii. 7,	ii. 15
x. 16,	i. 423	xxii. 15,	i. 445, ii. 15
xiv. 3, etc.,	ii. 74	xxii. 18,	ii. 15
xvi. 6,	i. 432	xxii. 31, LXX.,	ii. 71
xvi. 56,	i. 404	xxiii. 4,	ii. 140

INDEX OF TEXTS.

	VOL. PAGE		VOL. PAGE
Ps. xxiv. 7,	ii. 16	Ps. cxlviii. 5, 6,	i. 252
xxxii. 1, 2,	ii. 102	cxlix. 5,	ii. 51
xxxii. 11,	i. 324	Prov. i. 7,	i. 366
xxxiii. 6,	i. 85, 276	i. 20, 21,	ii. 109
xxxiii. 9,	i. 123	iii. 19, 20,	ii. 441
xxxiv. 1,	ii. 33	v. 22,	i. 280
xxxiv. 13, 14,	i. 429, ii. 28	viii. 15,	ii. 119
xxxv. 9,	i. 407	viii. 22-25,	i. 441
xxxviii. 11,	ii. 15	viii. 27-31,	i. 441
xl. 6,	i. 426	ix. 10,	i. 366
xlv. 2, 3, 4, 7,	ii. 13	xix. 17,	i. 436
xlv. 6,	i. 269	xxi. 1,	ii. 119
xlv. 11,	ii. 47	Isa. i. 2,	i. 379, ii. 51
xlv. 17,	i. 362, 387	i. 3,	i. 78
xlix. 12,	i. 385	i. 8,	i. 385
xlix. 20,	ii. 74	i. 8, 9,	ii. 16
xlix. 21,	ii. 52	i. 10, 16,	ii. 52
l. 1, 3,	i. 269	i. 11,	i. 427
l. 3, 4,	ii. 106	i. 14,	ii. 177
l. 9,	i. 427	i. 17-19,	ii. 28
l. 14, 15,	i. 427	i. 22,	i. 409
li. 12,	i. 334	i. 23,	i. 381
li. 17,	i. 426	ii. 17,	ii. 16
lviii. 3,	i. 282	ii. 34,	ii. 21
lviii. 3, 4,	ii. 52	iv. 4,	ii. 454
lxviii. 18,	i. 192	v. 6,	i. 335
lxix. 21,	i. 346, ii. 15	v. 12,	i. 197, 380
lxix. 26,	i. 297	vi. 1,	ii. 13
lxix. 27,	i. 360	vi. 5,	i. 445
lxxii. 1,	i. 269	vi. 10,	i. 474
lxxvi. 1,	i. 279, ii. 14	vi. 11,	ii. 149, 151
lxxviii. 5,	i. 326	vi. 12,	ii. 152
lxxx. 1,	i. 293	vii. 4,	i. 349
lxxxi. 9,	i. 270	vii. 10-17,	i. 355
lxxxii. 6,	i. 270	vii. 11,	i. 366
lxxxii. 6, 7,	i. 344, ii. 45	vii. 13,	i. 346, 355
lxxxiv. 16,	i. 471	vii. 14,	i. 346, 351, ii. 14
lxxxv. 11,	i. 266	viii. 3,	i. 327, ii. 14
lxxxvi. 23,	ii. 140	viii. 4,	i. 327
lxxxix. 11,	ii. 112	viii. 14,	i. 338
xci. 13,	i. 367	ix. 1,	ii. 168
xcv. 4,	i. 285	ix. 6,	i. 326, 346, ii. 14
xcv. 8,	i. 297	xi. 1,	i. 280
xcvi. 1,	i. 400	xi. 2,	i. 334, 336
xcvi. 2,	ii. 35	xi. 12,	ii. 6
xcvi. 5,	i. 270	xii. 2,	i. 284
xcviii. 2,	i. 284	xii. 4,	i. 386, ii. 7
xcix. 1,	ii. 16	xiii. 9,	ii. 151
cii. 25-27,	i. 383	xxv. 3,	i. 350
civ. 2, 4,	i. 231	xxv. 8,	ii. 83
cix. 8,	i. 191, 297	xxv. 9,	i. 401
cx. 1,	i. 226, 269, 287, 327	xxvi. 10,	ii. 151
cxviii. 22,	ii. 6	xxvi. 19,	ii. 14, 95, 148
cxxiv. 8,	i. 285	xxvii. 6,	i. 384
cxxx. 7,	ii. 163	xxviii. 16,	i. 357
cxxx. 11,	i. 279	xxix. 13,	i. 411
cxxxiv. 8,	i. 379	xxx. 1,	i. 433
cxlviii. 5,	i. 123	xxx. 25,	ii. 149

INDEX OF TEXTS.

	VOL. PAGE		VOL. PAGE
Isa. xxxi. 9,	ii. 150	Jer. vi. 17, 18,	ii. 28
xxxii. 1,	ii. 150	vi. 20,	i. 428
xxxiii. 20,	i. 350	vii. 2, 3,	i. 428
xxxv. 3,	ii. 14	vii. 3,	ii. 28
xxxv. 5, 6,	ii. 14	vii. 21,	i. 428
xl. 6,	ii. 147	vii. 25,	ii. 32
xl. 12,	i. 437	vii. 29, 30,	ii. 28
xl. 12, 22,	i. 231	viii. 16,	ii. 137
xl. 15,	ii. 134	ix. 2,	i. 460
xlii. 3,	i. 446	ix. 24,	i. 428
xlii. 5,	i. 379, ii. 83	x. 11,	i. 271
xlii. 10,	i. 400	xi. 15,	i. 429
xliii. 5,	i. 417	xv. 9,	ii. 16
xliii. 10,	i. 270, 386	xvii. 9,	i. 239, 345, ii. 14
xliii. 19, 27,	ii. 17	xxii. 17,	i. 413
xliii. 23, 24,	i. 429	xxii. 24, 25,	i. 357
xliv. 9,	i. 270	xxii. 28, etc.,	i. 357
xlv. 5, 6,	i. 23, 103	xxiii. 7, 6,	ii. 148
xlv. 7,	ii. 49	xxiii. 20,	i. 461
xlvi. 2,	i. 429	xxiii. 23,	i. 438
xlvi. 9,	i. 23, 143	xxxi. 10,	ii. 150
xlviii. 32,	i. 71	xxxi. 11,	i. 276
xlix. 16,	ii. 153	xxxi. 26,	ii. 3
l. 6,	ii. 15	xxxi. 31,	i. 400
li. 6,	i. 383	xxxi. 31, 32,	ii. 17
liii. 2,	i. 346	xxxiii. 29,	ii. 103
liii. 3,	ii. 6, 15	xxxv. 15,	ii. 32
liii. 4,	ii. 14	xxxvi. 30, 31,	i. 358
liii. 7,	ii. 6, 15	Lam. iv. 20,	i. 284
liii. 7, 8,	i. 305	Ezek. i. 1,	i. 407
liii. 8,	i. 224, 345	ii. 1,	i. 407
liv. 1,	i. 45	xx. 12,	i. 422
liv. 11-14,	ii. 151	xx. 24,	i. 419
lvii. 1,	ii. 21	xxvii. 1,	ii. 95
lvii. 16,	ii. 83	xxviii. 25, 26,	ii. 148
lviii. 8,	i. 155	xxxvi. 26,	ii. 17
lviii. 6,	i. 429	xxxvii. 12,	ii. 96, 148
lviii. 14,	ii. 149	Dan. ii. 33, 34,	ii. 126
lx. 17,	i. 464	ii. 34,	i. 356
lxi. 1,	i. 280, 334, 336, 456	ii. 41, 42,	ii. 126
lxi. 2,	i. 196	ii. 42, 43,	ii. 126
lxiii. 9,	i. 350	ii. 44, 45,	ii. 127
lxiv. 4,	ii. 157	iii. 19,	ii. 25, 67
lxv. 1,	i. 269, 279	iii. 26,	i. 448
lxv. 2,	ii. 15	vii. 4,	i. 448
lxv. 17, 18,	ii. 154	vii. 8, 23,	ii. 123
lxv. 18,	ii. 151	vii. 10,	i. 138
lxv. 22,	ii. 96	vii. 13,	i. 346, ii. 7, 13
lxvi. 1,	i. 381	vii. 13, 14,	i. 448
lxvi. 3,	i. 434	viii. 12, 23,	ii. 124
lxvi. 13,	ii. 95	ix. 27,	ii. 125
lxvi. 22,	ii. 156	xii. 3,	i. 462
Jer. i. 5,	ii. 97	xii. 4, 7,	i. 461
ii. 13,	370	xii. 9, 10,	i. 79
ii. 19,	ii. 41	Hos. i. 2, 3,	i. 449
iv. 22,	i. 381	i. 6-9,	i. 450
v. 3,	ii. 74	ii. 23,	i. 45
v. 8,	ii. 52	iv. 1,	i. 78

INDEX OF TEXTS.

	VOL. PAGE		VOL. PAGE
Hos. vi. 6,	i. 430	Matt. v. 14,	i. 395
vii. 27,	ii. 149	v. 16,	i. 142, ii. 37
ix. 10,	ii. 185	v. 17, 18,	ii. 19
xii. 10,	i. 310, 443	v. 18,	i. 13
xii. 13,	ii. 149	v. 20,	i. 413
Joel ii. 28,	i. 297	v. 21,	i. 243, 413
iii. 16,	i. 351, ii. 14	v. 22,	i. 425, ii. 27
Amos i. 2,	i. 351	v. 23, 24,	i. 431
v. 25, 26,	i. 420	v. 26, 27,	i. 95
viii. 9, 11,	ii. 15	v. 27, 28,	i. 413
ix. 11, 12,	i. 312	v. 28,	i. 425
Jonah i. 9,	i. 348	v. 33,	i. 413
ii. 2,	i. 348	v. 34,	i. 381
ii. 11,	ii. 66	v. 35,	i. 383, ii. 35
iii. 8, 9,	i. 347	v. 39,	i. 342, ii. 21
Mic. iv. 23,	ii. 21	v. 41,	i. 414
vii. 9,	i. 350	v. 44,	i. 342
Hab. ii. 4,	ii. 19	v. 45,	i. 142, 197, 372, 414,
iii. 2,	i. 330		ii. 34, 59, 129
iii. 3,	ii. 14	vi. 3,	i. 479
iii. 5,	i. 351	vi. 9,	i. 142
Zech. vii. 9, 10,	i. 429, ii. 28	vi. 12,	ii. 100
vii. 16, 17,	i. 429	vi. 19,	i. 422
viii. 17,	ii. 28	vi. 24,	i. 275
ix. 9,	i. 346, ii. 6, 15	vii. 1, 2,	i. 478
xii. 10,	ii. 13	vii. 5,	i. 478
Mal. i. 2,	i. 452	vii. 7,	i. 130, 181, 232
i. 10, 11,	i. 430	vii. 15,	i. 2
i. 11,	ii. 176	vii. 19,	ii. 78
ii. 10,	i. 440	vii. 25,	i. 219
iii. 1,	i. 290	viii. 9,	i. 31
iv. 1,	i. 385, ii. 7	viii. 11,	i. 397
Matt. i. 1,	i. 324	viii. 11, 12,	ii. 36
i. 1, 18,	i. 294	viii. 13,	ii. 39
i. 12-16,	i. 357	ix. 2,	ii. 101
i. 18,	i. 324, 354	ix. 6,	ii. 102
i. 20,	i. 279	ix. 8,	ii. 101
i. 20, etc.,	i. 456	ix. 17,	ii. 17
i. 23,	i. 279, 354	ix. 29,	ii. 39
ii. 2,	i. 279	x. 6,	i. 315, 382
ii. 15,	i. 279	x. 8,	i. 18, 246
ii. 16,	i. 328	x. 10,	i. 399
iii. 3,	i. 278	x. 15,	i. 472
iii. 7,	i. 278	x. 17, 18,	i. 341
iii. 9,	i. 395, 459, ii. 148	x. 20,	i. 334
iii. 10,	i. 399, ii. 30, 103, 172	x. 21,	i. 14
iii. 11,	i. 385	x. 24,	i. 14, 224
iii. 12,	ii. 7, 13	x. 25,	ii. 128
iii. 16,	i. 279	x. 26,	i. 2
iv. 3,	i. 392, ii. 112	x. 28,	i. 341
iv. 7,	ii. 115	x. 29,	i. 216, ii. 116
iv. 9,	ii. 119	x. 30,	i. 215
iv. 10,	ii. 113	xi. 9,	i. 281, 290
v. 5,	i. 359, ii. 77, 143	xi. 11,	i. 281
v. 8,	i. 401, 442	xi. 12,	ii. 40
v. 12,	ii. 12	xi. 19,	ii. 3
v. 13,	ii. 3	xi. 23, 24,	ii. 29, 30
v. 13, 14,	i. 25	xi. 25,	i. 379

INDEX OF TEXTS.

	VOL. PAGE		VOL. PAGE
Matt. xi. 25-27,	i. 80	Matt. xxii. 13,	ii. 32
xi. 27,	i. 133	xxii. 14,	ii. 33
xi. 28,	i. 80	xxii. 21,	i. 275
xi. 40,	ii. 140	xxii. 29,	i. 386, 387, ii. 9
xii. 5,	ii. 150	xxii. 33-41,	ii. 26
xii. 6,	i. 400	xxii. 42-44,	ii. 27
xii. 7,	i. 430	xxii. 43,	i. 357, ii. 9
xii. 18,	i. 292	xxiii. 2-4,	i. 410
xii. 25,	ii. 126	xxiii. 9,	i. 378
xii. 29,	i. 276, 342, 353, ii. 114	xxiii. 13,	ii. 52
xii. 31,	i. 236	xxiii. 24,	i. 341, ii. 10
xii. 36,	i. 184, 425	xxiii. 26,	i. 433
xii. 41,	ii. 9	xxiii. 27,	i. 433
xii. 41, 42,	i. 357	xxiii. 34,	i. 400
xii. 43,	i. 72	xxiii. 35,	ii. 92
xiii. 11-16,	i. 474	xxiii. 37,	ii. 35, 36, 39
xiii. 17,	i. 405, 454	xxiv. 15, 21,	ii. 122, 125
xiii. 25,	ii. 79	xxiv. 21,	ii. 16, 134
xiii. 30,	ii. 129	xxiv. 28,	i. 417
xiii. 34,	ii. 50	xxiv. 42,	ii. 29, 79
xiii. 38,	i. 461, ii. 51, 53, 145	xxiv. 45, 46,	i. 464
xiii. 40-43,	ii. 49	xxiv. 48,	i. 463, ii. 38
xiii. 43,	i. 243	xxv. 2,	i. 209
xiii. 44,	i. 461	xxv. 5,	i. 218
xiii. 52,	i. 399, 462	xxv. 13,	ii. 79
xiv. 19, 21,	i. 209	xxv. 14,	i. 336
xv. 3,	i. 409	xxv. 21,	i. 407
xv. 3, 4,	i. 403	xxv. 32, 34,	ii. 49
xvi. 6,	ii. 52	xxv. 34,	i. 436, 472
xvi. 13,	ii. 340	xxv. 35, 36,	i. 479
xvi. 16,	i. 345	xxv. 41,	i. 138, 243, 470, ii. 13, 48, 53
xvi. 17,	i. 315, 357, ii. 166	xxvi. 24,	i. 193, 472
xvi. 21,	i. 340	xxvi. 26,	i. 430
xvi. 24, 25,	i. 349	xxvi. 27,	ii. 144
xvii. 1, etc.,	i. 209	xxvi. 35,	ii. 154
xvii. 3, etc.,	i. 446	xxvi. 38,	i. 33, 360
xvii. 7,	i. 61	xxvi. 39,	i. 33
xvii. 27,	ii. 119	xxvi. 41,	ii. 76
xviii. 8, 9,	i. 470	xxvii. 46,	i. 33
xviii. 10,	i. 58	xxvii. 52,	ii. 171
xviii. 12,	i. 88	xxviii. 19,	i. 334
xix. 7, 8,	i. 420	Mark i. 1,	i. 326
xix. 17, 18,	i. 411	i. 24,	i. 392
xix. 21,	i. 414	iii. 27,	ii. 114
xix. 29,	ii. 144	iv. 28,	i. 435
xix. 30,	i. 362	v. 22,	i. 87
xx.	ii. 34	v. 31,	i. 13
xx. 1-16,	i. 6	vi. 42, 44,	i. 209
xx. 16,	i. 362, 420, 470	viii. 31,	i. 328
xx. 18,	ii. 186	ix. 2,	i. 67
xxi. 8,	i. 381	x. 17,	i. 79
xxi. 13,	i. 407	x. 38,	i. 81
xxi. 16,	i. 407	xiii. 32,	i. 224
xxi. 23,	i. 80	xiii. 33,	ii. 79
xxi. 31,	i. 451	xiv. 21,	i. 193
xxii. 1, etc.,	ii. 31	xvi. 19,	i. 287
xxii. 7,	ii. 33	Luke i. 2,	i. 318, 376
xxii. 10, 11,	ii. 156		

INDEX OF TEXTS.

	VOL. PAGE		VOL. PAGE
Luke i. 6,	i. 281	Luke x. 12,	ii. 30, 129
i. 8,	i. 281	x. 13,	ii. 121
i. 15,	i. 281	x. 16,	i. 258
i. 17,	i. 287, 290	x. 18,	i. 336
i. 26,	i. 282	x. 19,	i. 192, 367, ii. 121
i. 32,	i. 282, 327	x. 21,	i..379
i. 33,	i. 279	x. 22,	i. 389, 393, 396
i. 35,	i. 354, ii. 57	x. 35,	i. 336
i. 38,	i. 361	x. 60,	ii. 76
i. 42,	i. 357	xi.	i. 319
i. 46,	i. 282, 394	xi. 21, 22,	ii. 9
i. 68,	i. 283	xi. 40,	i. 225
i. 69,	i. 326	xi. 50,	ii. 92
i. 71, 75,	i. 442	xii. 20,	i. 319
i. 76,	i. 283	xii. 35, 36,	ii. 38
i. 78,	i. 283, ii. 101	xii. 37, 38,	i. 149
ii. 8,	i. 394	xii. 45, 46,	i. 463, ii. 38
ii. 11,	i. 284	xii. 47,	ii. 38
ii. 20,	i. 285	xii. 50,	i. 81
ii. 22,	i. 286	xii. 58,	i. 95
ii. 23,	i. 14	xiii.	i. 319, 320
ii. 28,	i. 35, 327	xiii. 6,	ii. 35
ii. 29,	i. 286, 327, 394	xiii. 15, 16,	i. 397
ii. 36,	i. 35	xiii. 16,	i. 204
ii. 38,	i. 286	xiii. 28,	i. 397
ii. 42,	i. 12	xiii. 32,	ii. 53
ii. 49,	i. 79	xiii. 34,	ii. 35
iii. 8,	ii. 142	xiv. 12,	ii. 144
iii. 11,	i. 479	xiv. 14,	ii. 157
iii. 17,	ii. 7	xiv. 27,	i. 14
iii. 23,	i. 6, 201	xv. 4,	i. 69
iv. 6,	ii. 116, 119	xv. 4-8,	i. 35
iv. 6, 7,	ii. 113	xv. 8,	i. 69
iv. 18,	i. 456	xv. 11,	ii. 34
v.	i. 319	xv. 22, 23,	i. 418
v. 20,	ii. 101	xvi.	i. 319
v. 31, 32,	i. 267	xvi. 9,	i. 479
v. 36, 37,	ii. 23	xvi. 11,	i. 253
vi. 3, 4,	i. 398	xvi. 16,	i. 385
vi. 13,	i. 12	xvi. 19,	i. 251, 380
vi. 24,	i. 319	xvi. 28,	i. 209
vi. 29,	i. 414	xvi. 31,	i. 380
vi. 40,	ii. 140	xvii.	i. 319
vi. 46,	ii. 38, 75	xvii. 5,	i. 319
vii.	i. 319	xvii. 24,	ii. 129
vii. 8,	i. 31	xvii. 26,	ii. 29
vii. 12,	ii. 87	xviii.	i. 319, 320
vii. 26,	i. 290	xviii. 2,	ii. 124
vii. 35,	i. 35	xviii. 8,	ii. 13
vii. 43,	i. 348	xviii. 10,	ii. 35
viii. 41,	i. 33	xviii. 18,	i. 79
viii. 51,	i. 209	xviii. 27,	i. 146, 442, ii. 67
ix. 13, 14,	i. 209	xviii. 29, 30,	ii. 144
ix. 22,	i. 328	xix.	i. 319
ix. 57, 58,	i. 33	xix. 5,	i. 34
ix. 60,	i. 34	xix. 8,	i. 412
ix. 61, 62,	i. 34	xix. 26,	i. 27
x. 1,	i. 194	xix. 42,	i. 80

INDEX OF TEXTS.

	VOL. PAGE		VOL. PAGE
Luke xxi. 4,	i. 432	John viii. 58,	i. 416, ii. 182
xxi. 34,	ii. 37	viii. 59,	ii. 182
xxi. 34, 35,	ii. 29	ix. 1,	i. 177
xxiii. 24,	i. 341	ix. 3,	ii. 96
xxiv.	i. 320	ix. 7,	ii. 97
xxiv. 25,	i. 328	ix. 30,	ii. 87
xxiv. 39,	ii. 60	xi. 25,	i. 387
xxiv. 44,	i. 328	xi. 54,	i. 199
John i. 1,	i. 288, 293, ii. 305	xii. 1,	i. 99
i. 1, 2, 3, 4,	i. 36	xii. 27,	i. 33
i. 3,	i. 85, 123, 276, 358, ii. 5	xii. 32,	i. 382
i. 5,	i. 37	xiii. 5,	i. 454
i. 6,	i. 290	xiv. 2,	i. 347, ii. 156
i. 10, 11,	i. 289, ii. 105	xiv. 6,	i. 266
i. 13,	i. 245, ii. 58, 106	xiv. 6, 7,	i. 395
i. 13, 14,	i. 325	xiv. 7, 9, 10,	i. 315
i. 14,	i. 284, 289, 290, ii. 10, 105	xiv. 11,	ii. 104
i. 15, 16,	i. 284	xiv. 16,	i. 295
i. 18,	i. 291, 444, 447	xiv. 28,	i. 227
i. 29,	i. 283	xv. 15,	i. 415
i. 47,	i. 292	xv. 16,	i. 417
i. 49,	i. 292	xvi. 7,	i. 335
i. 50,	i. 401	xvii. 5,	i. 416
ii. 3,	i. 291	xvii. 12,	i. 193
ii. 4,	i. 330	xvii. 16,	i. 27
ii. 19-21,	ii. 69	xvii. 24,	i. 417
ii. 23,	i. 198	xix. 11,	i. 434
ii. 25,	i. 280	xix. 15,	i. 452
iii. 5,	ii. 174	xix. 34,	ii. 7
iii. 14,	i. 382	xx. 17,	ii. 140
iii. 18-21,	ii. 130	xx. 20, 27,	ii. 140
iv. 6,	i. 360	xx. 22,	ii. 182
iv. 14,	ii. 29, 182	xx. 24,	i. 77
iv. 24,	ii. 176	xx. 25-27,	ii. 70
iv. 35,	i. 455	xx. 26,	ii. 182
iv. 37,	i. 460	xx. 31,	i. 328
iv. 41,	i. 382	Acts i. 7,	i. 362
iv. 50,	i. 198	i. 16,	i. 297
v. 1,	i. 198	i. 20,	i. 191
v. 5,	i. 204	ii. 22-27,	i. 297
v. 14,	ii. 33, 96	ii. 30-37,	i. 298
v. 28,	ii. 88	ii. 37, 38,	i. 298
v. 35,	ii. 180	ii. 41,	i. 457
v. 39, 40,	i. 403	iii. 6,	i. 299
v. 43,	ii. 124	iii. 12,	i. 300
v. 46,	i. 403	iii. 15,	i. 200
v. 46, 47,	i. 379	iv. 2,	i. 300
vi. 1,	i. 199	iv. 4,	i. 457
vi. 9,	i. 209	iv. 8, etc.,	i. 300
vi. 11,	i. 291	iv. 22,	i. 301
vi. 69,	i. 292	iv. 24.	i. 301
vii. 30,	i. 330	iv. 31,	i. 302
vii. 39,	ii. 105	iv. 33,	i. 302
viii. 34,	i. 275	v. 30,	i. 302
viii. 36,	i. 344	v. 42,	i. 302
viii. 44,	ii. 116, 118	vii. 2-8,	i. 308
viii. 56,	i. 388	vii. 5, 6,	ii. 142
viii. 56, 57,	i. 202	vii. 38,	i. 420

INDEX OF TEXTS.

	VOL. PAGE
Acts vii. 56,	i. 310
viii. 9-11,	i. 86
viii. 9, 18,	i. 246
viii. 20, 21, 23,	i. 86
viii. 27,	i. 456
viii. 32,	i. 405
viii. 37,	i. 405
ix. 15, 16,	i. 321
ix. 20,	i. 306
x. 1,	i. 303
x. 15,	i. 304
x. 28, 29,	i. 313
x. 34, 35,	i. 304
x. 37-44,	i. 304
x. 47,	i. 313
xiv. 15-17,	i. 307
xv. 14,	i. 312, 349
xv. 15,	i. 311
xvi. 8,	i. 316
xvi. 13,	i. 316
xvii. 24,	i. 307
xx. 5, 6,	i. 316
xx. 25,	i. 318
xxi.	i. 317
xxii. 8,	i. 321
xxvi. 15,	i. 321
xxvii.	i. 317
xxviii. 11,	i. 317
Rom. i. 1-4,	i. 326
i. 3, 4,	i. 360
i. 17,	ii. 19
i. 18,	i. 471
i. 21,	ii. 6
i. 25,	i. 143
i. 28,	i. 475
ii. 5,	ii. 18
ii. 27,	i. 412
iii. 8,	ii. 94
iii. 11,	i. 78
iii. 21,	ii. 19
iii. 23,	i. 468
iii. 30,	i. 455, ii. 115
iv. 3,	i. 396
iv. 12,	i. 395
v. 14,	i. 243, 360
v. 17,	i. 332
v. 19,	i. 244, 358
v. 20,	i. 368
vi. 3, 4,	i. 332
vi. 7,	i. 367
vi. 9,	i. 333
vi. 12, 13,	ii. 94
vii. 18,	i. 349, ii. 34
vii. 24,	i. 351
viii. 3,	i. 349
viii. 5,	ii. 80
viii. 8,	ii. 80
viii. 9,	ii. 73, 80

	VOL. PAGE
Rom. viii. 10,	ii. 80, 175
viii. 11,	i. 333, ii. 70
viii. 13,	ii. 80
viii. 15,	i. 270, 404, ii. 73
viii. 19,	ii. 142
viii. 21,	ii. 157
viii. 34,	i. 333
viii. 36,	i. 198, 422
ix. 5,	i. 326
ix. 10-13,	i. 452
ix. 13,	i. 452
ix. 25,	i. 44, 278
ix. 25, 26,	i. 450
x. 3, 4,	i. 411
x. 6, 7,	i. 338
x. 9,	i. 338
x. 15,	i. 314
xi. 16,	i. 34
xi. 17,	ii. 78
xi. 21, 17,	i. 468
xi. 26,	i. 382
xi. 32,	i. 44, 349
xi. 33,	i. 45
xi. 34,	i. 55
xi. 36,	i. 14
xii. 1,	ii. 176
xii. 3,	ii. 110
xii. 16,	ii. 115
xiii. 1,	ii. 119
xiii. 1-7,	ii. 34
xiii. 4,	ii. 119
xiii. 6,	ii. 119
xiii. 10,	i. 410
xiv. 9,	i. 338
xiv. 15,	i. 339
1 Cor. i. 18,	i. 15
i. 23,	i. 338
i. 26-28,	i. 189
i. 29,	i. 348
ii. 6,	i. 35, 259, ii. 68
ii. 9,	ii. 157
ii. 10,	i. 226
ii. 14,	i. 34, ii. 75, 175
ii. 15,	i. 34, ii. 6, 18
iii. 1,	ii. 75
iii. 2,	ii. 42
iii. 3,	ii. 43
iii. 7,	ii. 460
iii. 16,	ii. 69
iii. 16, 17,	ii. 178
iii. 17,	i. 399, ii. 70
iv. 4,	i. 401
v. 6,	i. 470
v. 11,	i. 470
vi. 9, 10,	i. 470
vi. 9-11,	ii. 81
vi. 11,	ii. 39
vi. 12,	ii. 38

INDEX OF TEXTS.

	VOL. PAGE		VOL. PAGE
1 Cor. vi. 13,	ii. 70	2 Cor. iv. 11,	ii. 91
vi. 20,	ii. 89	v. 4,	i. 188, ii. 32, 72, 89
vii. 5,	i. 420	vii. 2,	i. 464
vii. 6,	i. 420	viii. 1,	ii. 11
vii. 12,	i. 420	x. 5,	ii. 33
vii. 14,	i. 450	xii. 2, 3, 4,	i. 235
vii. 25,	i. 421	xii. 3,	i. 236, ii. 60
vii. 31,	i. 383, ii. 154, 155	xii. 4,	ii. 66
viii. 1,	i. 215	xii. 7-9,	ii. 61
viii. 4, etc.,	i. 272	xii. 9,	i. 347
viii. 11,	i. 339	xiii.	ii. 11
ix. 24,	ii. 40	xiii. 4,	ii. 179
x. 1, etc.,	i. 469	Gal. i. 1,	i. 315
x. 4,	ii. 182	i. 15, 16,	ii. 85, 97
x. 11,	i. 418	ii. 1, 2,	i. 315
x. 16,	i. 336, ii. 59	ii. 5,	i. 315
xi. 4, 5,	i. 296	ii. 8,	i. 314
xi. 10,	i. 33	ii. 12, 13,	i. 313
xii. 4, 5, 6,	i. 226	iii. 5-9,	i. 451
xii. 4-7,	i. 443	iii. 6,	ii. 143
xii. 28,	i. 291, 370, 464	iii. 13,	i. 339
xiii. 2,	i. 410	iii. 16,	ii. 143
xiii. 9,	i. 226, 227	iii. 19,	i. 274, ii. 110
xiii. 9, 10,	i. 401	iii. 24,	i. 382
xiii. 9, 12,	ii. 172	iv. 4,	i. 330, 358, ii. 111
xiii. 13,	i. 222, 410	iv. 5,	i. 326
xiv. 20,	i. 474	iv. 8,	i. 143
xv. 3. 4,	i. 339	iv. 8, 9,	i. 272
xv. 8,	i. 33	iv. 24,	i. 45
xv. 10,	i. 457	iv. 26,	ii. 153
xv. 11,	i. 314	iv. 28,	i. 395
xv. 12,	i. 339	v. 19,	ii. 81
xv. 13,	ii. 91	v. 21,	i. 26
xv. 20-22,	i. 362	vi. 14,	i. 15
xv. 22,	i. 368, ii. 58	Eph. i. 7,	ii. 93
xv. 25, 26,	ii. 156	i. 10,	i. 14, 42, 110
xv. 26,	i. 367	i. 13,	ii. 72
xv. 27, 28,	ii. 157	i. 21,	i. 438, 458
xv. 30,	i. 111	ii. 2,	ii. 121
xv. 36,	ii. 71	ii. 7,	i. 387
xv. 41,	i. 175	ii. 13,	i. 339, ii. 93
xv. 42,	ii. 71	ii. 15,	ii. 93
xv. 43,	ii. 71	ii. 17,	i. 268
xv. 44,	i. 188, ii. 72	ii. 20,	i. 459
xv. 45,	ii. 85	iii. 21,	i. 12
xv. 46,	ii. 82	iv. 5, 6,	ii. 5, 105
xv. 48,	i. 34, ii. 76	iv. 6,	i. 123, 440
xv. 49,	ii. 77, 83	iv. 8,	i. 192
xv. 50,	ii. 75, 79, 80	iv. 9,	i. 454, ii. 140
xv. 52,	ii. 87	iv. 9, 10,	ii. 182
xv. 53,	ii. 60, 80, 88, 91	iv. 25, 29,	ii. 38
xv. 54,	i. 44	v. 6, 7,	i. 470
xv. 54, 55,	i. 367	v. 13,	i. 37
2 Cor. ii. 15, 16,	i. 473	v. 30,	ii. 60
ii. 17,	i. 464	v. 32,	i. 35
iii. 3,	ii. 90	vi. 12,	i. 42
iv. 4,	i. 272, 475, ii. 179	Col. i. 14,	ii. 59
iv. 10,	ii. 90	i. 14, 15,	i. 326

INDEX OF TEXTS.

	VOL. PAGE
Col. i. 16,	i. 19
i. 18,	i. 200, 440
i. 21,	ii. 93
ii. 9,	i. 14
ii. 11,	i. 422
ii. 14,	ii. 102, 176
ii. 16,	ii. 177
ii. 18,	ii. 175
ii. 19,	ii. 5, 94
iii. 5,	ii. 85
iii. 9,	ii. 84
iii. 10,	ii. 85
iii. 11,	i. 14
iv. 14,	i. 317
Phil. i. 22,	ii. 85
ii. 8,	i. 458, ii. 96
ii. 9,	ii. 175
ii. 10, 11,	i. 42
ii. 15,	i. 388
iii. 2, 9,	ii. 89
iii. 11,	ii. 90
iv. 17,	i. 399
iv. 18,	i. 434
1 Thess. ii. 10-12,	ii. 69
v. 3,	ii. 137
v. 23,	ii. 69
2 Thess. i. 6-10,	i. 471
i. 9, 10,	ii. 13
ii. 4,	i. 272
ii. 8,	i. 274, ii. 123
ii. 11,	i. 475
1 Tim. i. 1,	ii. 175
i. 9,	i. 423
ii. 5,	ii. 100
iii. 15,	i. 293
iv. 2,	i. 196
vi. 4,	i. 308
vi. 4, 5,	ii. 175
vi. 20,	i. 89, 116
2 Tim. ii. 17, 18,	i. 241
ii. 23,	i. 376
iii. 6,	i. 56
iii. 7,	i. 402, ii. 109
iv. 3,	i. 195
iv. 10, 11,	i. 317
Tit. iii. 10,	i. 71, 263
Heb. i. 3,	i. 238
iii. 5,	i. 272
x. 9,	i. 426
xi. 13,	ii. 142
xiii. 15,	ii. 142

	VOL. PAGE
Jas. i. 18,	ii. 56
i. 21,	ii. 79
ii. 23,	i. 416, 423
1 Pet. i. 8,	i. 401, ii. 72
i. 12,	i. 177, ii. 19, 157
ii. 3,	ii. 175
ii. 5-9,	i. 398
ii. 16,	i. 425, ii. 38
ii. 23,	i. 333, 440
ii. 24,	ii. 170
iii. 20,	i. 76
iv. 14,	ii. 12
2 Pet. iii. 8,	ii. 118, 132
1 John ii. 1,	i. 336
ii. 18,	i. 339
v. 1,	i. 332
2 John 7, 8,	i. 331
11,	i. 71
Jude 3,	ii. 175
7,	ii. 30
Rev. i. 5,	i. 362
i. 12,	i. 448
i. 15,	i. 418
i. 17,	i. 448
ii. 6,	i. 98
ii. 17,	ii. 79
iii. 7,	i. 440
iv. 7,	i. 293
v. 6,	i. 449
v. 8,	i. 431, ii. 176
vi. 2,	i. 452
vii. 5-7,	ii. 137
xi. 19,	i. 436
xii. 14,	i. 242
xiii. 2,	ii. 131
xiii. 11, 14,	ii. 132
xv. xvi.	i. 480
xvii. 8,	ii. 138
xvii. 12,	ii. 125
xix. 11-17,	i. 449
xix. 20,	ii. 131
xx. 6,	ii. 149
xx. 11,	ii. 153
xx. 12-14,	ii. 154
xx. 15,	i. 154
xxi. 1-4,	ii. 154
xxi. 2,	ii. 153
xxi. 5, 6,	ii. 155
xxii. 17,	i. 264
xxii. 19,	ii. 136

II.—INDEX OF PRINCIPAL SUBJECTS.

AARON and Miriam, their sin against Moses, and its punishment, ii. 173.

Abel and Cain, the offerings of, i. 432.

Abominations, the, practised by the Valentinians, i. 26, etc.

Abraham, saw the day of Christ, 388, 394, etc.; vain attempt of Marcion to exclude him from Christ's salvation, 396, etc.; had faith identical with ours, 451; both covenants prefigured in, 459, 460; waited for the promises of God, ii. 142, 143.

Abraxas, Basilides' doctrine of, i. 93.

Acceptable year of the Lord, the, i. 197.

Achamoth, an account of, i. 16; origin of the visible world from, 17, etc.; shall at last enter the Pleroma, 28; asserted to be referred to in Scripture, 33-35.

Adam and Eve, the story of, according to the Ophites, i. 107, 108.

Adam, the first, made a partaker of salvation, i. 362; his repentance signified by the girdle which he made, 366; why driven out of Paradise, 367; in Paradise, ii. 66; sinned on the sixth day of creation, 116-118; death of, 118.

Adam, analogy between the first and the second, i. 359.

Æon, the twelfth, the sufferings of, not to be deduced from Scripture, i. 190; nor typified by the woman with the issue of blood, 203.

Æons, the thirty, of Valentinus, i. 4, etc.; English equivalents of the Greek names of, 5, 6, note; how the thirty are said to be indicated in Scripture, 12; the production of, 152, etc., 168, etc.; further inquiry into and refutation of the speculations respecting, 172-179; the theory of, further exposed, 180, etc., 184, etc.; the twelve apostles not types of the twelve, 194; the thirty, not typified by the baptism of Jesus in His thirtieth year, 196.

Agape, i. 212.

Αἰών, meaning of the term, i. 444.

Aletheia, the Æon so called, i. 5, 7; how her passion is said to be indicated in Scripture, 13; of Ptolemy, 49; revealed by Tetrad, 59, etc.

Aletheia, the numerical value of, does not square with Valentinianism, i. 212.

Anaxagoras, i. 162.

Anaximander, i. 162.

Angels, the world not made by, i. 120, 121; could not be ignorant of the Supreme God, 132.

Angels of the devil, ii. 50, etc.

Animal men, the, of the Valentinians, i. 25, 33.

Animals, clean and unclean, ii. 74.

Anthropos and Ecclesia, the Æons so named, i. 5, 7, 50, 106.

Antichrist, the fraud, pride, and tyranny of the kingdom of, ii. 121-125; concentrates in himself the apostasy, 131; the number of the name of, 135.

Antiphanes, the theogony of, i. 160.

Apator, i. 21.

Apocryphal Scriptures, the, of the Marcosians, i. 79.

Apostles, the twelve, not types of the twelve Æons, i. 194.

Apostles, the, did not begin to preach till endued with the Holy Spirit, i. 258; preached one God, 259; the doctrine of, 296-314; the labours of, lessened by their predecessors, 455.

Aquila and Theodotian, their interpretation of Isa. vii. 14 referred to, i. 351, 352.

Ark of the covenant, i. 207, ii. 163.

Autogenes, i. 102.

Axe, the, made to float by means of wood, ii. 171.

Axe, the, laid at the root, ii. 172.

Balaam, ii. 167; forbidden to curse Israel, 169; his ass a type, 169, 170; slain, 170.

Baptism of Jesus in his thirtieth year not a type of the thirty Æons, i. 196.

Barbeliotes or Borborians, the, i. 101.

Basilides, the doctrines of, i. 90, etc.; absurd notion of, as to the death of Jesus, 91; this notion of, refuted, 253.
Beast, the, ii. 131, etc., 134, etc.
Bishops, a succession of, in various churches, i. 261, etc.; first, of Rome, 261, 262.
Blandina, the martyr, ii. 165.
Blood, the, of Christ, redeems, ii. 58, 59.
Blood, the Christians accused of eating, how the calumny originated, ii. 165.
Bodies, the, of men, temples of the Holy Ghost, ii. 69; from the earth, 98.
Body and soul, the views of heretics respecting the future destiny of, refuted, i. 228.
Bread and wine in the Eucharist, ii. 59.
Breath of life, the, ii. 83.
Bythus, i. 4, 7, 49; absurdity of, 124.

Cain, i. 365; and Abel, the respective offerings of, 432.
Cainites, the doctrines of the, i. 113.
Carnal and spiritual, ii. 80, etc.
Carpocrates, the doctrines of, i. 93; the followers of, practised magic and incantations, 94; immorality of the system of, 94, 95; his views of the devil, 95; his followers branded with external marks, and have images of Jesus, etc., 96.
Centurion, the, of the Gospels, asserted by the Valentinians to be the Demiurge, i. 30.
Cerdo, the doctrines of, i. 98.
Cerinthus, the doctrines of, i. 97.
Christ, Valentinus' views of, i. 14, 25, 28, 29, 46, 51; the origin of, according to the Ophites, 104; the descent of, upon Jesus, according to the Ophites, 111, 112; the apostles of, their preaching, 266; and Jesus, the same, the only-begotten Son of God, 223-233; not, but the Holy Spirit, descended upon Jesus, 334; and Jesus of Nazareth proved from the writings of Paul to be one and the same, 337, etc.; did not flee away from Jesus at the cross, 340; did not suffer in appearance merely, 342; assumed actual flesh, conceived and born of the Virgin, 359, etc.; the advent of, foretold, 404; the advent of, foreknown and desired by righteous men, 405; did not abolish the law, 408; is the end of the law, 411; did not abrogate the natural precepts of the law, but removed the bondage, 412; came for the sake of men of all ages, 433, etc.; is the treasure hid in the field, 461; descended into regions beneath the earth, 467; foreseen and foretold by the prophets, ii. 13-17; the prophets referred all their predictions to, 18, etc.; alone able to redeem us, 55, etc.; took flesh, not seemingly, but really, 56; conferred on our flesh the capacity of salvation, 58-61; his resurrection a proof of ours, 70, etc.; the dead raised by, a proof of the resurrection, 87; fitting that He should take human nature and be tempted by the devil, 110, etc.; His victory over Satan, *ibid.*; temptation of, 111, etc.; His kingdom eternal, 127, 128; the resurrection of, 139, 140; how prefigured, 167, 168; testimony of the sacred books to, 182, 183, 184.
Christians, calumnies against the, ii. 165.
Church, the, her gifts, i. 246; performs nothing by incantations or curious arts, *ibid.*; of Rome, founded by Peter and Paul, 261; the catholic, the depository of truth, 264, etc.
Clean and unclean, ii. 74.
Colorbasus, the doctrines of, i. 49, etc.
Commandment, the first and greatest, i. 411.
Communion with God, ii. 129.
Cosmocrator, the, i. 23.
Covenant, the new, ii. 19, 20.
Covenants, one author and one end to both, i. 399, etc.; the oneness of both proved by Jesus' reproof of customs repugnant to the former, 408.
Created things, made after the image of invisible things, according to the Marcosians, i. 72, etc.
Created things, not images of Æons within the Pleroma, i. 134-140; not a shadow of the Pleroma, 140-142.
Creation, the, of all things out of nothing by God, i. 144-146.
Creator, but one, of the world, i. 142.

Creator, the, made all things, spiritual and material, i. 237, 239; is the Word, ii. 105.
Creator, the, could not be ignorant of the Supreme God, i. 132, 133.

Day, the, does not square with the theory of Valentinus, i. 211.
Day of retribution, the, i. 197.
Dead, the, raised by Christ, a proof of the resurrection, ii. 87.
Death, the, and life, ii. 82.
Decalogue, the, at first inscribed on the hearts of men, i. 419; not cancelled by Christ, 424, 425.
Demiurge, the, the formation of, according to Valentinus, i. 20; the creator of all things outside the Pleroma, 21; ignorant of what he created, 22; ignorant of the offspring of his mother Achamoth, 24; passes into the intermediate habitation, 28; instructed by the Saviour, 20; is the centurion of the Gospels, *ibid.*; views of the heretics respecting, exposed and confuted, 184, etc.; declared by the heretics to be animal, 231; if animal, how could he make things spiritual? 237, 239.
Devil, views of the Carpocratians respecting, i. 95.
Devil, practised in falsehoods, he tempted man, ii. 116, 117; his lie in regard to the government of the world, 119, 120.
Devil, the sons of the, ii. 51.
Deuteronomy, ii. 167.
Diatheses, the, of Ptolemy, i. 49.
Disciples, the true spiritual, ii. 6, etc.
Discriminating faculty, the, in man, ii. 45.
Disobedient, the, are the angels of the devil, ii. 49.
Duodecad, the, of Valentinus, how said to be indicated in Scripture, i. 12.
Dyad, the, of Valentinus, i. 45.

Earthly things, types of heavenly, i. 436.
Ebionites, the, i. 97; refutation of, who disparaged the writings of Paul, 320, etc.; strictures on, ii. 57.
Ecclesia, the, of the Valentinians, i. 24; of Ptolemy, 50.
Egyptians, the Israelites commanded to spoil the goods of, an exposition and vindication, i. 475-480.

Elements, the twenty-four, of Marcus, i. 64, etc.
Elijah, ii. 66.
Elisha, ii. 102.
Emanations, the, of Valentinus and others, an account of, 4-35, 45, etc., 49, etc., 64, etc.; ridicule poured on, 47, 48.
Encratites, the, i. 100.
Enmity, the, put between Eve and the serpent, i. 367.
Ennœæ, i. 4, 5, 49, 101, etc., 104.
Enoch, the translation of, ii. 65, 66.
Enthymesis, the, of Sophia or Achamoth, i. 9, 21; the absurdity of, 180, etc.; the treachery of Judas not a type of, 191-193.
Error, how often set off, i. 2.
Eucharist, the, i. 435, ii. 59.
Evanthas, ii. 137.
Eve and the Virgin Mary compared, ii. 106, etc.
Eve, the story of, according to the Ophites, i. 107.

Faith, the unity of the, in the universal church, i. 42, etc.
Faith of Abraham, the, the same as ours, i. 45.
Father, the, the world made by, through the Word, i. 120-123.
Father, the, how no one knows, but the Son, i. 389; reveals the Son, 391.
Fear produces (according to Valentinus) animal substances, i. 22, 23.
Five, the number, the frequent use of, in Scripture, i. 208-210.
Flesh, the, as nourished by the body of the Lord, incorruptible, i. 435; made capable of salvation, ii, 59-64; quickened, 84, etc.; saved by the Word taking flesh, 91; the saints having suffered in, shall receive their rewards in, 141, etc., 143, etc.
Flesh and blood, ii. 75-78.
Flesh, the works of the, ii. 80, etc.
Florinus, ii. 158.
Free-will, man endowed with, ii. 37-41.
Fruit of the belly and of the loins, i. 355.

Gentiles, the conversion of, more difficult than that of the Jews, i. 457-459.
Gideon, a type, i. 335, ii. 68.
Gifts, the, of the Holy Spirit, ii. 72.

Gnostics, the hypocrisy and pride of, i. 321.
God, but one, proved against Marcion and others, i. 117-120; the world made by, 120-123; created all things out of nothing, 144-146; not to be sought after by means of syllables and letters, 212, etc.; many things, the knowledge of which must be left in His hands, 221, 222; alone knows all things, 224; all things made by, 235; different names of, in the Hebrew Scriptures, 254, 255; one, proclaimed by Christ and the apostles, 266; the Holy Ghost throughout the Old Testament mentions but one, 268; objection to the doctrine of one, deduced from 2 Cor. iv. 5, answered, 273; objection from Matt. vi. 24 answered, 275; proved to be one and the same, the Creator, from the Gospel of Matthew, 277; from Mark and Luke, 281; from John, 287-292, 296, etc.; showed Himself to be merciful and mighty to save, after the fall of man, 347, etc.; His providential rule over the world, 371; just to punish and good to save, 371, 372; but one, who is the Father, 377, 378; the unity of, proved from Moses, the prophets, and Christ, 378-382; immutable and eternal, 382; the destruction of Jerusalem derogates nothing from His majesty, 383; but one, announced by the law and the prophets, whom Christ confesses as His Father, 386, etc.; has placed man under law for man's own benefit, 416, etc.; needs nothing from man, 426, 427; formed all things by the Word and Spirit, 439-444; declared by the Son, 444; seen by men, 426, 427; yet invisible, 446; not the author of sin, 471; the author of both testaments, ii. 4, etc.; attributes of, 43; the misery of departure from, 47; one and the same, inflicts punishments and bestows rewards, 48, etc.; His power and glory will shine forth in the resurrection, 61, etc.; those deceived who feign another, 64, etc.; the image of, in which man was made, 99; unity of, reaffirmed, 100; pardons our sins, 100, etc.; and the Word, formed all things by their own power, 103, etc.; declared by the law and manifested in Christ, 114, etc.; communion with, 129, 130; His infinitude, 162; always true and faithful, 170.
God of this world, the, i. 273.
Gods, the so-called, in the Old Testament, i. 270.
Good works not necessary for Valentinian heretics, i. 26.
Gospels, the four, there can be neither more nor fewer, i. 293; symbolized by the four living creatures, 293, 294; respective characteristics of, 294; those who destroy the form of, vain and unlearned, 295.
Government, civil, of God, and to be obeyed, ii. 119, etc.
Grain of mustard seed, the, ii. 172.
Greater and less, application of the phrase, i. 400-403.
Grief, evil spirits said by Valentinus to derive their origin from, i. 23.

Heaven, the, of Valentinus, i. 21, 22.
Heavens, the new, different abodes in, ii. 155, 156.
Helena and Simon Magus, i. 87, 88.
Henotes, i. 47.
Heresies, of recent origin, i. 265, 266.
Heretics, the, resort to Scripture to support their opinions, i. 11, 74, 78, 79; modes of initiation practised by, 28-84; deviation of, from the truth, 84, etc.; their perverse interpretations of Scripture, 144; have fallen into an abyss of error, 146, etc.; the first order of productions maintained by (viz. Æons), indefensible, 152, etc.; borrow their systems from the heathen, 160-168; miracles claimed to be wrought by, 241, etc.; blasphemous doctrines of, further exposed, 242, etc.; follow neither Scripture nor tradition, 259; refutation of, from the orderly succession of bishops in the churches, 260; tossed about by every wind of doctrine, 269-271; unlearned, ignorant, and divided in opinion, ii. 107; to be avoided, 108, etc.
Holy Spirit, the, descended on Jesus at His baptism, not Christ nor the Saviour, i. 334.
Holy Spirit, gifts of the, ii. 172.

Homer, laid under contribution by the Valentinians, curious instances of, i. 40, 41.
Hope, i. 211.
Horos and Stauros, i. 8, 9, 14.

Ialdabaoth, i. 106, 107.
I AM THAT I AM, i. 270.
Iao, i. 17.
Ignorance, human, of divine things, i. 219-228.
Image of God, the, in which man was created, ii. 99.
Immorality, the, of the Valentinian heretics, i. 26, 27.
Initiation, modes of, practised by the heretics, i. 82.
Intermediate state, the, ii. 140.
Isaac, the history of, symbolical, i. 451, 452; the blessing of, ii. 145.
Isaiah, his prophecy respecting the virgin conceiving, vindicated against Theodotian, Aquila, and the Ebionites, 351, etc.

Jacob, the actions of, typical, i. 452.
Jerusalem, the destruction of, derogates nothing from the majesty of God, i. 383, etc.
Jesus, the significance of the letters of the name, i. 215.
Jesus, how certain Æons are said to be indicated by the name of, i. 13; meaning of the letters of the name of, 60; the generation of, according to Marcus, 66; according to Basilides, was not crucified, but Simon of Cyrene in His stead, 91; descent of the Christ upon, according to the Ophites, 111, 112; His baptism when thirty years old, not a type of the thirty Æons, 197; passed through every stage of life, to sanctify all, 199; the ministry of, extended over ten years, 201, 202; lived at least till near fifty years old, 202; His teaching, 242, 243; the baptism of, 279, the same with Christ, the only-begotten Son of God, perfect God and perfect man, 323; with Him nothing incomplete — His time, 330, 331; neither Christ nor Saviour, but the Holy Spirit descended upon Him at His baptism, 334, etc.; and Christ, proved from the writings of Paul to be one and the same, 337, etc.; not a mere man, but very God, 344; became man so as to be capable of being tempted and crucified, 346; His birth foretold by Isaiah, 354; His reply to the Sadducees, 386, 387. [See Christ.]
John, and Cerinthus, a curious story relating to, i. 263.
Joshua, ii. 168.
Judas not an emblem of the twelfth Æon, i. 191-193.
Judgment, the future, by Jesus Christ, ii. 49, 128, etc.
Justin quoted against Marcion, i. 390.

Keltæ, the, i. 3.
Kingdom, the, of Christ, eternal, ii. 127, 128.
Kingdom, the earthly, of the saints after their resurrection, ii. 147-151; the prophecies respecting, not allegorical, 151, etc.
Knee, bending the, a symbol of the resurrection, ii. 163.
Knowledge, puffs up, i. 215; perfect, not attainable in this life, 219-228.
Knowledge, the true, ii. 11, 175.

Lateinos, ii. 137.
Law, the old and the new, has but one author, i. 399, etc.; Christ did not abrogate the natural precepts of, but removed the bondage of, 412, etc.; man was placed under, for his own benefit, 416; originally inscribed on the hearts of men, but afterwards, as the Mosaic, made by God to bridle the desires of the Jews, 419-421; perfect righteousness not obtained by, 421-425.
Letters and syllables, the absurd theories of Marcion respecting, i. 56-64, 65-71; absurdity of arguments derived from, 204; God not to be sought after by means of, 212, etc.
Levitical dispensation, the, not appointed by God for His own sake, i. 425, etc.
Life and death, ii. 82, etc.
Linus, bishop of Rome, i. 261.
Living creatures, the symbolic import of the four, i. 293.
Logos, the Æon so called, and Sige, i. 150; absurdity of the Valentinian account of the generation of, 175, etc., 224.

Lord, the, is one God, the Father, i. 377; testimony of Moses to, 378, etc.
Lot and his daughters, the typical import of the story of, ii. 1-3; the wife of, turned into a pillar of salt, 3, 4.
Luke, and Paul, i. 316; refutation of the Ebionites who tried to disparage the authority of Paul from the writings of, 320.

Magic, our Lord's miracles not performed by, i. 245.
Magical practices, the, of Marcus, i. 51, etc.
Man, the first, according to the Ophites, i. 104, 105.
Man, God's mercy to, after the fall, i. 347; the object of God's long-suffering, 348; needs a greater than man to save, 349, 350; why not at first made perfect, ii. 42, etc.; endowed with the faculty of distinguishing good and evil, 45; the whole nature of, has salvation conferred on it, 67, etc.; unfruitful, without the Holy Spirit, 78, etc.; all things created for the service of, 133; every, either empty or full, 170.
Man, the threefold kind, feigned by the heretics, i. 24; the respective destinations of the threefold kind of, 28, 33, 34.
Mansions, the many, ii. 156.
Marcion, the doctrines of, i. 98; mutilates the Gospels, *ibid.*; vain attempt of, to exclude Abraham from Christ's salvation, 396, etc.
Marcionites, the, refuted, in relation to prophecy, ii. 18, etc.
Marcosians, the, absurd interpretations of, i. 69-72; absurd theories of, respecting things created, 72-74; appeal of, to Moses, 74-77; cite Scripture to prove that the Father was unknown before the coming of Christ, 78; the apocryphal Scriptures of, 79; pervert the Gospels, 79, 80; views of, respecting redemption, 81-84; departure of, from the truth, 84-86.
Marcus, the deceitful arts and nefarious practices of, i. 51; pretends to confer the gift of prophecy, 52, 53; corrupts women, 54; hypothesis of, respecting letters and syllables, 56-64; pretended revelations of Sige to, 64-69.
Mary, would hasten on Jesus, but is checked by Him, i. 330; and Eve, compared, ii. 106.
Matter, ii. 173, 174.
Men possessed of free-will, ii. 36; not true that some are by nature good, and some bad, 37.
Men, spiritual, ii. 6, etc., 73-80, etc.
Men, the three kinds of, feigned by the heretics, i. 24-27.
Menander, successor to Simon Magus, i. 89.
Mercy, not to be exaggerated at the expense of justice, i. 471.
Metropator, i. 21.
Miracles claimed to be performed by heretics, i. 241; performed by Christ and His disciples, 245.
Moral faculty, the, in man, ii. 45.
Monogenes, the, of Valentinus, i. 5, 7; of Ptolemy, 49.
Monotes, i. 47.
Months, the, do not fall in with the Valentinian theories of Æons, i. 211.
Moses, ii. 172; Aaron and Miriam sin against, 173.
Mother, the, of the Valentinian heresy, i. 185-190.

Naaman cleansed of his leprosy, ii. 174.
Names of God, different, in the Hebrew Scriptures, i. 254, 255.
Names of our Lord, i. 205, 206.
New covenant, the, ii. 19, 20.
Nicolaitanes, the, i. 97.
Nous, or Monogenes, i. 5, 7, 49, 106.
Number of the beast, the, ii. 135-139.
Numbers and letters, the folly of deriving arguments from, i. 204-212.

Oblation, the new, instituted by Christ, ii. 76.
Oblations and sacrifices, i. 431, etc.
Ogdoad, the first, of Valentinus, i. 5, 21; John asserted to have set forth, 34-38, 45, 46, 47.
Old Testament, the, everywhere mentions and predicts the advent of Christ, i. 403.
Olive, the wild, the symbolical significance of, ii. 78, etc.
Ophites, the, i. 104.

Papias, quoted, ii. 146.
Parables, ii. 34, 35.
Parables, the proper mode of interpreting, i. 217.
Paschal solemnities, differences in the observance of, ii. 159, 160.
Passion of the twelfth Æon, how said to be indicated in Scripture, i. 13; not to be proved from Scripture, 190-193.
Passions, animal, produce, according to Valentinus, material substances, i. 22.
Pastors, the, to whom the apostles committed the churches, to be heard, ii. 108, etc.
Patriarchs and prophets foretold the advent of Christ, i. 455.
Paul, caught up into the third heavens, i. 335, 336; and Peter, founders of the church of Rome, 261; sometimes uses words not in their grammatical sequence, 273; knew no mysteries unrevealed to the other apostles, 316; refutation of the Ebionites who disparaged the writings of, 320, etc.
Perfect, why man was not made, ii. 42.
Persecution foretold, ii. 12.
Pharaoh's heart hardened, how, ii. 471.
Plato, quoted, i. 373.
Pleroma, the, of Valentinus, i. 5, 14; shown to be absurd, 124, 168, 170.
Polycarp, conversed with the apostles, i. 262, 263; his reply to Marcion, 263; the epistle of, 263, 264; Irenæus' testimony respecting, 158, 159.
Predictions of the prophets, the, ii. 12, etc.; all uttered under the same inspiration, 22.
Presbyters, the, ought to be obeyed, i. 462; false, 463; faithful, 463, 464.
Proarche, the, of Valentinus, i. 47.
Production, the first order of, maintained by heretics proved to be indefensible, i. 152, etc.; and absurd, 168, 180.
Prophets, the, refutation of the notion that they uttered their predictions under the inspiration of different gods, i. 254, ii. 22; their predictions, 12, etc.; referred all their predictions to Christ, 18, etc.; sent by the same Father who sent the Son, 26, etc.
Propator, the, of Valentinus, i. 4, 7; of Ptolemy, 50.
Protarchontes, i. 103.
Providence of God, the world ruled by, i. 371.
Prunicus, i. 104, 106, 107, 108.
Ptolemy the heresiarch, the doctrines of, i. 49, etc.
Ptolemy, the son of Lagus, procures a translation of the Jewish Scriptures to be made, i. 352, 353.
Pythagoras, the heretics borrow from, i. 164.

Redemption, the views of, entertained by heretics, i. 81, etc.
Resurrection, the, of the dead, asserted by Jesus against the Sadducees, i. 386, 387; of the flesh asserted, ii. 61, etc.; of the body, 64, etc.; various proofs of, from the Old Testament, 63, etc.; proved by the resurrection of Christ, 70, etc., 87, etc.; proofs of, from Isaiah and Ezekiel, 94; an actual, 155, etc.; illustrated, 164.
Retribution, the day of, i. 197.
Ridicule, poured upon the emanations and nomenclature of Valentinus, i. 47, etc.
Righteous, the, and the wicked, ii. 130.
Righteousness, perfect, not conferred by the law, i. 421-425.
Rod, the, of Moses, i. 357.
Roman empire, the dissolution of the, predicted, ii. 125.
Rome, the church of, founded and organized by Peter and Paul, i. 261; the first bishops of, 261, 262.

Sabaoth, i. 255 and note.
Sabbath-day, the law did not prohibit the hungry eating food ready to hand on the, i. 398.
Sacrifices, not required by God for their own sake, i. 426, 427-431; further remarks on, 431.
Sadducees, the reply of Jesus to the question asked by the, i. 387.
Samson, and the boy who guided him, types, ii. 171; further reference to, 178.
Satan, ii. 113; blasphemes God, 127, 128.

INDEX OF PRINCIPAL SUBJECTS.

Saturninus, the doctrines of, i. 89, 90.
Saviour, the, asserted by the Valentinians to be derived from all the Æons, i. 14, 25; various opinions of, among the heretics, 50.
Scriptures, the, appealed to by the heretics, i. 11, 15; how perverted by the heretics, 31, etc.; refutation of false interpretations of, 38, etc.; perverted by the Marcosians to support their absurdities, 74-80; perverse interpretations of the heretics, 144; proper method of interpreting the obscure passages of, 217-219; translation of the Hebrew, into Greek, 251; interpreted with fidelity by the LXX. translators, 253.
Seed, Valentinian absurdities respecting, exposed, i. 184-190.
Seeing God, i. 441, 442, 443, 444, 445, 446, 447.
Separatists, to be shunned, i. 463, 464.
Septuagint, the story of the origin of, i. 352, 353.
Serpent, the, cursed, i. 366; speculations respecting, ii. 165, 166.
Sethians, the doctrines of the, i. 104.
Shadrach, etc., in the fiery furnace, ii. 66.
Sige, i. 4 and note, 7; pretended revelation made by, to Marcus, 65; and Logos, mutually contradictory and repugnant, 150.
Simeon and Jesus, i. 327.
Simon of Cyrene, curious opinion of Basilides respecting, i. 91.
Simon Magus, i. 86; the pretensions of, 86, 87; honoured with a statue, 87; and Helena, 87, 88; the priests of, 88; succeeded by Menander, 89.
Sin, God not the author of, refutation of the Marcionites, 474, etc.
Sin, the pardon of, ii, 100, 101.
Sins of former times, recorded in Scripture for a warning to us, i. 465.
Son, meaning of the term, ii. 51.
Son of God, the, not made man in appearance only, i. 342-344; everywhere set forth in the Old Testament, 403, etc.
Son, the, reveals the Father, i. 390, 395; revealed by the Father, 391.
Sons of the devil, ii. 51.

Soul and body, views of the heretics relating to the future destruction of, refuted, i. 228, etc.
Souls, absurdity of the doctrine of the transmigration of, i. 247-250; existence of, after death, 250, 251; immortal, although they had a beginning, 251-253.
Soter, i. 205.
Sophia, the Æon so called, i. 6; her passion, 7, 8; another name of Achamoth, 16, 103; could have produced nothing apart from her consort, 149; exposure of the absurdity of the whole Valentinian theory respecting, 180, etc.
Spirit, the Holy, gifts of the, ii. 72.
Spiritual, the absurdity of heretics claiming to be, while they declare the Demiurge to be animal, i. 331.
Spiritual men, ii. 6, 73; and animal, 80, etc.
Spoiling the Egyptians, the act examined and vindicated, i. 475.
Stauros and Horos, i. 14, 15, 29.
Stesichorus, the story of, i. 87, 88.
Stone, the, cut out without hands, i. 356.

Tatian, the doctrines of, i. 100; refuted in his denial of the salvation of Adam, 368.
Teaching, the, of Jesus, opposed to the opinions of heretics, i. 242, 243.
Teitan, ii. 137.
Temptation, the, of Christ, ii. 111-113.
Testaments, the two, God the author of both, ii. 4.
Tetrad, the first, i. 5; of Marcus reveals Aletheia, 59.
Thamar, her labour typical, i. 459, 460.
Thelesis, i. 49.
Theodotian and Aquila, their interpretation of Isa. vii. 14 refuted, i. 351, 352.
Translation, the, of Enoch and Elijah, ii. 66.
Transmigration of souls, the, the absurdity of the doctrine of, i. 247-250.
Treasure hid in a field, the, i. 461.
Triacontad, the, of the heretics, i. 147.
Truth, the, to be found in the catholic church, i. 264.

Types, earthly, of heavenly things, i. 436, etc.

Unity, the, of the faith of the universal church, i. 42.
Unity, the, of God, i. 268, etc., ii. 100, 114.
Utter emptiness, the, of Valentinus, i. 48.

Vacuum, the absurdity of the, of the heretics, i. 125.
Valentinian views of Jesus refuted from the apostolic writings, i. 323.
Valentinians, the, their immoral opinions and practices, i. 26, 27; how they pervert Scripture to support their own opinions, 31, etc.; refutation of their false interpretations of Scripture, 38, etc.; quote Homer to support their views, 40, 41; the inconsistent and contradictory opinions of, 45, etc.
Valentinus, the absurd ideas held by, i. 4; his system derived from the heathen, with only a change of terms, 160-167; recapitulation of arguments against the views of, 239, etc.
Virgin, Jesus born of a, i. 346, 359-362; prophecy of Isaiah relating to, 351, etc.
Virgin Mary, the, and Eve, a comparison between, ii. 106.

Visions of God, i. 446, 447, 448, 449, 450.

Will, the freedom of the, in man, ii. 36, etc.
Wine, and water, the mixture of, ii. 57; and bread, in the Eucharist, 59
Woman, the, with the issue of blood not a type of the suffering Æon, i. 203.
Word, the, the world made through, i. 122; reveals the Father, 390, 391; always with the Father, 440; all things created by, 441; declares God, 444; takes flesh to save the flesh, ii. 91; the image of God, 99; the Creator, 105.
Works of the flesh, the, ii. 80.
World, the, not made by angels, but by God through the Word, i. 120, 123, 124, 125; not formed by any other beings within the territory contained by the Father, 129, etc.; the Creator of, one, 142; ruled by the providence of God, 371; to be annihilated, ii. 80.

Year, the divisions of, do not really suit the Valentinian theory of Æons, i. 210, 212.
Year of the Lord, the acceptable, ii. 197.

Zoe, i. 5.

THE END.

CPSIA information can be obtained at www.ICGtesting.com
Printed in the USA
LVOW032042300412

279663LV00004B/48/P